FOOD EDITORS'
FAVORITES
C·O·O·K·B·O·O·K

Two Volumes in One

FOOD EDITORS' FAVORITES
COOKBOOK

Two Volumes in One

Edited by
Barbara Gibbs Ostmann
and Jane Baker

For
The Newspaper Food
Editors and Writers
Association, Inc.

WEATHERVANE BOOKS
New York

This book was originally published as two separate volumes under the titles: *Food Editors' Favorites Cookbook* and *Food Editors' Hometown Favorites Cookbook*.

This 1986 edition is published by Weathervane Books, distributed by Crown Publishers, Inc., by arrangement with Hammond, Incorporated.

Printed and Bound in the United States of America

Library of Congress Cataloging in Publication Data

Main entry under title:

Food editors' favorites.

   Includes index.
   1. Cookery, American.   I. Ostmann, Barbara Gibbs.
II. Baker, Jane.   III. Newspaper Food Editors and
Writers Association (U.S.)
TX715.F669   1986   641.5   85-31573
ISBN 0-517-60521-X

h g f e d c b a

CONTENTS

Food Editors' Favorites
Cookbook   1

Food Editors' Hometown
Favorites Cookbook   151

Index   301

Volume One

FOOD EDITORS'
FAVORITES
C O O K B O O K

A WORD OF THANKS

This cookbook would not have been possible without the generous contributions from the food editors and writers of our organization who took the time to dig into their personal recipe files. We want to express special thanks to the following members for their help in planning and preparing the book:

Deni Hamilton, *Courier-Journal,* Louisville, Kentucky
Susan Manlin Katzman, St. Louis, Missouri
Karen Marshall, *Globe-Democrat,* St. Louis, Missouri
Eleanor Ostman, *Pioneer Press and Dispatch,*
    St. Paul, Minnesota
Mary Frances Phillips, *Mercury News,* San Jose, California
Marjorie Rice, *Evening Tribune,* San Diego, California
William E. Rice, *Food and Wine* magazine
Phyllis Singer, *Waterloo Courier,* Waterloo, Iowa
Betty Straughan, *News-Review,* Roseburg, Oregon

In addition, we are appreciative of the clerical assistance provided by Virginia S. Marshall and Marie Jalageas.

BARBARA GIBBS OSTMANN
St. Louis Post-Dispatch, St. Louis, Missouri

JANE BAKER
The Phoenix Gazette, Phoenix, Arizona
Chairpersons of the cookbook committee

Contents

Volume 1

Introduction   5

Appetizers   7

Soups   25

Salads   33

Main Courses   47

Vegetables   81

Breads   103

Desserts   119

Index   301

INTRODUCTION

What do food editors discuss when they get together at conferences? In addition to such serious topics as nutrition, consumerism, government regulations and food prices, the discussion usually gets around to recipes and what's new in various areas.

As food editors, we have our fingers on the culinary pulse of cities across the country, even the world. We are continually exposed to all sorts of food: some good, some not so good. Sooner or later, we all end up with bulging personal recipe files.

The idea of putting food editors' favorite recipes into a cookbook was bound to come up. Sure enough, it did, and since 1978 we've been collecting personal favorites from our members to be shared with people everywhere via this cookbook.

We would like to make clear that these recipes are our favorites; we make no claim that they are original (is there really such a thing?). When possible, we've given credit where credit is due. But in many cases, recipes just evolved, and it is hard, if not impossible, to say from where they came.

This book is also our way of introducing the Newspaper Food Editors and Writers Association (NFEWA) to you. The association was founded in 1974 to encourage communication among food editors and writers, to foster professional ethical standards, to share our knowledge about food and to promote a greater understanding among other journalists.

Incorporated in 1982, the association has more than 150 members around the world, including the United States, Canada, New Zealand and Mexico. We sponsor an annual meeting with seminars, speakers and self-help sessions, as well as frequent regional meetings.

Perhaps the most important aspect of the association is the enthusiasm and support shared among the members, helping each other to continually strive to do a better job of serving the reader and the public.

We hope this book will find a special place in your own kitchen library, as it will in each of ours.

BARBARA GIBBS OSTMANN
Past President, NFEWA
(1982-1984)

JANE BAKER
President, NFEWA
(1984-1986)

Appetizers

CHICKEN PATE

approx. 2 cups

¼ cup butter
1 medium onion, sliced
3 whole, uncooked chicken breasts, boned, skinned and cut into small pieces
1 cup tawny port wine, divided
1 package (3 ounces) cream cheese, softened

2 tablespoons evaporated milk
1¼ teaspoons crumbled leaf tarragon
1 teaspoon salt or to taste
¼ teaspoon pepper
1 package (2¾ ounces) slivered almonds, toasted
Paprika
Assorted crackers

Melt butter in skillet; add onion and chicken. Sauté over moderate heat, stirring frequently, until chicken loses its pink color on outside. Add ½ cup wine. Bring to boil. Cook over moderate heat at rolling boil, uncovered, until liquid is reduced by approximately half.

Purée mixture in blender or food processor. Add cream cheese, milk, tarragon, salt, pepper and remaining ½ cup wine to chicken mixture. Blend until smooth. Add almonds, reserving some for garnish.

Firmly pack pâté into decorative crock. Refrigerate, covered, 1 to 2 days before serving.

Garnish with reserved almonds and paprika. Serve with crackers.

Helen Dollaghan *The Denver Post* / Denver, Colorado

SPINACH FRITTATA

6 dozen appetizers

This vegetable-strewn omelet is excellent as an appetizer when cut into squares or diamonds. Cut in large rectangles, it makes an excellent accompaniment to an entrée.

4 bunches green onions (approx. 24), finely chopped
4 tablespoons butter
2 bunches (approx. 2 pounds) spinach, finely chopped
⅓ cup finely chopped fresh parsley
12 eggs

½ teaspoon salt
¼ teaspoon freshly ground pepper
⅛ teaspoon ground nutmeg (optional)
½ cup sour cream
1½ cups shredded Gruyère, Swiss or Cheddar cheese
¾ cup shredded Parmesan cheese, divided

Sauté the onions in butter until tender in large frying pan. Add spinach and sauté 2 minutes. Remove from heat; add parsley, then set aside.

Beat eggs in bowl until light; mix in salt, pepper, nutmeg, sour cream, shredded cheese, half the Parmesan cheese and the onion mixture. Pour into well-greased 15x10x1-inch jelly roll pan. Sprinkle with remaining Parmesan cheese.

Bake in preheated 350°F. oven 25 minutes, or until set. Cut into squares or diamonds. Serve hot.

Lou Pappas *The Peninsula Times Tribune* / Palo Alto, California

OLIVE-CHEESE BALLS

approx. 36 appetizers

This recipe makes delicious tidbits to offer with cocktails, or as treats for any occasion.

2 cups finely grated Cheddar cheese
½ cup butter, softened
¼ teaspoon hot pepper sauce
½ teaspoon salt

1 teaspoon paprika
1 cup all-purpose flour, unsifted
36 pimiento-stuffed green olives (approx.)

Mix thoroughly cheese, butter, hot pepper sauce, salt, paprika and flour. Form portion of dough around each well-drained olive. Bake in 400°F. oven about 15 minutes, or until golden brown.

Note: These cheese balls can be made ahead and frozen, then popped in the oven and cooked just before serving.

Beverly Daniel *The Bellingham Herald* / Bellingham, Washington

CRAB PUFFS

approx. 3 dozen appetizers

A little crab goes a long way in this recipe. The puffs look fancy even though the preparation is simple.

1 package (3 ounces) cream cheese, softened
¼ pound crab meat, fresh, canned or frozen
1 teaspoon finely minced garlic
Dash Worcestershire sauce
2 drops hot pepper sauce

¼ teaspoon salt
⅛ teaspoon white pepper
½ pound (approx.) wonton wrappers
Margarine
Vegetable oil for frying
Mustard powder
Water

Combine cream cheese, crab, garlic, Worcestershire, hot pepper sauce, salt and pepper.

Place ½ teaspoon (slightly rounded) crab filling in center of each wonton wrapper. Spread small amount margarine on two adjacent sides of wrapper. Fold one side over to form triangle. Press at edges to seal. (The margarine helps, since the wrappers are lightly floured and resist sticking.) Pinch in middle, then fold down opposite corners of triangle as though folding paper airplane, forming wings.

Deep fry in hot vegetable oil until golden. Drain on paper towels.

Serve with hot mustard made by mixing dry mustard powder and water to desired consistency.

Note: These can be assembled and refrigerated or frozen before frying. Be sure to keep them in an airtight container because the wonton skins dry out easily.

Barbara Durbin *The Oregonian / Portland, Oregon*

LOVE LETTERS
4½ to 5 dozen appetizers

I developed this recipe for a dinner that was sold at a local charity auction one year. The host paid $900 for the dinner, which I cooked for ten people; I thought he deserved something just a little different.

2 cups shredded cooked chicken	⅓ cup grated Parmesan cheese
1 can (4 ounces) chopped green chilies, drained	Dash each garlic powder and onion powder
4 large green onions, finely chopped	Dash salt
	1 package (16 ounces) wonton wrappers
	Vegetable oil for frying

Combine chicken, chilies, green onions, cheese, garlic and onion powders and salt in medium-size bowl; mix well.

Place a wrapper on counter with one corner facing toward you. Put about 1 teaspoon chicken mixture slightly below center of wrapper and fold bottom corner up. Fold sides in, points overlapping. Wet edges to seal. Fold final corner down, to resemble an envelope. Wet edges slightly to seal. Repeat with remaining chicken and wrappers.

Deep fry, a few at a time, until golden and crispy around edges. Drain on paper towels; serve hot.

Note: Love Letters are good plain, but they are also good served with sour cream and/or sweet-sour sauce.

These freeze beautifully. To prevent sticking, spread uncooked wontons on cookie sheets and set in freezer just until hard. Do not thaw before frying. If desired, they can be fried several hours before guests arrive; simply reheat in a 400°F. oven for 5 to 10 minutes.

Karen K. Marshall *St. Louis Globe-Democrat / St. Louis, Missouri*

HOT MUSHROOM SANDWICHES   *21 sandwiches*

When Helen Gurley Brown, editor of Cosmopolitan, *entertains, she told me she turns over the cooking "to one wonderful caterer" and concentrates on her guest list. "I work fiendishly hard about whom to combine. I like to have somebody interesting at each party, but I don't bring in someone from Mars. I mix up people that have quite a lot in common, but didn't know each other, although each guest should know at least two others besides the host and hostess," she said. This party hors d'oeuvre recipe, one of Ms. Brown's favorites, was shared by New York City caterer, Donald Bruce White.*

1½ cups finely minced
     fresh mushrooms
1 tablespoon thinly minced
     shallots or whites of
     scallions (green onions)
4 tablespoons butter,
     divided
3 tablespoons all-purpose
     flour

½ cup chicken stock
½ cup heavy cream
   Dash cayenne
   Dash ground nutmeg
   Dash salt
   Dash white pepper
   Splash Madeira
21 slices firm white bread,
     sliced thin

Mince mushrooms and shallots. Sauté in 2 tablespoons butter. Allow liquid from mushrooms to cook down.

Melt remaining 2 tablespoons butter in separate pan; stir in flour to make roux (paste). Add chicken stock, cream, cayenne, nutmeg, salt and white pepper. Cook until mixture becomes quite thick. (Don't let heat get too high.) When mixture is thick, add mushroom mixture. Add splash of Madeira.

Trim crusts from bread. Spread some mushroom mixture on one slice of bread, add second slice, more mushroom mixture, then add third and final slice of bread. Don't spread mushroom mixture to edges, or it will ooze out. (There should be enough mushroom mixture to make 7 triple-decker sandwiches.)

Preheat oven or toaster-oven to 400°F. Toast sandwiches 10 to 12 minutes, or until they are slightly golden in color. Cut each sandwich into three fingers and serve warm.

Note: These sandwiches could also be served for lunch or as part of a tea menu.

Barbara Burtoff Syndicated writer / Washington, D.C.

CURRY DIP

approx. 2 cups

This curry dip served with raw vegetables has become my price of admission to many friends' parties. The original version of this recipe came from the home economists at the Wisconsin Gas Company as part of a food story on nutritious appetizers for New Year's Eve.

2 teaspoons curry powder	2 tablespoons cider vinegar
1½ teaspoons garlic salt	1 cup sour cream
2 tablespoons granulated sugar	1 cup mayonnaise
2 teaspoons prepared horseradish	Cherry tomatoes
2 teaspoons grated onion	Raw vegetables in bite-size pieces

Mix curry powder, garlic salt, sugar, horseradish, onion and vinegar. Add sour cream and mayonnaise; mix well. Cover and chill several hours or overnight.

Serve with cherry tomatoes and bite-size pieces of other raw vegetables. Some of my favorites are cauliflower, broccoli, mushrooms, carrots, celery, green and red peppers, asparagus, kohlrabi and rutabaga.

Peggy Daum *The Milwaukee Journal* / Milwaukee, Wisconsin

VEGETABLE HOT DIP

approx. 1½ cups

4 medium tomatoes, finely chopped	2 tablespoons red wine vinegar
½ onion, finely chopped	¼ cup vegetable oil
½ cup finely chopped celery	1 teaspoon mustard seed
¼ cup finely chopped green pepper	Salt and pepper to taste
2 tablespoons chopped green chilies	Corn chips or raw vegetables

Combine tomatoes, onion, celery, green pepper, chilies, vinegar, oil, mustard seed, salt and pepper. Allow mixture to chill at least 2 hours before serving. If you like a hotter dip, add more chopped green chilies.

Serve with corn chips or an assortment of raw vegetables such as celery, carrots, mushrooms or green pepper.

Donna Morgan *Salt Lake Tribune* / Salt Lake City, Utah

POULTRY MOUSSE

approx. 3 cups

My friend Sue Sutker, who teaches cooking classes in Tampa, makes a liver mousse that is extremely simple, yet so good that every time I serve it, people ask for the recipe.

1 pound chicken livers,
  trimmed
1 cup chicken stock
½ cup sliced onions
  Salt and pepper

2 cups unsalted butter,
  softened, cut into 1-inch
  pieces
1 tablespoon (or more)
  cognac

Place chicken livers in large saucepan with stock, onion and salt and pepper to taste. Bring to boil, reduce heat and simmer 12 minutes. Strain, reserving poaching liquid. (I freeze it to use for the next batch.)

Put livers in food processor or blender; add butter and cognac and blend until smooth. Transfer to bowl.

Refrigerate, stirring occasionally, until mixture gets heavy. Put in terrine or other serving dish and cover with plastic wrap. Refrigerate until serving time.

Note: When adjusting the seasoning before refrigerating, I sometimes add lemon juice, hot pepper sauce and more cognac.

This recipe can be prepared ahead and frozen. Remove from freezer the evening before you expect to use it.

Ann McDuffie *The Tampa Tribune* / Tampa, Florida

SWISS CRUSTS

6 servings

Wine-soaked butter-browned bread rounds topped with a Gruyère sauce make a delightful hot first course for a cool meal. Assemble them in advance and pop them in to bake at the last minute.

6 slices egg bread or other
  rich white bread
6 tablespoons butter,
  divided
¼ cup dry white wine
¼ cup all-purpose flour
2 cups milk, heated

½ teaspoon salt
  Dash black pepper
  Dash ground nutmeg
3 egg yolks
1½ cups shredded Gruyère
  cheese

Remove crusts from bread and trim slices to fit ramekins. Brown bread in 2 tablespoons butter until golden, but still soft inside. Arrange in six buttered ramekins and saturate with wine.

14 APPETIZERS

Melt remaining 4 tablespoons butter in saucepan and stir in flour. Cook for 2 minutes. Gradually stir in milk, salt, pepper and nutmeg. Stirring constantly, cook until thickened. Beat egg yolks. Remove small quantity of sauce from pan and blend into beaten egg. Pour slowly into sauce, blending carefully. Add cheese and stir until cheese is melted. Spoon sauce over wine-soaked bread. Bake in 400°F. oven 10 minutes, or until golden brown.

Lou Pappas *The Peninsula Times Tribune / Palo Alto, California*

DILL DIP IN A BREAD BOWL   *approx. 3 cups*

This dill dip recipe appeared in my newspaper in a column written by Susan Manlin Katzman. It's easy to make, pretty to serve and delicious to eat. I serve it in a bread bowl, which is itself eaten.

1 large, round unsliced loaf Russian rye bread or other round loaf
1⅓ cups sour cream
1⅓ cups mayonnaise
2 tablespoons finely chopped fresh parsley
2 tablespoons grated onion

3 teaspoons chopped fresh dill leaf or 2 teaspoons dried dill weed*
2 teaspoons Beau Monde seasoning**

*Do not use dill seed.

**Available in most supermarkets.

With serrated knife, cut circle from center of bread, keeping sides intact; trim inside of bread to form bowl. Set bread bowl aside and cut remaining bread (part cut from center) into large, bite-size pieces. Set aside.

Combine sour cream, mayonnaise, parsley, onion, dill and Beau Monde. If you use dried dill weed, refrigerate dip overnight to let flavors develop and mingle.

Fill hollow portion of bread bowl with sour cream mixture just before serving. Place bread bowl on serving plate and surround it with cut bread pieces. Use bread as dippers.

Note: I usually double the amount of dip and use two loaves of bread, one for the "bowl" and the other to cut up in pieces. The dip is also good with assorted raw vegetables.

Barbara Gibbs Ostmann
St. Louis Post-Dispatch / St. Louis, Missouri

ZIPPY CHEESE BALL

There are enough cheese ball recipes to fill volumes. But this one, though it may appear as unremarkable as the next, has enough zip to make it disappear quickly at parties.

3 cups shredded Cheddar
  cheese
1 package (8 ounces) cream
  cheese, softened
2 tablespoons mayonnaise

2 tablespoons Worcester-
  shire sauce
1½ teaspoons onion powder
  Chopped nuts
  Crackers or fresh
  vegetables

   Mix thoroughly Cheddar cheese, cream cheese, mayonnaise, Worcestershire and onion powder. Blend well. Form into large ball. Roll in chopped nuts.
   Serve with crackers or fresh vegetables.

Barbara Durbin *The Oregonian* / Portland, Oregon

GOUGERE BOURGIGNON

Gougère is a light, ring-shaped pastry with a delicate cheese flavor. It is native to the Burgundy region of France, from which come many fine wines. Traditionally, gougère is served at wine tastings to clear the palate between samplings. It is equally enjoyable as an hors d'oeuvre at a holiday cocktail party or afternoon tea.

1 cup sifted all-purpose flour
½ cup water
2 tablespoons unsalted butter

1 teaspoon salt
3 eggs
¼ cup grated Gruyère cheese

   Measure flour and set aside. Put water, butter and salt into saucepan. Bring water to full rolling boil, letting butter melt completely. Remove from heat. Immediately add flour and mix thoroughly, using heavy wooden spoon.
   Beat 2 eggs; add gradually to flour mixture, beating well after each addition. When mixture is well blended, put into pastry bag with medium plain tip.
   Pipe mixture onto baking sheet, forming 6-inch circle. Pipe concentric second circle just slightly larger, touching first circle. Pipe third circle on top of first two circles, resting between them. (As they bake, the three rings will fuse into one.)

Beat third egg. Use pastry brush to gently brush some beaten egg on top circle. Sprinkle cheese over egg-glazed surface. Bake in preheated 425°F. oven 25 minutes, or until puffed, golden and slightly dry. Serve warm or cool.

Constance Quan
The Village Gazette / Old Greenwich, Connecticut

CURRIED CHICKEN ROLL-UPS   *2 dozen appetizers*

This appetizer goes over well with guests because it's refreshingly light.

4 chicken breast halves
2 cups chicken broth or
  bouillon
3 to 4 teaspoons curry
  powder
24 lettuce leaves (leaf or
  butter type)

1 cup sour cream
3 tablespoons finely
  chopped, toasted
  sunflower seeds
¼ cup finely chopped
  chutney
1 cup toasted coconut

Combine chicken breasts, broth and curry powder in medium-size saucepan. Bring to boil and simmer 30 minutes, or until chicken is tender. Remove from heat; refrigerate without draining, allowing chicken to cool in broth for several hours. In the meantime, wash lettuce leaves and pat dry.

Remove chicken breasts from broth; remove and discard skin and bones. Cut each half-breast into 6 to 8 fingers, each 2 to 3 inches in length and ½ inch wide. Place each strip of chicken on lettuce leaf; fold in sides of leaf and roll up. Secure with toothpick, if necessary. Refrigerate rolls for several hours before serving.

Dip for rolls: Combine sour cream, sunflower seeds and chutney. Refrigerate until serving time.

Arrange chicken rolls on large platter or tray with dip and toasted coconut in small bowls in center. To serve, dunk rolls in dip, then in coconut.

Alice Krueger *Winnipeg Free Press* / Winnipeg, Manitoba

EGG-SHRIMP DIVINE

approx. 2 cups

Sometimes the things that are the easiest to make are the most elegant. This is one of those recipes.

1 package (8 ounces) cream cheese
3 tablespoons mayonnaise
½ teaspoon curry powder
1 can (6 ounces) shrimp, drained

1 hard-cooked egg, chopped
¼ cup chopped green onions
1 tablespoon finely chopped celery
Paprika
Crackers

Mix cream cheese with mayonnaise and curry powder; beat until smooth. Press into shallow soup bowl. Mix thoroughly shrimp, egg, onions and celery. Press shrimp mixture into cheese mixture. Sprinkle with paprika. Chill to blend flavors. Serve with crackers.

Marilyn Hagerty
Grand Forks Herald / Grand Forks, North Dakota

SUMMER CRAB MOLD

16 to 20 servings

This is my husband's favorite appetizer. I wanted to call the dish "Crab Marshall" after him, but feared he would find the name a dubious compliment.

¼ cup butter
¼ cup all-purpose flour
1¼ cups milk
1 package (8 ounces) cream cheese
1 envelope unflavored gelatin
3 tablespoons water
¾ cup mayonnaise
⅔ cup chopped celery

1 cup canned or frozen crab meat, chopped and cleaned
1 small onion, grated
Beau Monde seasoning* to taste
Salt to taste
Hot pepper sauce to taste
Sesame seed crackers
*Available in most supermarkets.

Melt butter in saucepan and whisk in flour. Cook, stirring constantly, 1 minute. Gradually whisk in milk to make white sauce. When thickened, stir in cream cheese. Soften gelatin in water and add to hot mixture; stir to dissolve gelatin. Remove mixture from heat.

Stir in mayonnaise, celery, crab and onion. Add Beau Monde, salt and hot pepper sauce to taste.

Rinse 4- to 5-cup mold with cold water. Fill mold with crab mixture and chill until firm. Unmold and serve with sesame crackers.

Susan Manlin Katzman Free-lance writer / St. Louis, Missouri

MIMI'S ARTICHOKE SQUARES   *3 dozen appetizers*

Many recipes that have become my favorites came from people I have written about in the newspaper through the years. This recipe for Artichoke Squares is one example. It goes together fast with a food processor to chop the onion and artichoke and to make the bread crumbs and shred cheese.

2 jars (6 ounces each) marinated artichokes
1 onion, finely chopped
2 cloves garlic, crushed
4 eggs
¼ cup fine dry bread crumbs
¼ teaspoon salt
⅛ teaspoon pepper
⅛ teaspoon oregano
⅛ teaspoon hot pepper sauce
2 cups grated sharp Cheddar cheese
2 tablespoons (or more) minced fresh parsley

Drain marinade from 1 jar of artichokes into skillet. Drain second jar of artichokes. Chop artichokes; set aside. Add onion and garlic to marinade in skillet. Sauté until limp, about 5 minutes.

Beat eggs in bowl; add bread crumbs, salt, pepper, oregano and hot pepper sauce. Stir in cheese, parsley, artichokes and onion mixture. Pour into greased 11x7x2-inch baking pan. Bake in 325°F. oven for 30 minutes, or until set.

Let cool, then cut into squares. Serve cold or reheat in 325°F. oven for 10 to 12 minutes.

Note: The marinade from the second jar of artichokes can be reserved for use as a salad dressing.

Barbara Durbin *The Oregonian* / Portland, Oregon

LIME FRUIT DIP

approx. 2 cups

2 eggs
½ cup granulated sugar
4 teaspoons cornstarch
1 can (6 ounces) frozen
  limeade concentrate,
  undiluted

2 to 3 drops green food
  coloring
1 cup heavy cream, whipped
Fresh fruit, cut into sticks,
  and berries

Beat eggs and combine in top of double boiler with sugar, cornstarch and limeade concentrate. Cook until thickened, stirring frequently. Remove from heat and stir in food coloring. Cool. Whip cream and fold into cooled limeade mixture.

Transfer to bowl or individual serving dishes and serve with fresh fruit and berries.

Note: This mixture can be frozen, but it also keeps well in the refrigerator.

Donna Morgan *Salt Lake Tribune* / Salt Lake City, Utah

MUSHROOM APPETIZERS

2 dozen appetizers

24 thin bread slices, crusts
  removed, buttered on
  both sides
4 tablespoons butter
3 shallots, chopped
1 pound fresh mushrooms,
  chopped fine
2 tablespoons all-purpose
  flour
1 cup heavy cream

1 tablespoon Dijon mustard
½ teaspoon salt
⅛ teaspoon cayenne
1 tablespoon chopped fresh
  parsley or 1 teaspoon
  crushed dried parsley
1½ tablespoons chopped
  chives
2 teaspoons lemon juice

Grease small muffin tins (total 24 muffins); fit one bread slice into each mold. Trim edges of bread as necessary. Bake in 400°F. oven 10 minutes. Remove bread shells from muffin tins and cool on rack.

Melt butter in skillet and sauté shallots for a few minutes. Add mushrooms and cook, stirring often, until all moisture has gone. Stir in flour until well blended; add cream and cook, stirring, until thickened. Add mustard, salt, cayenne, parsley, chives and lemon juice, stirring to blend. Place cooled shells on cookie sheet and fill with mushroom mixture. Bake in 350°F. oven 10 minutes. Allow to cool slightly before serving.

Note: The unfilled bread shells may be frozen. It is not necessary to thaw them before filling with the mushroom mixture. The mushroom mixture may be made a day or two ahead of time.

Donna Anderson *Vancouver Sun* / Vancouver, British Columbia

SWEET AND SOUR MEATBALLS   *75 to 85 meatballs*

For many years, Mildred Albert, now in her seventies, owned the Hart Modeling Agency in Boston and had cause to entertain many international celebrities from the fashion world. No matter how elaborate a menu was presented by a local caterer, guests could always count on these scrumptious Sweet and Sour Meatballs (Ms. Albert's own specialty) being on the hors d'oeuvre table. As proof of their popularity, the meatballs were always the first dish to disappear.

1 clove garlic, minced	1 quart (32 ounces)
2 pounds ground beef	cocktail vegetable juice
2 eggs	1 box (1 pound) light
3 tablespoons chili sauce	brown sugar
2 tablespoons dried	1 cup white vinegar
parsley flakes	3 cloves garlic, halved
½ teaspoon salt	30 prunes, pitted
½ teaspoon pepper, divided	

Mash minced garlic with ground beef, eggs, chili sauce, parsley flakes, salt and ¼ teaspoon pepper. Shape meat mixture into 75 to 85 balls.

Combine vegetable juice, brown sugar, vinegar, garlic cloves and remaining pepper; bring mixture to boil.

Drop meatballs into juice mixture. Reduce heat to low; cook 40 minutes. Add prunes; cook 20 minutes more.

Drain off most, but not all, sauce before putting meatballs and prunes into chafing dish. Serve hot with toothpicks.

Note: A quart is 32 ounces; if you buy the 46-ounce can of cocktail vegetable juice, do not use the whole thing.

It is best to make these a day ahead, then refrigerate them. At serving time, you can skim off the fat on top of mixture before reheating.

To make 115 to 125 meatballs,, increase the meat mixture ingredients by half; leave the sauce ingredients as they are.

Barbara Burtoff Syndicated writer / Washington, D.C.

EGGPLANT APPETIZER

4 to 8 servings

This is great party fare. It's easy to make and can be prepared ahead of time. The only problem is there are never any leftovers—it's too good. I originally found the recipe in an Italian cookbook, but "perfected" it with different ingredients.

¼ cup olive oil
1 onion, chopped
4 cloves garlic, minced
1 medium eggplant, peeled and chopped
2 green peppers, seeded and chopped
1 cup chopped celery
1 can (8 ounces) pitted black olives, drained and chopped

1 cup chopped mushrooms
1 can (8 ounces) tomato sauce
2 tablespoons wine vinegar
¼ cup light brown sugar
¼ teaspoon basil, crushed
Salt and pepper to taste
Italian bread, cut into thick slices or cubes

Heat olive oil in large, heavy skillet. Add onion and garlic; sauté until tender. Add eggplant, green pepper and celery. Cook, covered, stirring occasionally, for about 15 minutes. Add olives, mushrooms and tomato sauce; mix thoroughly. Add vinegar, brown sugar and basil; simmer uncovered until all ingredients are tender, about 15 minutes. Season with salt and pepper to taste.

Serve at room temperature with Italian bread, or refrigerate until needed. This also can be served warm as a vegetable dish.

Jane Baker *The Phoenix Gazette* / Phoenix, Arizona

SHRIMP SPREAD

approx. 6 cups

1 can (10½ ounces) condensed tomato soup, undiluted
1 package (8 ounces) cream cheese, softened
1½ tablespoons unflavored gelatin
2 tablespoons water
1 cup mayonnaise

1 tablespoon Worcestershire sauce
Hot pepper sauce to taste
2 cans (4½ ounces each) shrimp, drained
½ cup chopped celery
½ cup chopped onion
Lettuce leaves
Crackers

Bring undiluted soup to boil in medium saucepan. Remove from heat and add cream cheese; stir until smooth. Soften gelatin in water. Add to hot soup mixture and stir until gelatin is dissolved. Add mayonnaise, Worcestershire and hot pepper sauce; mix well.

Refrigerate until slightly thickened. Add shrimp, celery and onion; mix well. Pour into lightly oiled 6-cup ring mold or other 6-cup gelatin mold. Refrigerate until firm.

Unmold onto platter lined with lettuce leaves. Serve with party crackers.

Note: The shrimp mixture also can be divided among several smaller molds to facilitate serving at large parties.

Jane Baker *The Phoenix Gazette* / Phoenix, Arizona

HOLIDAY ANTIPASTO
approx. 3½ quarts

This antipasto has earned a permanent place at my annual Christmas bash — a snack buffet for about 100 people. I alter it from year to year. This is the current version.

1 bottle (8 ounces) Italian salad dressing
4 cups sliced carrots
2 cups coarsely diced onion
1 cup sliced celery
1 cup sliced mushrooms
1 can (14 ounces) artichoke hearts, drained
1 jar (11 ounces) baby eggplants, drained
1 cup Greek olives, drained and pitted
1 jar (15½ ounces) dilled brussels sprouts or broccoli
2 jars (2 ounces each) chopped pimiento

Heat Italian dressing in large skillet. Add carrots; cover and cook 5 minutes. Add onion, celery and mushrooms; stir. Cover and cook 5 minutes longer. Vegetables should be hot through, but still colorful and crisp. Celery will eventually fade in color.

Uncover and let cool. Chill. Add artichokes, eggplants, olives, brussels sprouts or broccoli and pimiento. Chill until serving time.

Note: This recipe keeps at least a week in the refrigerator.

Dilled tomatoes can be used in place of the brussels sprouts or broccoli. The dilled vegetables should be easily obtainable at a Greek grocery.

Janet Beighle French *The Plain Dealer* / Cleveland, Ohio

SALMON ROLL

approx. 2 cups

Tina and Earl Isaacson, who now spend most of their time in Bradenton, Florida, were among the most hospitable people who ever lived in Grand Forks. This is one of Tina's recipes.

1 can (16 ounces) red salmon
1 package (8 ounces) cream cheese, softened
2 drops liquid smoke or Worcestershire sauce

½ cup chopped pecans
3 tablespoons chopped fresh parsley
Crackers

Combine salmon, cream cheese and liquid smoke or Worcestershire; mix well. Shape into ball or log. Roll in mixture of pecans and parsley. Roll up in plastic wrap or wax paper. Chill to blend flavors.

Serve with crackers.

Marilyn Hagerty
Grand Forks Herald / Grand Forks, North Dakota

BOWKNOTS

2 dozen appetizers

1 loaf fresh sandwich bread (white or whole wheat), thinly sliced
1 can (10½ ounces) condensed cream of mushroom soup, undiluted

12 bacon strips, uncooked, cut in half
24 toothpicks

Trim all crust off bread. Spread soup on one side of bread slices, being careful to cover edges. Roll each slice from one corner to opposite corner. Wrap bacon strip around middle of each roll and secure with toothpick. Place on cookie sheet and bake in 250°F. oven for 1 hour. The bowknots will be dry, crisp and delicious.

Note: Prepared bowknots may be frozen before baking. Place on a flat pan; when frozen solid, transfer to freezer bags. Bake without thawing, extending baking time about 15 minutes.

Other condensed soups such as cream of asparagus or chicken can be substituted for the mushroom soup.

Kathleen Kelly *Wichita Eagle-Beacon* / Wichita, Kansas

Soups

BEEFY VEGETABLE SOUP

approx. 6 quarts

Ve call this Mom's Presbyterian version of chicken soup. Although it can be made with a hearty stock and hunks of beef, this version is quicker and, I think, just as good.

2 to 3 carrots, chopped
2 large potatoes, chopped
1 large onion, chopped
4 ribs celery, preferably with tops, chopped
1 small head cabbage, coarsely shredded (approx. 3 cups)

1 to 2 pounds ground beef
2 teaspoons salt
1 teaspoon freshly ground pepper
1 quart tomato juice

Combine carrots, potatoes, onion, celery, cabbage, ground beef, salt and pepper in large stock pot and add enough water to cover. Add tomato juice. Bring to boil, then lower heat and simmer at least 1 hour, until meat is cooked and vegetables are tender. Stir occasionally to break up meat. Skim off fat and taste for seasoning.

Note: This soup freezes beautifully and generally tastes better the second or third day. The amounts of ingredients are flexible, but all of the ingredients should be fresh.

Karen K. Marshall *St. Louis Globe-Democrat* / St. Louis, Missouri

ZUCCHINI SOUP

approx. 4 servings

When summer melts into September, the days grow cooler and you have more zucchini than you know how to handle. Here's a simple, super zucchini soup. It's almost too easy to believe — and it is low in calories.

2 cups sliced zucchini
2 cups water

3 chicken bouillon cubes
1 cup milk

Add sliced zucchini to combined water and bouillon cubes in saucepan. Heat until zucchini is tender. Pour mixture into blender or food processor and purée. Return puréed mixture to pan and add milk. Heat to serving temperature.

Marilyn Hagerty
Grand Forks Herald / Grand Forks, North Dakota

GAZPACHO

This recipe came from a reader more than fifteen years ago and is the most filling and delicious gazpacho I have ever consumed.

1 small clove garlic, chopped and mashed
1 tablespoon granulated sugar
1½ teaspoons salt
1 can (46 ounces) tomato juice
¼ cup vegetable oil
2 tablespoons lemon juice
1 teaspoon Worcestershire sauce
3 tomatoes, finely chopped
1 cucumber, peeled and diced
1 green pepper, finely diced
1 cup shredded carrots
1 cup thinly sliced celery
¼ cup thinly sliced green onion

Combine garlic, sugar, salt, tomato juice, oil, lemon juice and Worcestershire in large bowl. Beat until well blended. Stir in tomatoes, cucumber, green pepper, carrots, celery and green onion. Cover and chill for several hours.

Note: This keeps 3 to 4 days in the refrigerator.

Calories can be cut by eliminating the vegetable oil. The texture will not be as thick, but the flavor will not be impaired.

Mary Hart Sorensen
Minneapolis Star and Tribune / Minneapolis, Minnesota

TOMATO MADRILENE
4 servings

This jellied soup also can be layered like a parfait with avocado purée and topped with a spoonful of whipped cream cheese. It makes a colorful first course.

½ cup cold water
1 tablespoon unflavored gelatin
2 cups tomato juice

Combine cold water and gelatin in small saucepan and let stand for about 5 minutes. Add 1 cup tomato juice and stir over heat until gelatin dissolves. Add second cup of tomato juice. Pour into bowl; stir well, then chill until firm.

Break into chunks with fork and serve in parfait glasses.

Ruth Gray *St. Petersburg Times* / St. Petersburg, Florida

CHILLED CUCUMBER SOUP

4 to 6 servings

This soup tastes fantastic after we have spent an afternoon in the sun. I also like to serve it in cups, as the first course for a dinner party, and my daughters like it for between-meal snacking.

2 tablespoons butter or margarine
½ cup chopped green onion, including some tops
2 cups diced seeded cucumber (approx. 1 large cucumber)
1 cup watercress or leaf spinach, chopped
½ cup peeled and diced potato (approx. 1 medium potato)
2 cups chicken broth
¾ teaspoon salt
½ teaspoon white pepper
1 cup light or heavy cream
Thinly sliced radishes for garnish

Melt butter in saucepan; add green onion and cook over moderate heat for 5 minutes, being sure not to brown butter or onions. Add cucumber, watercress, potato, broth, salt and pepper; bring to boil. Reduce heat to low and cook for 15 minutes, or until vegetables are tender. Cool slightly.

Purée in blender, adding 1½ cups of mixture at a time. Put in large bowl and stir in cream; cover and chill thoroughly for several hours or overnight.

When ready to serve, float several thin radish slices atop each serving.

Note: Other garnishes might be a sprinkle of paprika or curry powder, chopped chives or a cucumber slice.

Donna Segal *Indianapolis Star* / Indianapolis, Indiana

SQUASH SOUP

6 servings

4 cups chopped yellow squash
6 cups chicken broth
3 large carrots, chopped
3 medium onions, chopped
1 tablespoon butter
1 tablespoon vegetable oil
6 tomatoes, peeled, seeded and chopped
½ cup grated Parmesan cheese
1 cup plain yogurt
½ teaspoon dried thyme
Salt and pepper to taste

Pour broth over squash in large saucepan and cook until tender. Sauté carrots and onions in butter and oil in another pan until tender. Stir tomatoes into onion-carrot mixture and cook for 5 minutes; add to squash and broth and mix well.

Pour into blender container and blend until combined, but not smooth. Return to saucepan. Add cheese, yogurt, thyme, salt and pepper. Simmer until hot.

Anne Byrn Phillips
The Atlanta Journal-Constitution / Atlanta, Georgia

MINESTRONE SICILIANO

approx. 3 quarts

This Italian favorite — an array of fresh vegetables in beef stock seasoned to perfection — will rate rave reviews.

1 to 1½ pounds beef bones or small piece of beef chuck
2 teaspoons seasoned salt
6 cups water
1 can (15 ounces) butter beans, undrained
1 cup fresh green beans, cut in ½-inch slices, or 1 package (9 ounces) frozen green beans
3 medium carrots, peeled and diced
1 large potato, peeled and diced

2 medium tomatoes, coarsely chopped
1 small onion, chopped
1 tablespoon chopped fresh parsley
1½ teaspoons dried basil
Freshly ground pepper to taste
1 small head cabbage, chopped
1 package (10 ounces) frozen peas, partly thawed
1 large zucchini, sliced

Combine beef bones, seasoned salt, water, beans, carrots, potato, tomatoes, onion, parsley, basil and pepper in large soup pot. Cover and heat to boiling; reduce heat and add cabbage. Cover and simmer 1 hour.

Remove bones from soup, cut off any meat and return meat to soup. Stir in peas and zucchini; simmer 5 to 10 minutes longer.

Natalie Haughton *Daily News* / Van Nuys, California

FRENCH LEEK SOUP

8 servings

8 leeks (approx.) (white part only), minced
4 tablespoons butter
4 medium potatoes, thinly sliced
¼ cup chopped celery
1 tablespoon chopped fresh parsley
2 quarts chicken stock or canned bouillon

2 cups heavy cream
2 tablespoons sour cream
Salt, pepper and nutmeg to taste
2 tablespoons Madeira or sherry wine
1 teaspoon Worcestershire sauce

Sauté leeks slowly in butter in large, heavy saucepan until leeks are soft but not brown. Add potatoes, celery, parsley and chicken stock; simmer 30 minutes.

Rub soup through sieve or put through food mill. Return to pan and add heavy cream, sour cream, salt, pepper, nutmeg, wine and Worcestershire. Bring to serving temperature without boiling. Serve immediately.

Margaret Mallory   *Oakland Tribune / Oakland, California*

CHILLED BLUEBERRY SOUP

8 servings

My husband refused to eat cold soup. "Soup should be hot!" is his idea. After coaxing him into tasting this recipe, he polished off two bowls.

3 cups water
1 quart fresh blueberries, rinsed, stemmed and drained
¾ cup granulated sugar

Ground cinnamon to taste
2 tablespoons cornstarch
1½ to 2 tablespoons cold water
Sour cream or yogurt for garnish

Bring water to boil in saucepan. Add blueberries, sugar and cinnamon. Cook for several minutes, stirring to dissolve sugar. Set aside. In small bowl mix cornstarch with enough cold water to make paste. Stir into warm berry mixture and bring to boil again. Cool. Cover and refrigerate.

Serve well chilled with tablespoon of sour cream or yogurt atop each bowl of soup. Sprinkle with additional cinnamon.

Diane Wiggins   *St. Louis Globe-Democrat / St. Louis, Missouri*

BROWN MUSHROOM SOUP

approx. 6 servings

This recipe came from a native Parisian whom I met in Canada. It uses mature, brown mushrooms that give off a rich woodsy taste and often can be purchased at reduced prices.

1 pound mature* mushrooms, diced
½ cup diced celery
½ cup diced carrots

*Mature mushrooms are dry, not slimy.

¼ cup diced onion
3 cups water (approx.)
Rich chicken or beef stock
Salt and pepper to taste

Cover mushrooms, celery, carrots and onion with water in 2-quart heavy saucepan. Simmer, partially covered, for about 45 minutes. Add stock to make 6 cups of liquid. Season with salt and pepper to taste. Heat through.

Note: The soup is excellent served as is in the fine-chopped stage, but it is especially nice if processed or blended until smooth, then reheated and served with a tablespoon of sour cream and a tablespoon of dry sherry per serving.

Jeanne Cummins *Noblesville Daily Ledger* / Noblesville, Indiana

BUTTERNUT SQUASH SOUP

6 to 8 servings

1 medium butternut squash (approx. 1 pound)
3 tart green apples, peeled and coarsely chopped
1 medium onion, peeled and chopped
¼ teaspoon rosemary or marjoram (optional)
1 teaspoon salt

¼ teaspoon pepper
3 cans (10½ ounces each) chicken broth
2 soup cans of water
¼ cup heavy cream or half-and-half
Chopped fresh parsley for garnish

Peel squash and seed it; cut into chunks. Combine squash with apples, onions, rosemary, salt, pepper, broth and water in large, heavy saucepan. Bring to boil and simmer, uncovered, for 45 minutes.

Purée soup in blender or food processor. Return mixture to saucepan and bring just to boiling point, then reduce heat. Before serving, add cream. Serve hot, with chopped fresh parsley sprinkled on top.

Phyllis Hanes *The Christian Science Monitor*

CREAM OF FALL-VEGETABLE SOUP

6 servings

This is a lovely rose-colored soup that is delicately flavored with herbs and curry powder.

3 small beets, peeled and chopped
3 green onions, sliced
2 small yellow onions, chopped
3 carrots, peeled and sliced
1 potato, peeled and cubed
2 ribs celery, sliced
½ cup chopped fresh parsley
3½ cups chicken broth
2 teaspoons butter
2 teaspoons all-purpose flour
1 cup light cream or half-and-half
½ teaspoon curry powder
½ teaspoon salt

Combine beets, green and yellow onions, carrots, potato, celery, parsley and chicken broth in large saucepan. Cover and simmer for 25 minutes, or until potatoes and carrots are tender. Whirl in blender or food processor in batches until ingredients are minced, but not too smooth.

Melt butter in another large saucepan. Add flour and cook, stirring 1 minute. Add cream and cook, stirring with wire whisk until just at boiling point. Add vegetable mixture, curry powder and salt. Heat through.

Daisy Fitch *Trenton Times / Trenton, New Jersey*

Salads

ORANGE-TUNA-MACARONI SALAD *6 to 8 servings*

½ cup mayonnaise
1 teaspoon prepared mustard
¼ teaspoon salt
⅛ teaspoon black pepper
2 large oranges, peeled and
   cut into bite-size pieces

1 can (7 ounces) tuna,
   drained and flaked
2 cups cooked and drained
   macaroni, cooled
½ cup diced celery
¼ cup finely chopped onion

Blend mayonnaise, mustard, salt and pepper; mix with orange pieces, tuna, macaroni, celery and onion lightly but thoroughly.
Note: This salad can be made ahead and refrigerated overnight.

Kathleen Kelly *Wichita Eagle-Beacon* / Wichita, Kansas

GERMAN POTATO SALAD *20 to 25 servings*

This is a party-size potato salad, but it is easily reduced in size. You can make it a day ahead, but it suffers if made any sooner than that.

6 pounds new potatoes
  Salt
1 bunch celery, sliced very
  thin
3 medium-to-large red onions,
  sliced thin and separated
  into rings
1 pound bacon, fried crisp
  and crumbled

2 bunches fresh parsley,
  finely chopped
3 cups mayonnaise
4 tablespoons white or cider
  vinegar
2 tablespoons granulated
  sugar
  Salt and pepper to taste

Cook unpeeled potatoes until tender; slice as thin as possible without causing them to crumble. Place layer of sliced potatoes in very large bowl and sprinkle with salt. Top potatoes with layer of celery, then onions, then bacon, then parsley.

Combine mayonnaise, vinegar, sugar, salt and pepper. Spread several tablespoons of dressing mixture over parsley layer. Repeat layers several times, until all ingredients are used. Toss salad very gently, trying not to break up potato slices more than necessary. Chill, covered, until serving time.

Karen K. Marshall *St. Louis Globe-Democrat* / St. Louis, Missouri

CHINESE ASPARAGUS SALAD

6 to 8 servings

The nicest thing about spring is all the marvelous fresh asparagus. This is one of my favorite asparagus recipes.

2 pounds fresh asparagus
¼ cup soy sauce
½ teaspoon granulated sugar

½ teaspoon cider vinegar
½ teaspoon salt
2 teaspoons sesame oil

Wash and peel the asparagus with potato peeler. Cut spears diagonally in 1½-inch lengths. Cook asparagus pieces in boiling water for 1 minute; drain and rinse under cold water to stop cooking.

Combine soy sauce, sugar, vinegar, salt, and oil in large bowl. Add asparagus and toss. Chill well before serving.

Pat Hanna Kuehl *Rocky Mountain News* / Denver, Colorado

TANGY COLE SLAW

8 servings

1½ cups mayonnaise*
3 tablespoons bottled
   sandwich spread
¾ teaspoon dry mustard
2 tablespoons dried
   parsley flakes
1 medium head cabbage,
   shredded
   *Do not use salad dressing.

¾ cup drained sweet pickle
   relish
½ cup chopped celery
¾ cup chopped onion
   Paprika

Combine mayonnaise, sandwich spread, mustard and parsley. Mix well; set aside. Toss cabbage with relish, celery and onion. Add enough mayonnaise mixture to moisten all ingredients. Mix lightly but thoroughly. Sprinkle with paprika.

Note: Dressing can be stored tightly covered, in refrigerator, for a week or longer. Makes approximately 1½ cups.

Helen Dollaghan *The Denver Post* / Denver, Colorado

THE ORIGINAL CAESAR SALAD   *6 large servings*

In the spring of 1965, the following story was sent to me — before I was food editor of the Hollywood Sun-Tattler — *by Rosa Cardini of Los Angeles, who is a daughter of Caesar:*

In 1924, over a holiday weekend, Caesar's Place — a restaurant in Tijuana, Mexico — ran short of food. Caesar experimented, and that evening the first Caesar Salad was served. While the waiters kibitzed, Caesar demonstrated his creation. "Take everything to each table," he instructed, "and make a ceremony of fixing the salad. Plenty of fanfare. Let guests think they're having the specialty of the house." And the guests did.

You'll find many variations of Caesar Salad, but here Rosa Cardini shares her father's authentic recipe and salad know-how.

Garlic-flavored Olive Oil:
  1 cup olive oil or salad oil
    (or ½ cup of each)
  6 cloves garlic

Caesar Croutons:
  1 cup bread cubes (approx.)
    Grated Parmesan cheese

Salad:
  3 medium heads romaine,
    chilled, dry and crisp

2 to 3 tablespoons wine
  vinegar
  Juice of 1 lemon
1 or 2 one-minute coddled
  eggs
  Freshly ground pepper
  Salt
  Dash Worcestershire sauce
5 or 6 tablespoons grated
    Parmesan cheese
    (Anchovies for garnish,
    optional)

Garlic-flavored olive oil: Prepare one to several days early. Slice cloves of garlic lengthwise in quarters and let stand in olive oil.

Caesar croutons: Preheat oven to 225°F. Cut bread in strips one way, then across 5 times, to make cubes. Spread out on cookie sheet; pour small amount garlic-flavored oil over cubes. Heat in oven for 2 hours. Sprinkle croutons with grated Parmesan cheese. Store in jar and refrigerate to keep crispness.

Romaine: Wash 24 hours ahead if possible. Pat leaves dry with towel; wrap in fresh towels and refrigerate.

To prepare salad: Break romaine leaves in 2- to 3-inch widths. At last minute before serving, place romaine in chilled salad bowl. Drizzle about ⅓ cup garlic-flavored oil over greens, then vinegar, then lemon juice. Break in eggs. Grind flurry of pepper over all. Season with salt and dash Worcestershire. Sprinkle with cheese. Roll-toss (see Caesar Salad Helps below) 6 or 7 times, or until dressing is thoroughly combined and every leaf is coated. Add croutons; toss 1 or 2 times. Serve at once on chilled dinner plates.

Garnish with rolled anchovies, if desired.

Note: The anchovies, now a familiar ingredient in Caesar Salad, didn't become part of the recipe until some 10 years later.

Caesar Salad Helps:

Croutons: Slow toasting of bread insures that croutons will stay crunchy when tossed with greens and dressing. Cubes should be so dry they'd float on water.

Romaine: Wrapping washed and dried leaves in towels and refrigerating helps them to retain their crispness. Always break or tear leaves, never cut, or they may take on an unattractive brown edge. This method may be used for any salad greens.

Dressing the greens: For even distribution, always follow a Z-line as your pour oil, vinegar and lemon juice over salad. Always add oil first to coat leaves—salad stays crisper that way.

Roll-toss to mix: With salad spoon in right hand, fork in left, go down to bottom of bowl with one tool while going up and over with other. "Roll" salad until every leaf shines with dressing.

Serving art: Start with chilled bowl and chilled plates. Traditionally, Caesar Salad is served on dinner-size plates, whether for the main course at lunch, or in smaller helpings for an appetizer. Don't overlook the drama of handsome accessories—the giant bowl, spoon and fork for tossing, little bowls to hold ingredients, oil and vinegar cruets, tall pepper mill and salt shaker.

Bernie O'Brien *Hollywood Sun-Tattler* / Hollywood, Florida

CARROT SALAD

1 pound carrots, peeled and sliced
1 can (16 ounces) tomato sauce
1 cup granulated sugar
½ cup vegetable oil
¾ cup wine vinegar
Salt and pepper to taste
1 teaspoon dry mustard
1 teaspoon (or more) Worcestershire sauce
Dash hot pepper sauce (optional)
1 medium onion, chopped
1 medium green pepper, chopped
1 can (16 ounces) whole kernel corn, drained
½ cup chopped celery

Boil carrots in salted water just until tender; drain and place in 2-quart covered casserole. Combine tomato sauce, sugar, oil, vinegar, salt, pepper, mustard, Worcestershire and hot pepper sauce; mix well. Pour over carrots; add onion, green pepper, corn and celery. Cover and marinate overnight.

Note: This salad will keep in the refrigerator at least 1 week.

Lorrie Guttman *Tallahassee Democrat / Tallahassee, Florida*

ZIPPY ZUCCHINI SALAD

This recipe was created when I started to cook zucchini one night; then my plans changed and I went out to dinner. The zucchini was tossed into the refrigerator. The next night, I took it out and served it on salad greens instead of reheating it.

1 clove garlic
2 teaspoons olive oil
3 zucchini, sliced into ¼-inch rounds
1 teaspoon granulated sugar
½ cup black olives, sliced
¼ cup slivered almonds
3 tablespoons cider vinegar
⅓ cup chili sauce
⅓ cup bottled spicy, sweet French salad dressing
2 tablespoons minced fresh parsley
½ teaspoon dried tarragon
¼ teaspoon dried oregano
Salt and pepper to taste
Salad greens

Sauté garlic in olive oil. Add zucchini and stir-fry until just tender. Discard garlic. Remove zucchini from pan and place in bowl or other container. Add sugar to pan, then add olives, almonds, vinegar, chili sauce, salad dressing, parsley, tarragon, oregano, salt and pepper. Cook over moderate heat about 2 minutes to blend flavors.

Pour sauce over zucchini; cover and chill several hours or overnight.

Serve on salad greens.

Mary Scourtes *The Tampa Tribune* / Tampa, Florida

KIWIFRUIT SALAD

6 servings

Kiwifruit are perphaps the most well known of the many New Zealand fruits that are now appearing in California and other markets in the United States. Other popular fruits are passionfruit, tamarillos and feijoas. This attractive salad combines the familiar citrus fruits with the more exotic kiwi.

2 sweet oranges
1 grapefruit or 4 mandarin
  oranges
¾ cup granulated sugar

½ cup water
3 tablespoons rum
3 kiwifruit

Using potato peeler, thinly pare the outside rind from one orange and cut into fine slivers.

Using sharp knife, thickly peel oranges and grapefruit or mandarin oranges, then cut flesh into segments. Discard peels. (If mandarin oranges are used, peel and remove as much membrane as possible, then break flesh into segments.) During peeling and segmenting, work over basin to catch any juice.

Place slivered orange rind in cold water to cover, bring to boil and boil for 2 to 3 minutes, then drain off water.

Heat sugar and ½ cup water, stirring until syrup boils. Add slivered orange peel and simmer gently without stirring until rinds are tender, about 7 minutes.

Warm rum in small metal container or ladle; ignite with match and pour while still burning into syrup. When flames have died down, pour this syrup over prepared citrus fruits and any of their juice.

Peel kiwifruit and cut lengthwise into sections Add to citrus fruits, cover and refrigerate for 2 to 3 days before using to allow flavors to mature.

Note: Kiwifruit Salad can be served alone or over ice cream.

Tui Flower
New Zealand Newspapers Ltd. / Auckland, New Zealand

CHRYSANTHEMUM SALAD

6 servings

This is one for those who like to smell their flowers and eat them, too. Check to see if the flowers have been sprayed with anything harmful before buying them.

3 large chrysanthemums, 2 yellow and 1 mauve
½ cup white wine vinegar
1 teaspoon honey
1 teaspoon fresh, chopped tarragon or ½ teaspoon dried
Juice of 1 lemon

½ pound lettuce, broken into bite-size bits
1 bunch watercress, coarsely chopped
4 large pimiento-stuffed olives, sliced
½ cup olive oil
Salt and pepper to taste

Pull petals from flowers. Combine vinegar with honey, tarragon and lemon juice in small bowl. Marinate petals in mixture for 30 minutes. Drain petals and reserve marinade. Mix petals with lettuce, watercress and olives in large bowl.

Mix olive oil with 3 tablespoons of reserved marinade; add salt and pepper. Toss salad with dressing just before serving.

Bernie O'Brien *Hollywood Sun-Tattler /* Hollywood, Florida

ORIENTAL SHRIMP SALAD

3 servings

This recipe is an adaptation of the top winner several years ago in the Globe-Democrat's recipe contest.

2 cups peeled and cooked shrimp
1 cup bean sprouts, rinsed and drained
1 can (8 ounces) water chestnuts, drained and finely chopped
¼ cup finely chopped green onions

¼ cup finely chopped celery

Soy Mayonnaise:
¾ cup mayonnaise
1 tablespoon lemon juice
1 tablespoon soy sauce
¼ teaspoon ground ginger

1 cup chow mein noodles

If shrimp are large, cut into halves or thirds. Combine shrimp, bean sprouts, water chestnuts, green onions and celery in medium-size bowl.

Combine Soy Mayonnaise ingredients thoroughly; add to shrimp mixture and toss to mix well.

Refrigerate, covered, until serving time. Just before serving, add chow mein noodles and mix well.

Note: This recipe can also be made with cooked, chopped chicken.

Karen K. Marshall *St. Louis Globe-Democrat* / St. Louis, Missouri

MRS. POOLE'S FRESH CAULIFLOWER SALAD

6 servings

While in his teens, my brother often ate at the home of a friend named Pebble Poole. My brother would return raving about Mrs. Poole's pie or Mrs. Poole's stew or Mrs. Poole's bread. Everything Mrs. Poole made, according to my brother, was "sheer heaven." In fact, I heard so much about Mrs. Poole's luscious food that I called her and asked if she would share some of her recipes. She was generous, and now, like my brother, I think everything Mrs. Poole made must have been "sheer heaven." The following is her recipe. I have never met Mrs. Poole but I am deeply in her debt and would like to take this space to say, "Thank you, Mrs. Poole, for years and years of pleasure."

1 cup fine dry bread crumbs
3 tablespoons butter
13 ounces romaine lettuce
    (9 to 10 cups bite-size
    pieces)
1 cup mayonnaise
2 tablespoons grated
    Parmesan cheese

1 tablespoon fresh lemon
    juice
1 small clove garlic, mashed
    Salt and pepper to taste
½ head of cauliflower

Brown bread crumbs in butter and set aside to cool. Break lettuce into bite-size pieces and put in pretty salad bowl. Combine mayonnaise, Parmesan cheese, lemon juice and garlic. Season with salt and pepper. Pour mixture over lettuce and toss well. Top with bread crumbs; don't toss. Grate cauliflower and sprinkle over bread crumbs. Serve immediately without tossing.

Susan Manlin Katzman Free-lance writer / St. Louis, Missouri

MOLDED GAZPACHO SALAD

8 to 10 servings

When I entertain with a buffet, I like to include this molded gazpacho salad because it is easier to serve than a soup course.

2 envelopes unflavored gelatin
1 can (18 ounces) tomato juice
½ cup lemon juice
½ teaspoon hot pepper sauce
2 small cloves garlic, minced
1 medium onion, grated
½ teaspoon salt
1 large green pepper, finely chopped
1 large cucumber, peeled, seeded and finely chopped
2 medium tomatoes, peeled and chopped

Sprinkle gelatin over tomato juice in small saucepan and let stand for 5 minutes to soften. Place over low heat and stir constantly until gelatin is dissolved. Cool.

Combine lemon juice, hot pepper sauce, garlic, onion and salt in mixing bowl. Add tomato-gelatin mixture and mix well. Chill until slightly thickened, stirring occasionally.

Stir in green pepper, cucumber and tomato. Turn into lightly oiled 6-cup mold and chill until set.

Christine Arpe Gang
The Commercial Appeal / Memphis, Tennessee

NANA'S CUCUMBERS

4 to 6 servings

This is an old family recipe, similar to, but not exactly like, many other cucumber salad recipes. The difference lies in the onion rings and copious amounts of freshly ground black pepper.

3 cucumbers
1 medium white onion
White vinegar
Salt and sugar to taste
Freshly ground black pepper

Slice cucumbers paper thin (peeling or not as you wish). Slice onion into rings.

Place cucumber in clean dish towel; roll towel and squeeze — hard. Try to remove as much moisture from cucumbers as you can.

Place squeezed cucumbers in bowl; add onion rings. Cover with vinegar to which small amount of cold water and hint of sugar have been added. Add salt. Sprinkle freely with pepper.

Refrigerate and let stand several hours—the colder the better.

Note: This makes a wonderful accompaniment for cold meats.

Janice Okun *Buffalo News* / Buffalo, New York

SOUTHWEST SALAD
10 to 12 servings

This is an unusual approach to ordinary macaroni salad. I often take it to potluck suppers. You can substitute almost any vegetables you like. Best of all, it can be made several days in advance.

1 pound small shell macaroni, cooked al dente and drained
¾ cup red wine vinegar
¼ cup vegetable oil
1 cup sliced celery
½ cup chopped green pepper
6 green onions, sliced (with green tops)
¼ teaspoon Worcestershire sauce
Several dashes hot pepper sauce
2 to 3 tablespoons chopped green chilies
Salt and pepper to taste
1 can (16 ounces) garbanzo beans, drained
1 can (12 ounces) corn, drained
½ cup chopped black olives
⅓ cup mayonnaise (approx.)

Put cooked macaroni in large salad bowl. Pour vinegar over macaroni and let stand while preparing other ingredients. Add oil, celery, green pepper, onions, Worcestershire, hot pepper sauce, chilies, salt, pepper, beans, corn, olives and mayonnaise to macaroni mixture; mix well.

Cover and refrigerate for 2 to 3 days. Taste for seasonings before serving. (There should be a suggestion of the chilies and the tart tang of vinegar, but only a minimal amount of mayonnaise.)

Jane Baker *The Phoenix Gazette* / Phoenix, Arizona

HEARTS OF PALM, ENDIVE AND AVOCADO WITH CAPER VINAIGRETTE

2 servings

1 cup drained hearts
   of palm
1 ripe avocado
6 large leaves endive

Caper Vinaigrette:
   2 tablespoons good wine
      vinegar
   ½ teaspoon coarse salt
      Few grinds black pepper
   6 tablespoons fruity
      olive oil
   1 teaspoon drained capers

Coarsely dice hearts of palm. Peel, halve, quarter and slice avocado. Combine with hearts of palm. Line two plates with endive leaves. Divide mixture in 2 even portions and form mound in center of each salad plate.

Caper Vinaigrette: As if scrambling eggs, mix vinegar, salt, pepper and olive oil in small bowl. After blending well, stir in capers.

Spoon Caper Vinaigrette sparsely over mounded salad.

Elaine Corn *The Courier-Journal* / Louisville, Kentucky

MUSTARD RING

12 servings

I knew Dorothy Doss in Dallas, Texas. Although she said she didn't like to cook, her buffets always were marvelous. My favorite memory is of a piquant mustard ring, which she served with baked ham.

4 eggs
¾ cup granulated sugar
2 tablespoons dry mustard
1 package (1 tablespoon)
   unflavored gelatin
1 tablespoon water

½ cup white vinegar
½ cup water
Dash salt
1 cup heavy cream,
   whipped

Beat eggs well. Combine sugar and dry mustard; beat into eggs. Soften gelatin in 1 tablespoon water and dissolve over low heat; add to egg mixture with vinegar and ½ cup water. Add salt.

Cook mixture in top of double boiler over simmering, not boiling, water, stirring constantly, until thickened. Cool by stirring over pan of cold water.

When mixture is cool, fold in whipped cream. Spoon mixture into oiled 1½-quart ring mold. Chill until firm.

Note: For a more piquant flavor, use 1 cup white vinegar in place of ½ cup vinegar and ½ cup water.

Nancy Millard *Muncie Star* / Muncie, Indiana

BROCCOLI SALAD

6 to 8 servings

I have served this to people who usually don't like broccoli and they've loved it.

2 bunches (2 pounds) fresh
broccoli, cut into flowerets
1 cup mayonnaise
Juice of ½ lemon
½ teaspoon anchovy paste or
to taste

1 small red onion, sliced thin
1 pound fresh mushrooms,
sliced
Freshly ground pepper to
taste

Cook broccoli in boiling water about 3 minutes and then plunge into cold water. Mix mayonnaise with lemon juice and anchovy paste. Mix drained broccoli flowerets, sliced onions (separated into rings) and mushrooms. Toss with mayonnaise mixture. Add pepper to taste.

If made in advance, let broccoli marinate in mayonnaise mixture in refrigerator, but wait until just before serving to add mushrooms and onions.

Note: Variations include using a little fresh raw spinach in addition to broccoli and adding sliced water chestnuts.

Christine Arpe Gang
The Commercial Appeal / Memphis, Tennessee

CONTINENTAL CAULIFLOWER SALAD   *8 servings*

I prefer salads that can be made ahead. This one is a great hit with guests because it's such a nice change from the usual tossed salad. I sometimes use red pepper and skip the pimiento.

4 cups thinly sliced cauliflower
½ cup coarsely chopped ripe pitted olives
1 green pepper, seeded and chopped
1 can (3¼ ounces) chopped pimiento
½ cup chopped onion

½ cup vegetable oil
3 tablespoons lemon juice
3 tablespoons red wine vinegar
1 teaspoon salt
½ teaspoon granulated sugar
¼ teaspoon pepper

Combine cauliflower, olives, green pepper, pimiento and onion in large salad bowl. Combine oil, lemon juice, vinegar, salt, sugar and pepper in small bowl; mix well. Pour dressing over vegetables. Toss to combine. Cover and refrigerate 4 hours, or overnight.

Barbara McQuade *Vancouver Sun* / Vancouver, British Columbia

PEANUT CRUNCH SALAD   *6 to 8 servings*

One of my closest friends gave this recipe to me because she knows my strong liking for peanuts. It's a good accompaniment for charcoal-cooked steaks or baked ham.

4 cups shredded cabbage
1 cup finely chopped celery
½ cup sour cream
½ cup mayonnaise
1 teaspoon salt
¼ cup chopped green onion
¼ cup chopped green pepper

½ cup chopped cucumber
1 tablespoon butter
½ cup coarsely chopped dry roasted peanuts
2 tablespoons grated Parmesan cheese

Toss cabbage and celery together. Chill. Combine sour cream, mayonnaise, salt, onion, green pepper and cucumber in small bowl. Chill.

Just before serving, melt butter in small skillet. Add peanuts and heat until lightly browned. Immediately stir in cheese.

Toss chilled vegetables with dressing. Sprinkle peanut mixture on top and serve.

Beverly Daniel *The Bellingham Herald* / Bellingham, Washington

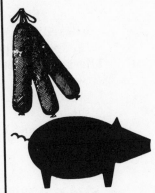

Main Courses

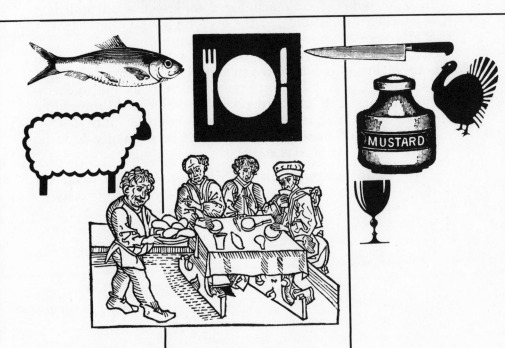

SWEET-SOUR PINEAPPLE CHICKEN   *approx. 4 servings*

Sweet-sour recipes of all sorts rank high in popularity with readers. This is one of my favorites, and it goes together in a breeze. It makes a good company offering, too, with plenty of hot rice.

2 whole chicken breasts or 4 chicken breast halves (approx. 1¾ pounds)
1 large onion, cut in thin wedges
1 green pepper, cut in ¾-inch squares
4 tablespoons vegetable oil, divided

2 tablespoons vinegar
1 tablespoon cornstarch
1 can (20 ounces) pineapple chunks in juice
2 tablespoons ketchup
2 tablespoons light brown sugar
1 large tomato, cut in eighths
Salt or soy sauce to taste
Hot cooked rice

Skin and bone chicken breasts. With sharp knife, cut chicken into 1-inch squares. Sauté onion and green pepper in 2 tablespoons hot oil in large skillet, stirring until vegetables are crisp-tender; remove to dish and set aside.

In same skillet, heat remaining 2 tablespoons oil until hot. Add chicken pieces and stir-fry over high heat until chicken cooks through and turns white, 5 to 7 minutes.

Mix vinegar and cornstarch; combine with juice drained from pineapple, ketchup and brown sugar. Stir into chicken in skillet. Cook, stirring constantly, until sauce clears, boils and thickens. Return onions and green pepper to skillet. Add pineapple chunks. Cover and cook a few more minutes, until heated through. Stir in tomato. Season with salt or soy sauce to taste. Serve over hot cooked rice.

Natalie Haughton   *Daily News / Van Nuys, California*

STEVE'S FAVORITE LASAGNA

8 servings

Whenever I ask my son, who is twenty-one and a student at Cal Poly, San Luis Obispo, what he wants when he comes home from school, it is always the same — lasagna. Now, however, he can whip it up as well as I can. He says this is better the second day.

2 pounds lean ground beef
1 medium onion, chopped
1 clove garlic, chopped
1 can (16 ounces) tomatoes
2 cans (8 ounces each) pizza
   sauce
1 teaspoon salt
½ teaspoon dried basil,
   crumbled

1 teaspoon dried oregano,
   crumbled
1 package (8 ounces) lasagna
   noodles, cooked and drained
1 cup small curd cottage
   cheese
2 cups grated Mozzarella
   cheese
½ cup grated Parmesan cheese

Brown beef, onion and garlic in large frying pan. Separate beef into chunks; pour off drippings. Add tomatoes, pizza sauce, salt, basil and oregano. Cover and cook over low heat for 20 minutes.

Reserve 1 cup meat sauce for top of lasagna. Place 1 cup sauce in bottom of greased 13x9-inch baking dish. Top with half the noodles, cover with half the remaining meat sauce, ½ cup cottage cheese, 1 cup Mozzarella cheese and ¼ cup Parmesan cheese.

Repeat with remaining noodles, meat sauce, cottage cheese and Mozzarella — no Parmesan cheese. Put reserved meat sauce over top of assembled dish. Sprinkle with remaining Parmesan cheese. Bake in 350°F. oven 30 minutes. Let stand 10 minutes to make slicing easier.

Mary Frances Phillips
San Jose Mercury and News / San Jose, California

SPINACH LASAGNA

8 servings

It pays to advertise. I first tasted this recipe at the annual potluck at my son's grade school. When I wrote about it in my Sunday column, a reader who had contributed it to the potluck volunteered to share its secret. This very rich and buttery lasagna, now a favorite in many Minnesota homes, is even better reheated.

8 ounces lasagna noodles, cooked and drained

2 packages (10 ounces each) frozen chopped spinach, cooked and drained

2 pounds cottage cheese

2 eggs

1 tablespoon chopped fresh parsley or 1 teaspoon crushed dried parsley

½ cup butter, softened

Salt, pepper and garlic powder to taste

1 pound Monterey Jack cheese, grated

1 cup grated Parmesan cheese

Cook noodles according to package directions; drain. Cook spinach according to package directions; drain. Mix cottage cheese, eggs, parsley, butter, salt, pepper and garlic powder in bowl. Grease lasagna pan or 13x9x2-inch rectangular baking dish. Place layer of noodles in pan, followed by layers of cottage cheese mixture, Monterey Jack cheese, spinach and Parmesan cheese. Repeat layers. Bake in 350°F. oven 30 minutes.

Variation: For a less buttery version, omit butter from cottage cheese mixture. After arranging layers, drizzle with about 2 tablespoons melted butter, then bake as directed.

Eleanor Ostman
St. Paul Pioneer Press and Dispatch / St. Paul, Minnesota

CHICKEN CASSEROLE

8 servings

This is an old favorite that I have made often because it serves eight generously.

¾ cup chopped celery
1 to 2 tablespoons chopped onion
1 tablespoon chopped green pepper
2 tablespoons butter or margarine
2 cups soft bread crumbs
4 cups diced cooked chicken
1 cup cooked rice
2 tablespoons chopped pimiento
1 teaspoon salt
4 eggs
1½ cups milk
1½ cups chicken broth

Mushroom Sauce:

6 tablespoons all-purpose flour
¼ cup melted butter
2 cups chicken broth
1 can (4 ounces) sliced mushrooms, drained
1 teaspoon chopped fresh parsley
1 teaspoon salt
½ teaspoon paprika
1 teaspoon lemon juice
1 cup light cream or half-and-half

Sauté celery, onion and green pepper in butter. Combine sautéed vegetables with bread crumbs, chicken, rice, pimiento and salt in large mixing bowl. Beat eggs in medium-size bowl, then add milk and broth. Stir liquid mixture into chicken mixture. Spread in lightly greased 13x9x2-inch baking dish. Bake in 350°F. oven 50 to 60 minutes. To serve, cut into squares and top with Mushroom Sauce.

Mushroom Sauce: Stir flour into melted butter in skillet. Slowly add chicken broth; stir over low heat until mixture thickens. Stir in mushrooms, parsley, salt, paprika, lemon juice and cream. Gently stir mixture over low heat until hot.

Spoon sauce over portions of Chicken Casserole.

Ellen Carlson
St. Paul Dispatch and Pioneer Press / St. Paul, Minnesota

PORK LOIN WITH SAUSAGE MOUSSE   *4 servings*

Although this recipe looks complicated, it is amazingly simple when you consider the results. It is perfect for that special occasion when you really want to impress someone. This recipe is the work of a good friend and exceptional chef, Pierre Pollin, owner of Le Titi de Paris, a French restaurant in Palatine, Ill. But you know how chefs cook: a little of this and that, cook it until it looks right. So one Saturday morning I followed Pierre around his kitchen. As he prepared the recipe, I faithfully measured what he so nonchalantly tossed into the pot. Here is the result.

7 tablespoons unsalted
   butter, divided
3 tablespoons chopped
   shallots, divided
1 tablespoon dry white wine
8 medium mushrooms,
   finely chopped
1 cup peeled and diced
   carrots
⅓ cup chopped celery
⅓ cup peeled and diced
   turnip
5 Chinese pea pods or snow
   peas, chopped
3 ounces lean ground veal,
   chilled

½ teaspoon salt
⅓ cup plus 3 tablespoons
   heavy cream
1½ ounces bulk sweet Italian
   sausage
2 teaspoons chopped chives
⅛ teaspoon dried thyme
2 boneless pork loins
   (10 ounces each), trimmed
   of all fat
1 tablespoon vegetable oil
1 cup Burgundy wine
2 cups beef stock
2 tablespoons water
   (optional)

Melt 1 tablespoon butter in medium-size skillet. Add 1 tablespoon shallots and wine. Cook over moderate heat until shallots are golden, stirring occasionally. Add chopped mushrooms and cook, continuing to stir occasionally, until mixture is dry. Remove from heat and set aside.

Melt 2 tablespoons butter in large skillet; add carrots, celery, turnip, pea pods and 1 more tablespoon shallots. Stir-fry over high heat until tender-crisp. Combine half this mixture with mushroom mixture and chill. Set remaining stir-fried vegetables aside.

Place veal and salt in food processor. Using steel blade, process for 2 seconds to combine. With machine running, add ⅓ cup cream and process until smooth and light, about 10 seconds. Add sausage and process until combined, about 5 seconds. Remove meat mixture from processor and stir into chilled mushroom mixture. Add 1 more tablespoon heavy cream, chives and thyme. Stir to combine.

Along length of each pork loin, make cut two-thirds of the way through each pork loin lengthwise; open meat flat.

Place one loin between two pieces of plastic wrap and lay on cutting board. Using flat side of meat hammer, pound to spread loin until meat is about ¼-inch thick and forms rectangle. Remove top pieces of plastic wrap and set meat aside. Repeat with other piece of meat.

Preheat oven to 350° F. Spread each piece of pork evenly with half the meat-mushroom mixture. Starting with longer edge of each piece, roll up meat. Cut each roll in half to form 4 rolls. Fold and tuck in ends of each roll as well as possible. Tie with string to create 4 neat bundles.

Melt 1 more tablespoon butter in medium-size oven-proof skillet. Add 1 tablespoon oil and heat until foamy. Add meat rolls. When meat is browned on all sides, place pan in oven and bake 15 to 20 minutes. Meanwhile, prepare sauce.

Sauce: Melt 1 more tablespoon butter in heavy saucepan; add remaining shallots and sauté until golden. Add wine. Reduce over high heat until ⅛ cup of mixture remains. Add beef stock and reduce to ¼ cup. Add reserved stir-fried vegetables. Bring mixture to boil and add remaining butter in small pieces. Stir to combine. Remove from heat. If sauce is salty, add remaining cream and water.

When meat is done, remove from oven, cover and let stand until sauce is ready (at least 5 minutes). Remove strings from meat rolls, slice rolls crosswise into ¼-inch pieces.

Note: This is good served atop sautéed cabbage, rice, noodles or mashed potatoes and garnished with sauce.

Deborah Hartz *The Daily Herald* / Arlington Heights, Illinois

STIR-FRY CHICKEN WITH BROCCOLI *4 servings*

I always was a big fan of Chinese cooking, but never tried it until my sister gave me a wok for Christmas several years ago. Since then, it's become a passion, and much of my cooking has acquired an Oriental style. While not a classic Chinese dish, this is both fun to make and tasty.

1 bunch (approx. 1 pound) fresh broccoli
Peanut oil
½ cup whole almonds, blanched or unblanched
2 to 3 cloves garlic, minced
1 to 2 teaspoons minced fresh ginger
3 scallions, minced

1 large chicken breast, skinned, boned and cut into strips
2 tablespoons soy sauce
3 tablespoons white wine, chicken broth, or water
2 tablespoons cornstarch
3 tablespoons water
Hot cooked rice

Cut flowerets off broccoli; reserve. Slice stem horizontally into 2-inch sections; then slice sections vertically into ⅛-inch strips.

Heat ¼ cup peanut oil in wok or large skillet. Stir-fry almonds until golden but not burned. Remove. Stir-fry garlic, ginger and scallions quickly in hot oil for a few minutes, then add chicken strips and cook until chicken is white all the way through. Remove.

If necessary, add another tablespoon of oil to wok and heat, then add broccoli stems. Stir-fry 2 minutes. Add soy sauce, wine and broccoli flowerets. Cover and cook 2 minutes more over moderate heat.

Dissolve cornstarch in water. Add to wok with chicken and almonds. Heat and stir until sauce thickens and everything is hot.

Serve over hot cooked rice.

Kathy Lindsley *Rochester Times-Union* / Rochester, New York

NO-NOODLE SPAGHETTI

2 servings

Mother Nature has a good ploy for the pasta-crazed dieter. It's called spaghetti squash. It can be boiled or baked, but I prefer baking. The "spaghetti" will remain a mystery until the squash is cut.

1 small spaghetti squash	2 tablespoons olive oil
1 small onion	2 ripe tomatoes, cored and
6 to 8 large fresh basil leaves	chopped
or 1 teaspoon dried crushed	Salt and pepper to taste
leaves	Grated Parmesan cheese

Preheat oven to 350°F. Place spaghetti squash on cookie sheet and bake in oven 1 hour, or until fork pierces skin with relative ease.

Meanwhile, peel and chop onion. Mince basil leaves. Heat olive oil in medium-size skillet. Add onion and basil; sauté 5 minutes. Add tomatoes and simmer another 10 minutes. Season to taste with salt and pepper. (The sauce will taste milder when mixed with the squash.) Remove from heat and set aside.

When squash is tender, remove from oven. Use pot holder or towel to hold hot squash; cut squash vertically in two. Scoop out seeds and dark yellow pulp; run fork along inside squash flesh — it will separate into spaghetti-like strands. Keep working with fork until skin is reached. Repeat with second half.

Spoon spaghetti squash into skillet with tomato sauce. Toss over moderate heat briefly to heat through. Taste and adjust seasonings, if necessary. Sprinkle about 2 tablespoons grated Parmesan cheese on each helping before serving.

Bev Bennett *Chicago Sun-Times*

SHERRIED BEEF TENDERLOIN

6 servings

If I were to choose my "trademark" recipe, it surely would be Sherried Beef Tenderloin. It was shared by a close friend, who first served it to our couples' duplicate bridge club — part of my pre-employment "other life." I have served it since for family reunions, dinner parties and any occasion where I need a foolproof, easy-to-prepare entrée.

1 beef tenderloin (2 to 3 pounds), trimmed	2 tablespoons soy sauce
¼ cup butter, divided	1 teaspoon Dijon-style mustard
¼ cup finely chopped green onion	¾ cup dry sherry
	Freshly ground pepper

Preheat oven to 400°F. Place tenderloin on rack in shallow roasting pan, folding "tail" of tenderloin under to make a uniform thickness. Rub top surface of tenderloin with 2 tablespoons softened butter. Insert meat thermometer in thickest part of meat. Place pan in lower part of oven and roast, uncovered, 20 minutes.

Meanwhile, melt remaining butter in small saucepan over moderate heat. Add onion and cook until soft. Stir in soy sauce, mustard, sherry and generous amount of pepper. Bring mixture to boil, but do not burn butter.

After meat has roasted for 20 minutes, begin basting meat with sherry sauce. Baste every 5 to 10 minutes while continuing to roast meat 20 more minutes, or until meat thermometer registers 130° to 140°F. internal temperature.

Remove tenderloin to serving platter and cover with foil to keep warm while roast rests for 10 minutes before carving. Pour pan drippings and any remaining sauce into small saucepan. Boil down sauce over high heat to desired consistency. Spoon lightly over meat.

Note: I frequently serve a Greek-style pilaf (see page 90) with the tenderloin. I also have teamed it with thin spaghetti dressed with sesame oil, soy sauce, garlic and fresh herbs and scattered with lightly sautéed pea pods.

Marge Hanley *Indianapolis News / Indianapolis, Indiana*

BEEF STEAK AND KIDNEY PIE

8 servings

Beef Steak and Kidney Pie may not be everyone's cup of tea, but I think it is the best thing I have ever put in my mouth. The origin of the recipe is unusual. When a meeting of the International Wine and Food Society was held in England a few years ago, the group went from London to Torquay. On the return trip, lunch was served aboard the train. A waiter came out of the kitchen carrying a pie. He stopped at the first table and spooned an opening into the top of the pie. Fragrant steam literally poured out. Members of the society, who had been feasting for days, almost swooned over the goodness of the pie. When I returned to the States, I wrote for the recipe, never expecting to get it. It came. I tried it on a rainy Sunday afternoon, and it was every bit as good as that one on the train.

¾ pound calf kidney (or beef liver)
Salted water
2 tablespoons all-purpose flour
1 teaspoon salt
¾ teaspoon freshly ground black pepper
2 pounds beef steak, cut into bite-size pieces
4 tablespoons butter
4 shallots, finely chopped
1 cup beef bouillon

1 bay leaf
1 teaspoon chopped fresh parsley
Pinch ground cloves
Pinch marjoram, crushed
½ pound fresh mushrooms, sliced and sautéed
Splash dry sherry or Madeira
1 tablespoon Worcestershire sauce
Pastry for 10-inch top crust

Clean and split kidney; remove fat and large tubes. Soak in salted water 1 hour. Dry and cut into ¼-inch slices. Mix flour, salt and pepper; roll kidney and beef pieces in flour mixture. Melt butter in heavy pot and sauté shallots. When shallots have taken on a little color, add beef and kidney; brown lightly, turning. Add bouillon, bay leaf, parsley, cloves and marjoram. Stir; cover and simmer 1 to 1¼ hours, or until meat is tender. Add mushrooms, sherry and Worcestershire. If liquid is too thin, thicken with smooth paste of flour and water.

Grease deep 10-inch baking dish. Place pie funnel in center. Add meat mixture and allow to cool in refrigerator.

Meanwhile, prepare pastry. Place pastry over meat, sealing pastry edges to edge of dish. Make vents in pastry to allow steam to escape. Bake in 450°F. oven 8 to 10 minutes; lower heat to 375° and continue baking 15 minutes, or until crust is golden.

Elizabeth Sparks
Winston-Salem Journal / Winston-Salem, North Carolina

TRAIL RIDE EGGS
(Huevos Mexicanos)

The spring roundup of range cattle was a tradition in Texas for nearly a hundred years. Nowadays, the annual Rodeo and Stock Show revives memories of the good old days in San Antonio, Fort Worth and other Texas cities. Early in February, groups of trail riders set out a week or so in advance from surrounding areas and converge on San Antonio. This typical campfire breakfast would be easy to reproduce anywhere.

2 tablespoons butter or margarine
4 eggs, lightly beaten
Salt to taste
1 whole canned green chili, sliced

1 tomato, peeled, seeded and chopped (optional)
½ cup grated sharp Cheddar cheese

Melt butter in skillet. Add eggs and scramble, making certain eggs remain moist. Add salt to taste. Add sliced green chili and toss lightly with eggs. If using tomato, add after green chili. Stir in gently just to heat through. Remove to serving plate and top with grated cheese.

Billie Bledsoe
San Antonio Express and News / San Antonio, Texas

POACHED COD FILLETS

This cod recipe is dedicated to those who hate cod. The combination of butter and wine tends to tone down the strong fish flavor. This is one of those "no time to cook" recipes.

⅓ cup butter
1 pound cod fillets
1 to 1¼ cups white wine

¾ cup seasoned bread crumbs
Chopped fresh parsley for garnish

Melt butter in skillet just large enough to hold fillets. Add fish; add enough wine to almost cover fillets. Sprinkle bread crumbs over fillets. Cover and cook over medium-low heat until fish flakes easily. Sprinkle with chopped parsley.

Linda Giuca *The Hartford Courant / Hartford, Connecticut*

PAELLA

I like to serve paella buffet-style for a crowd. It feeds a big group and seems more special than most chicken and rice casseroles.

¼ cup olive oil
1 pound chicken breasts, boned and cut into large pieces
1 pound chicken thighs, boned
1 meaty pork chop, diced
1 medium onion, sliced
1 clove garlic, chopped
4 cups chicken broth or stock
1½ cups uncooked rice (preferably Spanish or Italian rice)
1 can (16 ounces) tomatoes, undrained

2 teaspoons salt
1 tablespoon paprika
½ teaspoon pepper
⅛ teaspoon saffron
½ teaspoon cayenne
1 pound cleaned and peeled raw shrimp
2 pounds cleaned mussels or clams
1 package (10 ounces) frozen peas
1 jar (2 ounces) sliced pimientos

Heat oil in Dutch oven or large paella pan until hot. Brown chicken and pork about 15 minutes. Remove meat from pan.

Preheat oven to 350°F. Add onion and garlic to fat in pan and cook until onion is tender. Drain fat. Stir in chicken broth, rice, tomatoes, salt, paprika, pepper, saffron and cayenne. Add chicken and pork to rice mixture and heat to boiling. Bake uncovered in oven 20 minutes.

Remove from oven, stir in shrimp and tuck mussels into rice with opening-side up. Stir in peas. Bake 10 to 15 minutes longer, or until mussels open and shrimp are cooked. Garnish with pimiento.

Christine Arpe Gang
The Commercial Appeal / Memphis, Tennessee

CRAB MEAT CASSEROLE

4 to 6 servings

1 can (20 ounces) artichoke
hearts, drained
1 pound crab meat
½ pound fresh mushrooms,
sautéed in butter
¼ cup butter
2½ tablespoons all-purpose
flour
1 cup light cream or half-
and-half

½ teaspoon salt
1 teaspoon Worcestershire
sauce
¼ cup medium-dry sherry
Paprika, cayenne and
black pepper to taste
¼ cup grated Parmesan
cheese

Place artichokes in bottom of 9-inch square baking dish. Spread on layer of crab meat. Add layer of sautéed mushrooms. Melt butter in saucepan. Add flour, cream, salt, Worcestershire, sherry, paprika, cayenne and black pepper, one at a time, stirring well after each addition, to form smooth sauce. Pour sauce over artichokes, crab and mushroom layers. Top with Parmesan cheese. Bake in 350°F. oven 20 minutes.

Anne Byrn Phillips
The Atlanta Journal-Constitution / Atlanta, Georgia

CHICKEN SAUTE WITH ARTICHOKES

4 servings

This recipe is my version of a dish that was created in San Francisco many years ago and called by a much more glamorous name.

1 frying chicken (3 pounds),
cut in serving pieces
Salt and pepper to taste
2 tablespoons butter
2 tablespoons olive oil
4 fresh medium artichokes

1 clove garlic
1½ cups dry white wine
2 egg yolks
1 cup heavy cream
1 teaspoon lemon juice

Dust chicken pieces lightly with salt and pepper; sauté in butter and oil in heavy skillet just until evenly golden brown all over.

Cut artichokes in quarters, lengthwise, and remove chokes and any tough outer leaves. Cut off tops of artichokes about two-thirds of way down and discard.

When chicken is browned, add artichoke pieces and garlic. Stir a few times to start artichokes cooking. Add wine, cover pan and cook very slowly until artichokes and chicken are tender, about 30 minutes. Remove artichokes and chicken pieces from pan and keep warm. Discard garlic clove.

Beat egg yolks with cream. Add a little hot liquid in pan to egg mixture, then add mixture to pan, stirring constantly with wire whisk, not allowing to boil but just to heat and thicken sauce. Stir in lemon juice quickly and correct seasoning, if necessary. Pour sauce over chicken and artichokes and serve immediately.

Jane Benet *San Francisco Chronicle*

BAKED CHICKEN BREASTS
WITH GRUYERE AND MUSHROOMS   *4 servings*

The first "company dish" I learned when I moved into my first apartment is still a favorite. It can be made ahead, then warmed to serving temperature while cocktails are being served. I serve this recipe with rice pilaf, fresh asparagus with lemon butter, and a green salad with a spiced peach half for garnish.

2 to 3 chicken breasts, boned and skinned	½ pound fresh mushrooms, sliced
4 eggs, well beaten	4 ounces Gruyère cheese, shredded
½ teaspoon salt	1 cup chicken stock
1 cup fine bread crumbs	Juice of 1 lemon
8 tablespoons butter	

Cut boned breasts into strips. Marinate in egg and salt mixture for 1 hour. Roll chicken in bread crumbs to coat. Brown lightly in butter in small pan. Transfer to 1½-quart casserole. Slice mushrooms over chicken. Sprinkle cheese over mushrooms. Pour chicken stock over all. Bake in 350°F. oven 30 minutes, or until heated through. Pour fresh lemon juice over casserole just before serving.

Pat Hanna Kuehl *Rocky Mountain News / Denver, Colorado*

SAFFRON MUSSELS

approx. 6 servings

Fresh mussels are at their best when scrubbed, steamed in a small amount of water, then served in the shell with melted butter and garlic for dipping, much like steamed clams. They are also good cold, having been stuffed with a well-seasoned mixture, such as in this recipe.

1 small onion, chopped
1 leek, chopped
3 tablespoons olive oil
1 tomato, peeled and seeded
2 garlic cloves

1 sprig fresh thyme, or ¼ teaspoon dried thyme, crumbled
½ bay leaf
1 teaspoon powdered saffron
1 cup water
36 mussels

Sauté chopped onion and leek in oil in large pot. Add tomato, garlic, thyme, bay leaf, saffron and water. Cook slowly until almost all liquid has evaporated.

Add mussels which have been scrubbed and washed. Cook until shells open, from 12 to 15 minutes. Remove and discard one half shell of each mussel. Add ½ teaspoon sauce to each mussel. Chill thoroughly.

Phyllis Hanes *The Christian Science Monitor*

BRUNCH SOUFFLE

8 servings

This recipe finds its way to many a brunch party in northwestern Ohio because it not only can, but must, be made the night before.

1 pound mild pork sausage
6 eggs
2 cups milk
1 teaspoon salt, or to taste

1 tablespoon dry mustard
6 slices white bread, cubed
(crusts removed, if desired)
1 cup grated Cheddar cheese

Brown sausage; drain and cool. Crumble sausage into bowl.

Beat eggs in another bowl and add milk, salt, mustard and bread cubes; mix well. Add cheese and sausage; mix again. Spoon into 12x8x2-inch glass baking dish. Cover and refrigerate overnight.

Remove dish from refrigerator. Bake in 350°F. oven 45 minutes, or until egg mixture is set. Cut into squares to serve.

Mary Alice Powell *The Blade / Toledo, Ohio*

PATE AMERICAIN

The French call it pâté. We call it meat loaf — ugh!

Filling:
- 1 garlic clove, minced
- 1 tiny onion, minced
- 8 mushrooms, coarsely chopped
- 1 tablespoon vegetable oil
- 1½ pounds ground beef
- ½ pound ground pork
- ½ pound bulk sausage
- 1½ cups fresh bread crumbs
- 2 eggs
- 2 teaspoons salt
- 4 leaves fresh sage, minced, or ½ teaspoon dried sage
- 1 teaspoon summer savory
- 1 teaspoon minced fresh thyme or ½ teaspoon dried thyme
- 2 tablespoons chopped fresh parsley
- ½ teaspoon ground cumin
- ½ teaspoon black pepper

Dough:
- 10 sheets phyllo dough
- ½ cup butter, melted
- ¾ cup fresh bread crumbs

Filling: Sauté garlic, onion and mushrooms in oil until softened. Mash beef, pork and sausage with bread crumbs, eggs, salt, sage, savory, thyme, parsley, cumin and pepper. Add sautéed vegetables. Continue mashing until mixture is very smooth.

Mound mixture in round cake pan, 8 or 9 inches in diameter. Bake in 350°F. oven 1 hour. Drain off as much fat as possible. Cool. Drain again. Leave in pan until ready to wrap with dough.

Dough: Lay first sheet of phyllo dough on buttered cookie sheet. Stroke butter on dough with pastry brush; dust with bread crumbs. Lay next sheet of phyllo over, but slightly askew, as if forming a pinwheel. Repeat with butter and bread crumbs. Continue layering phyllo in pinwheel design with butter and bread crumbs until all sheets are used.

Unmold meat. Place in center of dough. Carefully pull up ends of dough to form topknot or flower design. Generously brush ends and surface with butter. Finish baking, on cookie sheet, in 375°F. oven 20 to 30 minutes, or until crust is golden. Slice after cooling.

Elaine Corn *The Courier-Journal* / Louisville, Kentucky

CHICKEN SALAD WITH CHAMPAGNE DRESSING

8 to 12 servings

I have written a number of articles on champagne for wedding, anniversary and holiday parties. And champagne is a personal favorite. But I was surprised to read at the end of a champagne story in our magazine section, "Carol Brock is a food reporter for the Daily News and after five each evening enjoys a glass of champagne." This recipe for chicken salad was a tremendous hit when I developed it in the newspaper test kitchen for one of those champagne features. But there was no space for it in the story. As so often happens, once an item gets off the track it never appears elsewhere. And that's a pity.

1 roasting chicken
  (5½ pounds)
1 teaspoon salt
1 large onion, sliced
1 large bunch scallions
¾ cup minced celery
1 cup mayonnaise
¼ cup heavy cream
1 teaspoon salt

½ teaspoon coarse pepper
1 teaspoon dried
  tarragon (optional)
½ cup champagne
Toasted sliced almonds
  for garnish
1 bunch green grapes
  for garnish

The day before serving, put chicken in kettle or Dutch oven. Add water to cover, 1 teaspoon salt and onion. Bring to boil, then lower heat and simmer 65 minutes, or until fork tender. Let chicken cool in broth. Discard skin and bones; cut meat into large pieces. Place chicken in bowl and cover with a bit of broth.

Slice white part of scallions to equal 1 cup. Combine sliced scallions with celery, mayonnaise, cream, 1 teaspoon salt, pepper, tarragon and champagne. Drain broth off chicken; add scallion mixture to drained chicken. Toss well and chill, covered, overnight.

To serve, arrange on platter and sprinkle with almonds. Surround with grapes.

Carol Brock *Daily News* / New York, New York

PORTUGUESE PORK AND CLAMS

8 servings

James Beard had this at my house the first time I made it. I wasn't very pleased with the results: The clams were tough and dry and the entrée didn't have enough flavor. Beard suggested cooking the clams separately and adding mussels for contrast. He also thought adding some cumin might be a good idea. This version is the result.

3 cups dry white wine
5 teaspoons Hungarian paprika
½ teaspoon salt (optional)
⅛ teaspoon freshly ground black pepper
3 medium cloves garlic, minced
3 small bay leaves
3 pounds lean boneless pork, cut in ½-inch cubes
¼ cup vegetable oil
3 medium onions, sliced

2 tomatoes, seeded and chopped
3 large cloves garlic, pressed
1 piece (2 inches) dried red chili, seeds removed and broken up
1½ teaspoons ground cumin
24 small clams (cherrystone) and/or mussels, soaked and scrubbed
⅓ cup minced fresh coriander (cilantro) leaves
¼ cup chopped fresh parsley
1 lemon, cut into 8 wedges

Combine wine, paprika, salt, pepper, minced garlic and bay leaves; mix well. Add pork and marinate in mixture for 8 hours or overnight. Mix occasionally.

Drain pork and reserve marinade, discarding bay leaves. Heat oil in large skillet. Sauté onion and pork over high heat in oil until onions are soft and pork is brown. Add tomatoes, pressed garlic cloves, chili, cumin and reserved marinade. Cover and simmer until pork is tender, about 1 hour.

When pork is tender, steam clams and mussels 8 minutes, or until shells open. (Discard any shells which do not open.) Spoon pork into serving dish; arrange clams and mussels on top. Sprinkle with coriander and parsley. Garnish with lemon wedges.

Note: If fresh coriander is not available, add 1 teaspoon ground coriander to pork mixture before simmering. Garnish with ½ cup chopped fresh parsley instead of ¼ cup.

Marian Burros *The New York Times*

MYSTERY CHICKEN

6 to 8 servings

This rich and elegant dish is easy to prepare and can be made ahead of time. It's a company favorite at our house.

4 thin slices baked ham, cut in half
4 whole chicken breasts, split, boned and skinned
1 can (10¾ ounces) condensed cream of mushroom soup, undiluted

1 cup sour cream
½ cup Irish Mist liqueur
1 cup sliced fresh mushrooms
Hot cooked brown or wild rice

Preheat oven to 300°F. Arrange slices of ham in 8x12-inch baking dish. Place one half chicken breast on each slice of ham. Mix soup, sour cream, liqueur and mushrooms well. Spoon over chicken, covering completely. Bake in oven 1½ hours.

Serve with brown or wild rice.

Diane Wiggins *St. Louis Globe-Democrat* / St. Louis, Missouri

CHEESE IN A CHICKEN POCKET

4 servings

Chicken is a favorite at our house partly because it lends itself so well to experimentation. My husband came up with this delicious rendition.

2 whole chicken breasts, split and boned with skin left on
½ cup diced Mozzarella cheese

⅓ cup bread crumbs made from Italian or French bread
5 tablespoons unsalted butter
4 teaspoons diced cooked ham

Cut pocket in each chicken piece and stuff generously with cheese. Tuck and shape each piece until you have small loaf with skin on top. Wrap individually in foil and steam 20 minutes. Remove foil and discard skin from chicken.

Toast bread crumbs until golden in 2 tablespoons melted butter; set aside. Heat ham in remaining butter. Dress chicken with bread crumbs and ham. Serve immediately.

Evelyn Wavpotich
Island Packet / Hilton Head Island, South Carolina

TURKEY DIVAN
4 generous servings

More years ago than I like to remember, before World II, I lived in New York City. One of my mother's and my favorite restaurants for lunch was the Divan Parisienne on either 44th or 45th Street in Manhattan. Whether Turkey (or Chicken) Divan was an original dish or not for the midtown restaurant, I don't know, but it was delicious. Since that time I have seen many versions of it, most of them using mushroom soup and asparagus in place of broccoli, but the one that follows is as close to the one the restaurant served as I can remember from my teen-age years. It is a good company dish because everything except the baking can be done ahead of time. Fresh broccoli is better than frozen in this particular casserole.

2 packages (10 ounces each) frozen broccoli spears or one large bunch fresh broccoli, cooked
4 tablespoons melted butter, divided
4 ounces dry sherry, divided
1 pound (approx.) cooked turkey,* sliced, preferably white meat only
Freshly grated Parmesan cheese

White Sauce: *2 cups*
6 tablespoons butter
6 tablespoons all-purpose flour
2 cups milk
Salt and white pepper to taste
Dash Worcestershire sauce (optional)

*Chicken may be substituted for turkey.

White Sauce: Melt butter in saucepan over low heat. Add flour and blend 3 to 5 minutes. Slowly stir in milk. Cook and stir with wire whisk or wooden spoon until thickened and smooth. Season with salt and white pepper to taste, and Worcestershire, if desired.

Casserole:
Preheat oven to 400°F.
Cover bottom of 9x12-inch casserole with cooked broccoli. Drizzle over it half the melted butter and half the sherry. Cover broccoli generously with sliced turkey or chicken. Drizzle remaining butter and sherry over meat. Top with white sauce, spreading to edge of casserole to seal. Top with Parmesan cheese. Bake in oven 20 to 25 minutes, or until sauce is bubbly and browned.

Jean Thwaite
The Atlanta Journal-Constitution / Atlanta, Georgia

MAGGIE STEFFEN'S TURKEY POT PIE *6 servings*

I remember with special delight the Christmas food at my grandmother's farm. Granny was a wonderful cook who believed everything she served during the holidays should be like Christmas itself, rich and sumptuous. By Christmas Eve, when we arrived for our family reunion, her house bulged with holiday treats. For me, though, the best dishes came at noon on Christmas Day, after the presents and before the journey home. We would sit in the parlor around a fire and feast on hot, yeasty pan rolls, ice-cold cranberry relish and succulent turkey pot pie freshly made from Christmas Eve's turkey. The pie bubbled with chunks of sweet home-grown vegetables and generous mouthfuls of tender turkey. I found this recipe while sorting through Granny's "holiday box," and I offer it in tribute to a lovely woman and an extraordinary cook.

5¼ cups chicken broth
 3 carrots, pared and cut into 1-inch pieces
 1 small onion, diced
 ¼ pound fresh mushrooms, sliced
 ⅔ cup frozen peas, thawed
 ¾ cup butter
 ⅔ cup all-purpose flour
   Salt and pepper to taste
 4 cups cooked turkey, cut into large, bite-size pieces

Crust:
 1 cup all-purpose flour
 ½ teaspoon salt
 7 tablespoons solid shortening
 3 tablespoons ice water

 1 egg yolk
 1 tablespoon light cream or milk

Bring chicken broth to boil in large saucepan. Add carrots and onion and cook until almost tender. Add mushrooms and peas; cook 5 minutes. Remove vegetables from broth. Reserve vegetables. Strain broth and set 4 cups aside.

Melt butter and whisk in flour. Cook, stirring constantly, 2 minutes. Gradually whisk in reserved hot chicken broth. Cook until mixture thickens and bubbles 1 minute. Season to taste with salt and pepper.

Spoon ¼-inch layer of sauce into bottom of 2-quart baking dish. Place same amount of sauce in small bowl and set aside. Mix turkey, vegetables and remaining sauce. Put turkey mixture in baking dish and cover with reserved sauce. Refrigerate until cool.

Crust: Mix flour and salt. Add shortening and mix lightly with fingertips to form coarse crumbs. Add water, 1 tablespoon at a time, and mix with fork until pastry is moist enough to hold together. Knead on lightly floured surface until dough is smooth, about 20 strokes. Wrap in wax paper and chill 1 hour.

Preheat oven to 400°F. Roll pie crust dough about ¼-inch thick. Cut dough to fit top of baking dish, allowing for 1-inch overhang. Fit dough over turkey filling, tucking edges under. Press dough against side of dish with fork to seal. Cut 1½-inch circle from center of dough as steam vent. If you like, decorate top of pie with excess dough. (Stick decorations on dough with water.) Combine egg yolk and cream; brush top of pie. Bake in oven 40 minutes, or until crust is brown and filling is bubbly.

Susan Manlin Katzman Free-lance writer / St. Louis, Missouri

BROILED SHRIMP WITH ROSEMARY   *2 servings*

1 cup olive oil
6 cloves garlic, minced
1 tablespoon dried rosemary
    or 2 tablespoons fresh
    rosemary
¼ teaspoon cayenne
¼ cup finely minced fresh
    parsley

1 cup fresh lemon juice
1 tablespoon freshly grated
    lemon rind
1 dozen raw jumbo shrimp,
    shelled and deveined (10 to
    15 per pound)

Mix oil, garlic, rosemary, cayenne, parsley, lemon juice and rind in nonmetallic bowl. Add shrimp. Cover and refrigerate 4 to 24 hours. Stir occasionally.

Remove shrimp from marinade. Broil as close to heat source as possible about 4 minutes per side. Baste shrimp with marinade once during cooking. Serve at once, or refrigerate and serve cold.

Note: As a first course, this will serve 4 to 6.

Anne Byrn Phillips
The Atlanta Journal-Constitution / Atlanta, Georgia

BAY SCALLOPS WITH FRESH CORIANDER

6 servings

½ cup (approx.) all-purpose flour
Salt and freshly ground white pepper to taste
2 pounds bay scallops or sea scallops, quartered, washed, drained and dried thoroughly
¼ cup peanut oil

¾ cup unsalted butter, cut into small pieces, divided
1½ cups dry white wine
¼ cup chopped fresh coriander (cilantro) leaves
¼ cup chopped fresh parsley
¼ cup thinly sliced scallion rings

Mix flour, salt and pepper together on plate or in bowl. Dust scallops lightly with mixture and set aside.

Heat oil and 2 tablespoons butter in large skillet. Add scallops and sauté for 2 or 3 minutes over medium-high heat, stirring frequently. Remove from pan and pour off excess fat.

Add wine and deglaze pan by scraping up browned bits on bottom with wooden spoon. Bring to boil and whisk in remaining butter, one small piece at a time. Return scallops to pan over medium-high heat and add coriander, parsley and scallions. Cook 1 to 2 minutes longer, or just until scallops are heated through. (Do not overcook or sauce will become gluey.) Adjust seasonings. (If sauce begins to separate, add a few drops of wine to hold it.)

Marian Burros *The New York Times*

RAVE-BRINGING BEEF RIBS

4 servings

I invented this recipe when I first noticed beef plate ribs (the steer's spare ribs) in my supermarket. They were very inexpensive and I couldn't pass them up. But there weren't any recipes for them in any of my cookbooks. Of course, beef plate ribs can be barbecued just like pork spare ribs, but I wanted something without gooey, sweet tomato sauce.

4 to 5 pounds beef plate ribs
1 cup double-strength coffee
1 tablespoon liquid smoke
1 tablespoon light brown sugar
1 tablespoon Worcestershire sauce

Preheat oven to 350°F.

Score ribs on both sides between bones, or cut all the way through. Lay ribs in bottom of roasting pan with tight-fitting lid.

Combine coffee, liquid smoke, sugar and Worcestershire; pour over ribs. Cover and bake in oven 2 hours, or until ribs are almost tender. Remove cover and continue baking until ribs are browned and tender, another 20 minutes or so. Ribs may be turned over after 10 minutes to brown other side.

Deni Hamilton *The Courier-Journal* / Louisville, Kentucky

SWEET-SOUR POT ROAST

6 servings

The flavor of the meat in this recipe is extraordinarily good. It also makes delicious leftovers.

1 tablespoon solid shortening
4 pounds chuck or rump beef roast
2 onions, sliced
¼ teaspoon pepper
¼ teaspoon ground cloves
¼ cup honey
¼ cup granulated sugar
Juice of 2 lemons
1 teaspoon salt or to taste

Heat shortening in Dutch oven or heavy skillet with tight-fitting lid. Add meat and onions; brown, turning frequently. Add pepper, cloves, honey, sugar, lemon juice and salt. Cover tightly. Simmer slowly over low heat or bake in oven at 300°F. 3 to 3½ hours, until meat is tender.

Charlotte Hansen
The Jamestown Sun / Jamestown, North Dakota

BAKED BOSTON BLUEFISH

6 servings

6 bluefish fillets
  Salt and pepper to taste
1 teaspoon dried tarragon
1 teaspoon dried thyme

1 teaspoon dried oregano
1½ teaspoons chopped fresh
  parsley
  Olive oil

Sprinkle fish with salt and pepper to taste and place in baking dish. Combine tarragon, thyme, oregano and parsley; sprinkle over fish. Sprinkle all with olive oil. Bake in 350°F. oven 20 minutes, or until fish flakes easily with fork.

Phyllis Hanes *The Christian Science Monitor*

BUDGET BEEF BURGUNDY

4 to 6 servings

This recipe is an easy one that I frequently give to those who ask me, "What can I cook for company?" It has really been a lifesaver for me, too. There are just four ingredients, but you can add ingredients to create your own variations. Prepared several days ahead, it gains flavor.

1 envelope dry onion soup
  mix
1 cup red wine
1 can (10¾ ounces)
  condensed golden
  mushroom soup*
*Do not use cream of mushroom soup.

2 pounds beef cubes, fat
  removed

Preheat oven to 350°F. Combine soup mix, wine, soup and beef in 2-quart baking dish. Bake, covered, in oven 1 hour. If mixture is runny, remove cover 30 minutes before end of cooking time and allow to cook down.

Serve with buttered noodles sprinkled with poppy seeds, or baked potato or just toast.

Note: This dish freezes well.

Ruth Gray *St. Petersburg Times / St. Petersburg, Florida*

LAKE GEORGE SHRIMP

A veterinarian who fishes as a hobby introduced me to this interesting recipe. It makes use of perch, a common fish in the lakes and ponds east of the Rockies. It's called Lake George Shrimp because, after being cooked, the perch resembles the seafaring crustacean both in taste and appearance.

2 dozen perch fillets, cut in ½ x 3-inch strips 4 quarts boiling water	¼ cup salt Ice water Cocktail sauce

Put perch strips into sieve or colander and immerse in boiling water to which salt has been added. Allow strips to boil about 3 minutes, or until they become white and flaky and curl up.

Lift fish-filled sieve out of water and place immediately in an ice water bath. Leave until fish has cooled.

Arrange cooled fish pieces on platter and serve with cocktail sauce.

Note: The fish also is good served warm, with tartar sauce. When warm, it tastes remarkably like lobster.

Bass, pike, pickerel or blue gill can be used in place of perch.

The large amount of salt is necessary to give shrimp-like flavor.

Kingsley Belle *The Chronicle* / Glens Falls, New York

PORK SATAY

4 servings

I learned how to make this Indonesian recipe from my Swiss aunt.

2 tablespoons smooth peanut
butter
2 tablespoons ground
coriander
⅛ teaspoon cayenne
¼ teaspoon freshly ground
black pepper
1 clove garlic, chopped

2 tablespoons finely
chopped onion
1 teaspoon salt
1 tablespoon light brown
sugar
3 tablespoons lemon juice
¼ cup soy sauce
1½ pounds lean pork
Olive oil or melted butter

Mix peanut butter, coriander, cayenne, black pepper, garlic, onion, salt, sugar, lemon juice and soy sauce in bowl to make marinade. Cut pork into cubes and toss with marinade. Cover bowl with plastic wrap and refrigerate all day or overnight.

Skewer meat and broil over charcoal fire 20 to 25 minutes or bake in oven at 375°F. about 40 minutes. Baste often with olive oil or butter.

Note: This goes well with a rice pilaf and spinach salad.

Nancy Pappas *The Louisville Times* / Louisville, Kentucky

BROILED SEA BASS WITH FENNEL BUTTER

4 servings

¼ cup butter, melted
3 tablespoons chopped fresh
fennel or 2 tablespoons
fennel seeds, crushed
¼ teaspoon salt
1 tablespoon fresh lemon
juice

Freshly ground pepper
1 sea bass or other fish (2 to
2½ pounds), cleaned and
ready to cook
Parsley and lemon for
garnish

Combine butter with fennel, salt, lemon juice and freshly ground pepper. Rinse fish and pat dry. Brush inside and out with fennel butter. (Some will be left for basting.)

Place on oiled broiler rack. Broil 8 to 10 minutes on each side, about 5 inches from heat. Baste several times with fennel butter. Garnish with parsley and lemon.

Note: If you have fresh fennel, you may also put several whole sprigs of washed fennel into the cavity of the fish. Fresh dill weed may be substituted for fennel.

Rice pilaf is an excellent accompaniment.

Donna Lee
The Providence Journal and Bulletin / Providence, Rhode Island

OVEN-FRIED CHICKEN   *6 servings*

For baseball or football games, we like to pack up oven-fried chicken, a fresh fruit salad, rolls and butter and a bottle of white California wine — Riesling or Gewurztraminer.

6 chicken breasts, split in half
⅓ cup corn flake crumbs
2 teaspoons salt
2 teaspoons paprika
¾ teaspoon dried dill weed
2 teaspoons chopped fresh thyme leaves or ¼ teaspoon dried thyme, crumbled
2 tablespoons butter
2 tablespoons vegetable oil
¾ cup Riesling or Chenin Blanc

Preheat oven to 400°F. Toss chicken pieces with crumbs, salt, paprika, dill and thyme in paper or plastic bag. Melt butter with oil and put in shallow glass baking pan. Arrange seasoned chicken, skin-side down, in single layer in pan. Bake, uncovered, in oven 30 minutes. Turn chicken, add wine to pan and continue baking until chicken is tender, about 25 or 30 minutes longer. Serve warm, or refrigerate and serve cold.

Note: Potato salad goes especially well with this.

Mary Frances Phillips
San Jose Mercury and News / San Jose, California

MARINATED BROILED CHICKEN   *4 servings*

This is probably my favorite chicken recipe. Broiled chicken is easy and low in calories, and this marinade, made from things usually found around the kitchen, gives it a real tang. The recipe is even better (if possible) when charcoal grilled.

½ cup dry white wine
½ cup soy sauce
½ cup orange juice
¼ teaspoon ground ginger

¼ teaspoon garlic powder
1 frying chicken (2 to 3 pounds), cut up
Vegetable oil

Combine wine, soy sauce, orange juice, ginger and garlic powder; mix well. Pour over chicken pieces in a ceramic or glass bowl. Turn pieces every 30 minutes for 2 hours in refrigerator. Remove chicken and pat dry.

Brush chicken well with vegetable oil and broil or grill about 4 inches from heat source until done, turning when browned on each side. Total cooking time should be about 45 minutes.

Note: Marinade can be refrigerated in a closed jar and kept for reuse within a week or two.

Deni Hamilton *The Courier-Journal* / Louisville, Kentucky

WINE-ROASTED VENISON BACKSTRAP   *4 to 6 servings*

Venison backstrap (loin) (2 to 3 pounds)
Slivers of garlic
Red wine
Seeded canned jalapeno peppers, sliced

Bacon
Beef broth
Flour (optional)
Salt and pepper to taste

Stud backstrap with garlic. Marinate overnight in red wine.

Remove backstrap from refrigerator. Pour off wine and dry meat. Place in roasting pan and arrange sliced peppers over backstrap and wrap with bacon, securing with toothpicks or string. Roast in 325°F. oven 25 to 30 minutes per pound to medium doneness.

Remove venison and discard bacon and peppers. Place back strap on serving platter and keep warm. Deglaze roasting pa with a little additional red wine and beef broth. Cook pan juices over high heat to reduce by half. If desired, thicken gravy slight-with flour. Adjust seasoning with salt and pepper.

Dotty Griffith *The Dallas Morning News* / Dallas, Texas

RED DEVIL FRANKS

8 to 10 servings

This is an ordinary recipe, but it's great when raising a bunch of hungry kids.

1 cup finely chopped onion	1½ tablespoons prepared mustard
2 cloves garlic, minced	
4 tablespoons margarine	1½ teaspoons granulated sugar
½ teaspoon salt	
⅛ teaspoon pepper	½ cup chili sauce
1½ tablespoons Worcester-shire sauce	1 pound frankfurters (8 to 10)
	Frankfurter buns (8 to 10)

Cook onion and garlic in margarine over low heat until onion is tender, about 10 minutes. Stir frequently. Add salt, pepper, Worcestershire, mustard, sugar and chili sauce. Continue heating until flavors are well blended, about 5 minutes.

Split frankfurters lengthwise and arrange split-side up in shallow pan. Spoon sauce over frankfurters and heat under broiler until frankfurters are hot and sauce is bubbly, 3 to 5 minutes.

Serve hot on split, toasted frankfurter buns. Spoon on extra sauce.

Bernie Arnold *Nashville Banner* / Nashville, Tennessee

GERMAN-STYLE VENISON ROAST   *4 to 8 servings*

My husband is a hunter. He hunts everything — deer, wild turkey, rabbits, ducks, squirrel, elk, bear, antelope, quail. And everything he hunts, we eat. When my family comes to visit, they always examine the main course suspiciously and ask if it is something weird. I've converted even the most die-hard venison-haters with this recipe. They always ask for seconds. A German couple shared this recipe with me.

1 roast of venison (4 to 5 pounds)	1 cup hot water
6 strips bacon	½ cup sour cream
¾ cup butter	½ cup all-purpose flour
Salt and pepper to taste	½ cup half-and-half or light cream

Lard well-trimmed roast with bacon strips. Melt butter in skillet. Brown meat lightly on all sides. Sprinkle generously with salt and pepper. Place meat in roasting pan along with melted butter. (Layer the bacon over the roast at this point instead of larding it, if you prefer.) Rinse skillet with 1 cup hot water and pour over meat. Cover and bake in 350°F. oven 2 to 2½ hours. Baste with juices several times during cooking. About 30 minutes before it is done, remove roast from oven and make gravy.

Gravy: Combine sour cream, flour and half-and-half; stir until smooth. Pour mixture into meat juices in pan. (It may be necessary to remove meat in order to stir mixture into juices; return meat to pan.)

Return pan to oven, reduce oven heat to 325°F. and continue baking for last 30 minutes of cooking time, basting roast with gravy occasionally.

Note: I often use a clay cooker for the roasting pan; I think it is even better in the clay cooker.

I like to serve this with boiled potatoes, red cabbage and cranberry relish, with a red or white wine.

Barbara Gibbs Ostmann
St. Louis Post-Dispatch / St. Louis, Missouri

DOVE OR QUAIL IN MADEIRA SAUCE

2 to 3 doves per person or 2
    quail per person
Seasoned flour
Butter and vegetable oil
Madeira wine

Sauce:
1 jar (10 ounces) plum jelly
½ teaspoon salt
1 teaspoon ground ginger
½ cup Madeira wine

Rinse birds and pat dry. Lightly dredge in seasoned flour. Heat mixture of half butter and half oil in large pan and sauté birds until brown. Place in shallow baking dish with mixture of half Madeira wine and half water to depth of ⅛ to ¼ inch. Cover with aluminum foil and bake in 300°F. oven 1 hour. Meanwhile, prepare sauce.

Sauce: Combine jelly, salt, ground ginger and wine in small saucepan and cook over low heat until jelly melts.

During the last 20 minutes of cooking, remove foil and baste with sauce to glaze birds.

Dotty Griffith *The Dallas Morning News* / Dallas, Texas

SMELTS BAKED IN ORANGE SAUCE *6 to 8 servings*

Smelts are small, slender, silvery fish with a transparent olive-green coloration along their backs. They rarely grow longer than ten inches. But what they lack in size, they more than make up for in flavor.

2 pounds smelts, thawed and
    dressed
Salt and pepper to taste
¼ cup butter or margarine,
    melted

¼ cup orange juice
1 teaspoon grated orange
    rind

Arrange smelts in greased baking dish. Sprinkle with salt and pepper. Combine melted butter with orange juice and rind. Pour over fish. Bake in 450°F. oven 10 minutes.

Note: Smelts are inexpensive and can be cooked in the same ways as other fish — breaded and fried in butter, dipped in batter and deep-fried or cooked in a sauce with vegetables.

Claire Barriger Free-lance writer / Ottawa, Ontario

BROILED FISH FILLETS AMANDINE

4 to 6 servings

1½ to 2 pounds fish fillets (any mild-flavored fish)
¼ cup quick-mixing flour
2 teaspoons paprika
1½ teaspoons salt
1 to 2 tablespoons vegetable oil

Lemon-Butter Sauce:
3 tablespoons butter or margarine
2 teaspoons lemon juice
3 or 4 drops hot pepper sauce

Toasted Slivered Almonds:
2 tablespoons butter per serving
1 tablespoon slivered almonds per serving

Rinse fish fillets and pat dry with paper towel. Combine flour, paprika and salt; mix thoroughly. Coat fillets with flour mixture. Lightly oil shallow baking pan or casserole. Arrange flour-coated fillets in bottom of pan in one layer.

Lemon-Butter Sauce: Melt butter, lemon juice and hot pepper sauce in small pan.

Brush fillets with sauce. Broil fish 4 to 5 inches from source of heat, basting occasionally with additional sauce, until slight crust forms on surface, or until fish becomes opaque and flesh flakes easily when tested with fork. While fillets are broiling, prepare Toasted Almonds.

Toasted Almonds: Melt butter in small skillet over medium-high heat. When foaming subsides, add slivered almonds. Toss nuts in hot fat with fork until nuts and butter are golden brown, watching carefully that they do not burn. Lift nuts from fat with slotted spoon and drain on paper towel to crisp. Reserve butter and keep hot.

Pour hot butter over fillets when done and sprinkle with toasted almonds.

Note: Do not overcook fish, and do not turn fillets while broiling unless they are very thick.

Flounder, sole, turbot, red snapper, mackerel, bluefish and whitefish are among my choices for this dish.

Marilyn McDevitt Rubin
The Pittsburgh Press / Pittsburgh, Pennsylvania

Vegetables

MOTHER'S SCALLOPED POTATOES

8 servings

My mother makes wonderful scalloped potatoes, so when I decided to do a food page featuring potatoes, I thought Mom's recipe should be included. And I thought a simple long-distance phone call home would do it. "Oh, my," she said. "There is no recipe. I just make them. My Aunt Mary taught my mother and she taught me, but, of course, we've all made changes over the years." I suggested we make them, hypothetically, right then, over the phone. "How many potatoes?" I asked. "What pan are we using?" came her reply. Twenty minutes and a hefty phone bill later, we thought we had it figured out. "If it works," Mom said, "would you send me the recipe?" It took two tries to get enough "oh, medium, I guess" white sauce "to cover the potatoes," but here it is.

5 to 6 medium to large potatoes
⅓ cup all-purpose flour
2 tablespoons butter
2 cups milk

¾ pound processed cheese spread or ¾ pound longhorn cheese, chopped or shredded
1 jar (4 ounces) pimientos, drained and chopped
Salt and pepper to taste

Peel and cook potatoes in boiling, salted water. Cool slightly; dice coarsely and set aside.

Make white sauce by combining flour and melted butter in saucepan to form roux. Slowly stir in milk. Continue to stir, cooking over low heat until sauce thickens.

Mix sauce with potatoes and stir in cheese, mixing until cheese melts. Blend in pimientos. Check for seasoning. Pour into 13x9x 2-inch shallow baking dish and bake in 350°F. oven 30 to 40 minutes, or until top bubbles and browns slightly.

Karen K. Marshall *St. Louis Globe-Democrat* / St. Louis, Missouri

STIR-FRY BROWN RICE WITH VEGETABLES

4 to 6 servings

This recipe was one of the "year's favorite" recipes for our food section. Leftovers reheat well in a microwave oven, making this a perfect dish to tote to the office for lunch. Sometimes I make it just as described, but usually I throw in water chestnuts or vary the vegetables according to what I have on hand. This provides a lot of "chew" satisfaction for dieters.

1 cup brown rice, uncooked
1 tablespoon chicken bouillon granules
3 tablespoons vegetable oil, divided
1 cup thinly sliced carrots
3 green onions (including some tops), sliced

1 medium clove garlic, minced, or dash of garlic powder
1 large green pepper, sliced in thin strips
1 cup thinly sliced zucchini
1 cup thinly sliced fresh mushrooms
½ cup slivered almonds
4 to 5 tablespoons soy sauce

The day or morning before serving, cook rice according to package directions, adding chicken bouillon granules to water. Cool rice completely in refrigerator.

Heat about 1 tablespoon oil in wok or skillet over high heat. Add carrots; stir 1 minute. Add onions, garlic and green pepper; stir-fry 1 minute, adding more oil as needed to prevent sticking. Add zucchini, mushrooms and almonds; stir-fry for about 2 minutes, or until all vegetables are barely crisp-tender. Add rice and stir to separate grains and heat through. Season to taste with soy sauce. Serve at once.

Note: Do not omit slivered almonds. Canned mushrooms may be substituted for fresh mushrooms, if necessary.

Barbara Gibbs Ostmann
St. Louis Post-Dispatch / St. Louis, Missouri

MASHED POTATO STUFFING

6 to 8 servings

This mashed potato stuffing recipe is my family's traditional Thanksgiving stuffing recipe. We've always referred to it as stuffing, although I can't ever remember it used for stuffing the turkey.

6 medium potatoes
1 pound sweet or spicy
  Italian sausage
  Red wine (optional)
½ cup butter
⅔ cup milk (approx.)
⅔ cup shredded American
  cheese

⅓ cup grated Parmesan
  cheese
  Turkey giblets, cooked
  and chopped (optional)
2 eggs
  Chopped parsley
  Salt and pepper to taste

Wash potatoes, pare and remove blemishes. Cook in boiling water until tender. While potatoes are cooking, fry sausage in skillet until thoroughly cooked; add some red wine to pan, if desired. Remove sausage from pan and cool slightly. Slice sausage into ½-inch rounds and then into quarters; set aside.

Mash potatoes, mixing in butter and milk. Add cheeses, stirring well. Add sausage bits and chopped, cooked turkey giblets, if desired, and mix well. Beat eggs well and blend into potato mixture. Add parsley, salt and pepper to taste. If cheeses are especially salty, omit extra salt. (The consistency of the mixture should be smooth and slightly loose, like a thick pudding. If mixture seems too thick, thin slightly with more milk.)

Pour into greased 1½-quart casserole and bake in 350°F. oven 30 minutes, or until stuffing is set and top is nicely browned.

Linda Giuca *The Hartford Courant / Hartford, Connecticut*

SWEET POTATO CASSEROLE

8 to 10 servings

A good friend, Sidney Fiquette, brought this sweet potato casserole to a potluck picnic at our house a few years ago, and I fell in love with it. She said it was just something her family had always made. I have added it to the Thanksgiving menu, and sometimes sneak it in for other occasions. It is too sweet to serve often. In fact, you could argue in favor of serving it for dessert instead of as a vegetable.

3 cups cooked mashed sweet
    potato
1 cup granulated sugar
¼ cup butter or margarine,
    softened
¼ teaspoon salt
½ cup evaporated milk

Topping:
¾ cup light brown sugar
¼ cup all-purpose flour
¼ cup butter or margarine,
    softened
1 cup pecan halves

Combine mashed sweet potatoes, sugar, butter, salt and evaporated milk, mixing until creamy. Turn mixture into buttered 1½-quart casserole.

Topping: Combine brown sugar, flour, butter and pecans.

Crumble mixture by hand and spread over casserole. Bake in 350°F. oven for 45 minutes.

Note: You can use canned sweet potatoes and mash them, but it is best when made with fresh sweet potatoes that have been baked and mashed. Chopped pecans can be used, but pecan halves make it more special.

Barbara Gibbs Ostmann
St. Louis Post-Dispatch / St. Louis, Missouri

BAKED ONIONS
6 to 8 servings

Cream, Cheddar cheese and sherry give elegance to onions.

2 pounds small onions, peeled
1 cup light cream or half-and-half
¼ cup sherry
½ teaspoon salt
⅛ teaspoon pepper
3 tablespoons butter
½ cup grated sharp Cheddar cheese

Cook onions in boiling, salted water until just tender. Drain and arrange in shallow 1½-quart baking dish. Combine cream, sherry, salt and pepper. Pour over onions; dot with butter and sprinkle with cheese. Cover and bake in 350°F. oven for 20 minutes.

Claire Barriger Free-lance writer / Ottawa, Ontario

BROCCOLI-TOMATO CASSEROLE
8 to 10 servings

This broccoli casserole was shared by Frida Gustafson, a long-time Cleveland caterer. It has been a holiday favorite with the Plain Dealer *food staff, because preparation is done ahead.*

3 packages (10 ounces each) frozen broccoli, thawed and drained
3 large fresh tomatoes, peeled and sliced (1 quart)
2 cups mayonnaise
1 can (3 ounces) grated Parmesan cheese (approx. ⅔ cup)

Arrange broccoli in 10-inch round, buttered casserole. Top with tomato slices. Combine mayonnaise and Parmesan cheese, reserving a little cheese to sprinkle on top. Spread mayonnaise mixture over tomato slices and sprinkle with reserved cheese. Cover and refrigerate until ready to bake.

Preheat oven to 325°F. Bake casserole, uncovered, 50 to 60 minutes, or until nicely browned.

Janet Beighle French The Plain Dealer / Cleveland, Ohio

SKILLET CABBAGE

6 servin

4 cups shredded cabbage
1 green pepper, diced
2 cups diced celery
2 large onions, sliced
2 tomatoes, chopped, or
  1 can (16 ounces)
  stewed tomatoes

¼ cup bacon drippings
2 teaspoons granulated sugar
Salt and pepper to taste

Combine cabbage, green pepper, celery, onions, tomatoes, drippings, sugar, salt and pepper in large, covered skillet. Cook, covered, over moderate heat about 30 minutes.

Charlotte Hansen
The Jamestown Sun / Jamestown, North Dakota

PETE'S GRITS CASSEROLE

6 servings

I always like getting recipes from male cooks. Pete Peterson, a retired pilot, omitted salt from his grits recipe purposely. He, along with so many others, is trying to limit his salt intake. There are many grits recipes, but this one is special.

4 cups water
1 cup quick-cooking grits
1½ cups shredded sharp
    Cheddar cheese

½ cup butter or margarine
½ cup milk
3 eggs, well beaten
2 to 3 cloves garlic, minced

Preheat oven to 350°F. Bring water to boil in medium-size saucepan. Add grits; return to boil. Reduce heat and cook for 5 minutes, stirring occasionally. Add cheese, butter, milk, eggs and garlic, stirring until cheese is melted, about 5 minutes more. Pour into lightly greased 2-quart casserole or baking dish. Bake in oven 1 hour.

Evelyn Wavpotich
Island Packet / Hilton Head Island, South Carolina

FETTUCINE FLORENTINE

4 to 6 servings

½ cup butter
1 pound fresh spinach or 1 package (10 ounces) frozen spinach, cooked and chopped
¾ pound bacon, cooked crisp, drained and crumbled
¼ pound prosciutto or smoked ham, chopped (optional)

2 eggs, beaten
½ to ¾ cup freshly grated Parmesan cheese
1½ to 2 cups heavy cream
1 pound fettucine, cooked al dente
Salt and pepper, if needed

Melt butter in large pot. Add spinach, bacon and prosciutto or ham; mix well and heat. Meanwhile, combine eggs, cheese and cream in small bowl.

When spinach-bacon mixture is hot, add fettucine and mix thoroughly to coat all strands. Add egg mixture and heat, stirring constantly, until slightly thickened. Do not boil. Adjust seasoning, if necessary. Add additional cream if mixture is too dry. Serve immediately.

Jane Milza Staten Island Advance / Staten Island, New York

SWEET POTATO BALLS

8 servings

This recipe is good with holiday fare like baked ham or roast turkey. You can make it weeks in advance, freeze it, then simply place it in the oven 20 minutes before serving time.

3 cups cooked yams or sweet potatoes
¼ cup butter or margarine
¾ cup light brown sugar
2 tablespoons milk
¼ teaspoon salt

½ to 1 teaspoon grated orange rind
8 regular-size marshmallows
1 cup corn flakes, crushed, or 1 cup ground pecans

Mash sweet potatoes. Add butter, sugar, milk, salt and orange rind. Scoop up about ¼ cup potato mixture with tablespoon, and shape mixture around each marshmallow, using more as needed to cover. Roll each ball in crushed corn flakes or ground nuts. Place potato balls in buttered baking dish, cover with foil and freeze.

When ready to serve, preheat oven to 350°F. Take balls directly from freezer, place on pan and put in preheated oven. (Thawing them will make them soggy.) Bake 20 minutes, or until marshallows begins to ooze.

Diane Wiggins *St. Louis Globe-Democrat* / St. Louis, Missouri

POTATOES WITH MUSTARD AND CURRY

6 servings

¼ cup butter or margarine
6 medium potatoes, cooked and cut in quarters
1 green pepper, finely chopped

2 medium onions, finely chopped
½ teaspoon curry powder
½ teaspoon dry mustard
Salt and pepper to taste

Melt butter in large skillet; add potatoes, green pepper and onions. Sprinkle with curry powder, mustard, salt and pepper; toss to mix well. Fry gently, turning often until potatoes are well browned.

Vicki Fitzgerald *The Patriot Ledger* / Quincy, Massachusetts

CORN PUDDING

Given to me by my friend Susan Manlin Katzman at a recipe shower when I was married, this delicious vegetable dish has been a favorite ever since. I usually include it on the Thanksgiving table. It is so sweet it could almost be a dessert. When made with fresh corn from the garden, it is out of this world.

½ cup butter
¼ cup granulated sugar
 3 tablespoons all-purpose
   flour
½ cup evaporated milk

2 eggs, beaten
1½ teaspoons baking powder
2 packages (10 ounces each)
  frozen whole kernel corn,
  thawed

Preheat oven to 350°F. Melt butter in saucepan. Mix sugar and flour; stir into melted butter. Stir in milk, eggs and baking powder. Mix well. Stir in corn. Pour mixture into 2-quart buttered casserole or two 1-quart baking dishes. (I usually make it in two dishes and freeze one for later). Bake in oven until top is golden brown and center is set, about 45 minutes.

Note: This recipe can be prepared in the microwave oven, as well. I melt the butter, then cook the finished dish on high (100 percent) power about 10 to 15 minutes. It will not brown, but will have a great fresh taste. If I am going to freeze it, I only cook it partially, so it will finish cooking when I reheat it.

Barbara Gibbs Ostmann
St. Louis Post-Dispatch / St. Louis, Missouri

GREEK-STYLE PILAF

This is good with Sherried Beef Tenderloin (see page 56).

½ cup butter
 6 green onions, chopped
 1 cup sliced fresh mushrooms
¾ cup uncooked brown rice
¾ cup orzo (Greek pasta
   product)
 3 cups chicken stock

Generous pinch of dried
oregano to taste
Salt and freshly ground
black pepper to taste
1 tablespoon chopped fresh
  parsley
½ cup pine nuts

Melt butter in large, heavy saucepan over moderate heat. Add onions and cook until soft. Stir in mushrooms and cook until lightly browned. Stir in rice and orzo. Cook several minutes, stirring occasionally, until well coated with butter mixture. Stir in stock, cover and bring to boil. Reduce heat to very low and cook until rice is tender and liquid has been absorbed, 40 to 50 minutes. Mixture will hold well if necessary.

Add oregano, salt (depends upon seasoning in stock) and generous amount of pepper, stirring well. Stir in parsley and pine nuts. Remove from heat, or hold over very low heat several minutes to blend flavors.

Marge Hanley *Indianapolis News* / Indianapolis, Indiana

RATATOUILLE

4 to 6 servings

I like this version of ratatouille because it is layered rather than "scrambled." It also cooks in the oven rather than on top of the stove. This is a good party dish that can be made ahead of time and refrigerated for several days.

1 medium summer squash, cubed	½ teaspoon oregano
1 medium zucchini, cubed	3 medium onions, thinly sliced
1½ teaspoons salt	2 medium green peppers, cut into thin strips
3 large cloves garlic, mashed or minced	½ teaspoon dried marjoram
⅓ cup olive oil	4 medium firm-ripe tomatoes, peeled and thinly sliced
2 cups peeled, cubed eggplant	¼ teaspoon dill seed

Butter 2½-quart casserole. Cover bottom with cubes of unpeeled summer squash and zucchini. Sprinkle with one-third the salt, garlic and oil. Add layer of eggplant, again adding one-third salt, garlic and oil; add oregano. Add layer of onion slices and layer of green pepper. Sprinkle with remaining salt, garlic and oil; add marjoram. Cover casserole and bake in 350°F. oven for 45 minutes. Remove from oven and add layer of tomato slices; sprinkle with dill seeds. Continue baking, uncovered, for 10 minutes. Serve hot or chilled.

Gail Perrin *The Boston Globe* / Boston, Massachusetts

SPAGHETTI PRIMAVERA

4 to 6 servings

Spaghetti Primavera is a lush and lovely dish to serve as a first course at a splendid dinner, or as a main course at a wonderful lunch.

1 cup sliced zucchini
Salt
2 tomatoes, peeled and chopped
3 tablespoons olive oil, divided
3 cloves garlic, mashed, divided
Salt and pepper to taste
10 fresh mushrooms, sliced
8 tablespoons butter, divided
1½ cups broccoli pieces, blanched

1½ cups snow peas, blanched
6 asparagus stalks, blanched and sliced
1 pound spaghetti, uncooked
1 cup heavy cream, warmed
Chopped basil to taste (fresh, if available)
½ cup grated Parmesan cheese
Chopped parsley
Sautéed whole cherry tomatoes

Put zucchini in colander and sprinkle with salt. Set aside 20 minutes. Rinse with cold running water and drain. Pat dry with paper towels.

Sauté chopped tomatoes in 1 tablespoon oil with 1 mashed garlic clove, salt and pepper, until tomatoes render their juice.

In another pan, lightly sauté mushrooms with remaining garlic in 2 tablespoons butter and remaining oil. Add zucchini, broccoli, snow peas and asparagus; cook only until heated through.

Cook spaghetti al dente and drain. Melt remaining butter. Toss spaghetti with butter and warm cream. Add basil, salt and pepper to taste. Toss with cheese and vegetables. Sprinkle with parsley. Garnish with cherry tomatoes.

Susan Manlin Katzman Free-lance writer / St. Louis, Missouri

MARINATED CARROTS

6 to 8 servings

This is nice for a covered-dish supper or buffet dinner.

2 pounds carrots
½ to ¾ cup granulated sugar
½ cup vegetable oil
½ cup white vinegar
1 can (8 ounces) tomato sauce

½ can (6 ounces) tomato cocktail
1 onion, sliced and separated into rings
1 green pepper, thinly sliced

Scrape carrots; slice and cook in boiling water until tender-crisp. Drain. Combine sugar, oil, vinegar, tomato sauce and tomato cocktail; mix until sugar is dissolved. Pour over cooked carrots, onion rings and pepper slices in large bowl. Marinate in refrigerator for several hours, or overnight.

Harriett Aldridge Arkansas Gazette / Little Rock, Arkansas

CANDIED CARROTS

4 servings

The cranberry glaze in this recipe gives a butterscotch flavor that is delightful.

5 medium carrots
¼ cup butter
¼ cup canned jellied cranberry sauce

2 tablespoons light brown sugar
½ teaspoon salt

Scrape carrots and slice crosswise on bias about ½-inch thick. Cook, covered, in small amount of boiling water, until just tender, 6 to 10 minutes.

Combine butter, cranberry sauce, brown sugar and salt in skillet. Heat slowly and stir until cranberry sauce melts. Add drained carrots; heat, stirring occasionally, until nicely glazed on all sides, about 5 minutes.

Charlotte Hansen
The Jamestown Sun / Jamestown, North Dakota

SPICY MINCED WATERCRESS

4 servings

This makes a nice accompaniment to shrimp.

2 bunches watercress, minced
1 teaspoon salt
3 tablespoons vegetable oil

1 large, dried red chili
pepper
2 teaspoons sesame oil

Rinse watercress in cold water; shake dry. Mince both leaves and stems. Put minced watercress in bowl, sprinkle with salt and toss well. Refrigerate 30 minutes. Squeeze dry.

Heat large skillet over high heat until hot; add oil, swirl and turn heat to medium low. Brown chili pepper in oil about 40 seconds, flipping and pressing. Turn heat to high, scatter in watercress and stir-fry rapidly with scooping motions for 30 seconds. Add sesame oil, give a few sweeping turns and pour into serving dish. Refrigerate until watercress is thoroughly cold.

Carol Haddix *Chicago Tribune*

GOLDEN STUFFED BAKED POTATOES

The color and crunch of grated carrots in these baked potatoes make them unusual.

4 baked potatoes
1 cup grated raw carrots
¼ cup chopped fresh parsley
¼ cup minced onion or chives
½ teaspoon horseradish
⅔ cup plain yogurt or sour
cream

¼ cup melted butter or
margarine
Salt and pepper to taste
Grated Parmesan or
Cheddar cheese
Paprika

Halve baked potatoes and scoop out pulp. Whip pulp with carrots, parsley, chives, horseradish, yogurt and butter. Season to taste with salt and pepper. Refill potato halves. Top with grated cheese and paprika. Bake in 350°F. oven 15 minutes, or until cheese melts and mixture is hot.

If desired, filled potato halves can be refrigerated. When ready to serve, remove from refrigerator and top with cheese and paprika. Bake in 350°F. oven 20 to 25 minutes, or until hot.

Donna Lee
The Providence Journal and Bulletin / Providence, Rhode Island

DILLED CUCUMBERS

6 servings

These cucumbers taste especially good with roast turkey or chicken.

2 cucumbers (8 inches each), peeled
2 tablespoons butter or margarine
2 tablespoons all-purpose flour
¾ cup half-and-half
2 tablespoons dried dill weed
1 teaspoon granulated sugar
½ teaspoon salt
Dash white pepper

Cut peeled cucumbers in half lengthwise and scrape out seeds with spoon. Cut cucumbers in ½-inch cubes. Sauté in butter in large, heavy pan until tender but still firm, about 2 minutes. Sprinkle with flour and stir to blend. Add half-and-half, dill, sugar, salt and pepper. Cook over moderate heat until thickened, stirring constantly. If serving is delayed and sauce becomes too thick, add a little more cream.

Claire Barriger Free-lance writer / Ottawa, Ontario

CARROT SOUFFLE

4 to 6 servings

This is a delicious and easy dish that even carrot-haters will eat.

1 pound carrots, cooked
3 eggs
⅓ cup granulated sugar
2 tablespoons all-purpose flour
1 teaspoon baking powder
1 teaspoon vanilla extract
½ cup butter, melted
Dash ground nutmeg
Dash ground cinnamon

Topping:
¼ cup corn flake crumbs
3 tablespoons light brown sugar
2 tablespoons butter
¼ cup chopped nuts

Preheat oven to 350°F. Purée cooked carrots in blender. Add eggs to puréed mixture and blend well. Add sugar, flour, baking powder, vanilla, butter, nutmeg and cinnamon. Purée until smooth. Pour into greased 1½-quart soufflé dish.

Topping: Combine crumbs, brown sugar, butter and nuts. Sprinkle over casserole. Bake in oven 1 hour.

Rosemary Black *The Record* / Hackensack, New Jersey

CARROTS, GINGER AND CUMIN

4 to 6 servings

1 pound carrots
6 tablespoons butter, divided
2 teaspoons cumin seed
1 tablespoon chopped fresh
  ginger

2 cloves garlic, chopped
2 tablespoons lemon juice
½ cup low-fat or regular milk
Salt and freshly ground
  pepper to taste

Scrape carrots and cut into medium slices, or slice in food processor. Cook carrots in boiling, salted water until just tender, about 5 minutes, depending on thickness of carrots. Drain and rinse under cold water to stop cooking.

Meanwhile, melt 1 tablespoon butter in pan and sauté cumin about 30 seconds. Add ginger and garlic and sauté 1 minute longer. Combine cooked drained carrots with cumin-garlic mixture, lemon juice, remaining butter and milk.

Process in blender or food processor with steel blade, in batches, until smooth. Season with salt and freshly ground pepper. To serve, heat through.

Marian Burros *The New York Times*

SQUASH PUFF

6 servings

Serve this casserole with ham or sausage.

3 cups mashed cooked
  winter squash (approx.
  4 pounds)
½ cup chopped onion
2 tablespoons butter or
  margarine
2 eggs, beaten

¼ cup light cream or half-and-
  half
3 tablespoons all-purpose
  flour
1 teaspoon baking powder
¾ teaspoon salt
Dash pepper
⅓ cup buttered bread crumbs

Cook squash; mash. Sauté onion in butter until transparent. Add to squash. Beat in eggs and cream, then stir in flour, baking powder, salt and pepper. Turn into greased 1½-quart baking dish and top with crumbs. Bake in 375°F. oven 25 minutes, or until lightly browned.

Claire Barriger *Free-lance writer / Ottawa, Ontario*

POTATO CASSEROLE AU GRATIN   *10 to 12 servings*

I've had lots of requests for this recipe. Our congressman's wife liked it so much she put it in "The Congressional Club Cook Book."

6 medium potatoes
¼ cup butter or margarine
¼ cup all-purpose flour
1 cup chicken broth
⅓ cup light cream or half-and-half
1¼ teaspoons salt, divided
Dash pepper
½ cup finely chopped celery
⅓ cup finely chopped onion
¼ cup chopped pimiento, drained
1 cup grated Cheddar cheese
½ cup butter or margarine, melted
1 carton (8 ounces) sour cream
½ cup corn flake crumbs

Boil potatoes with jackets on until almost tender, about 15 minutes. Drain and let cool.

Melt ¼ cup butter in saucepan. Stir in flour. Slowly add chicken broth and cook, stirring constantly, until mixture thickens and is bubbly. Stir in cream, ¼ teaspoon salt and pepper. Remove from heat, cover and let cool.

Peel and grate potatoes. Combine with celery, onion, pimiento, cheese, melted butter and remaining salt. Stir in sour cream, then fold sauce into grated potato mixture. Turn into 9x13x2-inch baking dish. Sprinkle with corn flake crumbs. (Casserole can be refrigerated at this point, if desired.) Bake in 325°F. oven for 1 hour.

Sue Dawson *Columbus Dispatch / Columbus, Ohio*

ROSEMARY PARSNIP CASSEROLE
6 to 8 servings

12 parsnips (approx. 2 pounds)
2 tablespoons butter
¼ teaspoon fresh or dried rosemary
2 tablespoons all-purpose flour
¼ cup grated Parmesan cheese
2 cups light cream or half-and-half
½ cup cracker crumbs
¼ cup melted butter

Peel parsnips. Cook in boiling, salted water until tender. Drain and cut each in half lengthwise, or slice in rounds if parsnips are large. Arrange half the parsnips in bottom of greased 1½-quart baking dish. Dot with half the butter, sprinkle with half the rosemary, flour and cheese. Drizzle with half the cream. Repeat layers. Mix cracker crumbs with melted butter and sprinkle over casserole. Bake, uncovered, in 400°F. oven for 20 minutes.

Kathleen Kelly *Wichita Eagle-Beacon / Wichita, Kansas*

OKRA GUMBO
6 servings

4 cups diced okra
3 well-ripened medium tomatoes
3 strips bacon
2 small onions, finely chopped
1 green pepper, finely chopped
1 clove garlic, minced (optional)
Salt and pepper to taste

Wash okra, cut crosswise and dice fine. Peel tomatoes and chop fine. Fry bacon in skillet until crisp; remove bacon, drain and crumble.

Put okra, onions, green pepper and garlic into skillet with bacon drippings and cook until just tender. Add tomatoes; cook slowly, covered, about 30 minutes, stirring frequently. When done, season to taste with salt and pepper. Sprinkle with bacon and serve.

Note: This is delicious served over toast points or fluffy steamed rice, or in a small bowl as accompaniment to an entrée.

Clara Eschmann
The Macon Telegraph and News / Macon, Georgia

SPINACH CASSEROLE

4 to 6 servings

Three of my seven sisters are vegetarians, and this quick spinach casserole has become a standing item on our Thanksgiving table and at other family dinners. It's nutritious enough to be a main dish, but it's equally good as a vegetable accompaniment. My two-year-old daughter loves it.

2 eggs, well beaten
6 tablespoons all-purpose flour
1 package (10 ounces) frozen chopped spinach, thawed

1½ cups cottage cheese
1½ cups grated Cheddar cheese
½ teaspoon salt

Preheat oven to 350°F. Beat eggs and flour in bowl until smooth. Stir in spinach, cottage cheese, Cheddar cheese and salt; mix well. Pour into greased 1-quart casserole. Bake in oven for 1 hour.

Rosemary Black *The Record* / Hackensack, New Jersey

SQUASH AND TOMATOES

8 servings

½ pound bacon, coarsely diced
3 large onions, cut in half and sliced in thin moons
2 green peppers, cut in half and coarsely diced
1 cup chopped parsley, divided

¼ cup chopped fresh basil or 2 teaspoons dried basil
7 ripe tomatoes, peeled, seeded and chopped
10 to 12 small yellow squash, trimmed and diced
Salt and freshly ground pepper to taste

Place bacon in large, heavy skillet and heat. When half-cooked, stir in onion and green pepper; let sizzle about 3 minutes. Add ½ cup parsley, basil, tomatoes, squash, salt and pepper. Cook, stirring and tossing until squash is tender-crisp but not mushy. Garnish with remaining parsley.

Anne Byrn Phillips
The Atlanta Journal-Constitution / Atlanta, Georgia

CARROTS THE GOOD WAY

4 servings

I've met lots of people who don't eat cooked carrots unless they are in a stew. For some reason, they like raw carrots, but not cooked. This is the one recipe I've found that everybody likes. And I'm especially pleased with it because there's no sugar in it.

1 pound carrots, sliced
   in ¼-inch rounds
2 tablespoons horseradish*
1 small onion,
   finely chopped
   *Do not use horseradish sauce.

½ teaspoon salt
   Pinch pepper
½ cup mayonnaise
¼ cup dried fine
   bread crumbs
2 tablespoons butter,
   melted

Place carrots in saucepan with just enough water to cover; simmer until just tender. Drain well, but reserve about ¼ cup cooking liquid. Mix reserved cooking liquid with horseradish, onion, salt, pepper and mayonnaise.

Arrange carrots evenly over bottom of buttered 9-inch pie plate. Pour horseradish mixture over carrots. Mix bread crumbs with butter and sprinkle over top. Bake in 375°F. oven 20 minutes, or until crumbs are nicely browned.

Deni Hamilton *The Courier-Journal* / Louisville, Kentucky

THE POTATO PANCAKE PRINCIPLE *8 to 10 pancakes*

Recently, when demonstrating how to make potato latkes for Hanukkah, I discarded my recipes and put together a ratio of potatoes to other ingredients. I call it the potato pancake principle.

2 medium unpeeled baking
   potatoes (or 1 potato and
   1 beet or 1 zucchini)
1 medium onion
2 eggs
   Salt and freshly ground
   pepper to taste

1 handful fresh parsley,
   diced
½ cup (approx.) matzo meal
   Vegetable oil for frying
   Sour cream or
   applesauce (optional)

Cut potatoes (or potato and beet or zucchini) and onion into eighths; grate in food processor. Combine grated vegetables with eggs, salt, pepper and parsley. Add enough matzo meal to hold mixture together.

Shape 2 tablespoons potato mixture with hands to make each pancake. Fry pancakes, a few at a time, in ½ inch hot oil in heavy skillet. When brown, turn and fry on other side. Drain well. Serve pancakes with sour cream or applesauce, if desired.

Note: I recommend making the pancakes early in the day, letting them drain all day long (do not refrigerate), then crisping them again just before eating. To crisp pancakes, place them on ungreased cookie sheet in 350°F. oven until just warm.

Joan Nathan Free-lance writer / Chevy Chase, Maryland

CORN CUSTARD

6 servings

2 cups fresh or canned corn kernels, drained
¼ cup all-purpose flour
1 teaspoon granulated sugar
1 teaspoon salt
¼ teaspoon pepper
3 eggs, well beaten
2 cups milk
2 tablespoons butter or margarine, melted

Combine corn with flour, sugar, salt and pepper in bowl. Stir in eggs, milk and butter. Spoon or pour into 6 buttered custard cups or 1½-quart casserole. Set in pan of hot water and bake in 350°F. oven for 45 minutes for custard cups, or 1 hour for casserole, or until knife inserted in center comes out clean. Individual custards can be unmolded, if desired.

Claire Barriger Free-lance writer / Ottawa, Ontario

Breads

GRANDMA'S GRAHAM BREAD

2 loaves

1 package active dry yeast
½ cup warm water
1 quart water or milk

1 cup molasses
2 teaspoons salt
8 cups graham or whole
  wheat flour

Dissolve yeast in warm water. Combine water or milk and molasses, then warm them. Pour into large bowl and add yeast mixture, salt and graham or whole wheat flour. Stir well and set in cool place overnight.

In morning, stir well again. Mixture will be runny. Pour into 2 greased 9x5x3-inch loaf pans and let rise 1 hour in warm place.

Preheat oven to 450°F. Bake bread 10 minutes; lower heat to 400° and bake about 50 minutes more, or until done. (Sometimes it takes a bit less than full time.)

Gail Perrin *The Boston Globe* / Boston, Massachusetts

MOTHER'S MOLASSES RAISIN RYE BREAD *3 loaves*

My mother invented this bread by drawing on several Scandinavian recipes. It was an essential at our home during the holidays. After she died, I found a scrap of paper on which I'd written just the ingredients one day early in my marriage. I'd never made the bread while she was alive, but now I've reconstructed the recipe and it tastes just as good as my memories of it.

2 packages active dry yeast
½ cup warm water
3½ cups liquid (milk, water or
  a combination)
2 cups raisins
2 cups rye flour
1 cup rolled oats

¼ cup honey
2 tablespoons
  caraway seeds
5 to 6 cups all-purpose flour
½ to ¾ cup molasses
½ cup vegetable oil
4 teaspoons salt

Dissolve yeast in warm water. Combine yeast mixture, liquid, raisins, rye flour, oats, honey and caraway seeds. Add enough all-purpose flour, about 2 cups, to make batter of sponge consistency. Let rise until fluffy.

Stir in molasses, oil and salt. Add enough additional all-purpose flour, 1 cup at a time, to make workable dough. Knead until soft and elastic. Divide dough into three parts. Form into round loaves and place on greased baking sheets. Let rise, covered, in a warm place 1 hour, or until doubled in bulk.

Preheat oven to 375°F. Bake bread 10 minutes, reduce heat to 350°F. and bake an additional 35 to 40 minutes. Cool on wire racks.

Eleanor Ostman
St. Paul Pioneer Press and Dispatch / St. Paul, Minnesota

JOE'S GARLIC BREAD

This is a standard in my recipe repertoire. I haven't had any leftovers yet. Purchase the best Italian or French bread you can find. The bread can be prepared ahead and frozen.

Butter and margarine, softened (approx. 1 cup per loaf)
Garlic cloves, peeled and minced (2 to 3 per loaf)
Honey (optional)

1 loaf (or more) Italian or French bread
Basil
Paprika
Olive oil

Blend softened butter and margarine (half and half, or any proportion desired) with minced garlic. If you wish, beat in a tablespoon or two of honey.

Slice bread in half lengthwise. Spread butter-garlic mixture thickly on both cut sides of bread. Sprinkle lightly with basil, then paprika. Coat outside of loaf lightly with olive oil. Close up.

Preheat oven to 350°F. Wrap loaves in foil and bake in oven 20 minutes, or until inside of bread is hot and garlic is soft. Slice in large hunks and serve hot.

More informally, allow guests to rip off hunks according to appetite. This goes well with lasagna.

Note: If you plan to make garlic bread ahead and freeze it, be sure to ask at the bakery for plastic bags large enough to store the loaves. Wrap loaves in a double thickness of aluminum foil; seal completely and fit back into the plastic bags.

Bake frozen loaves at 350°F. about 30 minutes. Remove from foil, raise temperature to 375°F. Return bread to oven to crisp.

Joe Crea *Florida Times-Union* / Jacksonville, Florida

WHOLE WHEAT HONEY BREAD

2 loaves

4 cups whole wheat flour,
divided
½ cup nonfat dry milk
1 tablespoon salt
2 packages active dry yeast

3 cups water
½ cup honey
2 tablespoons vegetable oil
4 to 4½ cups all-purpose
flour

Combine 3 cups whole wheat flour, nonfat dry milk, salt and yeast in large bowl. Heat water, honey and oil in saucepan over low heat until warm; pour warm liquid over flour mixture. Blend with electric mixer at low speed 1 minute and at medium speed 2 minutes. Add remaining whole wheat flour and blend with mixer. Stir in about 4 cups all-purpose flour by hand.

Turn onto floured board and knead, adding flour as necessary to keep dough from being too sticky, until dough is smooth and elastic (about 5 minutes). Place dough in greased bowl, turning greased side up. Cover and let rise 45 to 60 minutes, until dough is light and doubled in bulk.

Punch down and divide in half. Roll each half into 14x7-inch rectangle. Starting with 7-inch side, roll up jelly-roll fashion. Place each loaf in greased 9x5-inch pan, tucking sides under. Cover loaves; let rise 30 to 45 minutes, or until light.

Preheat oven to 375°F. Bake bread 40 to 45 minutes, until loaf sounds hollow when lightly tapped. Remove from pan; cool thoroughly on wire rack before slicing. Bread slices even better the next day.

Lorrie Guttman *Tallahassee Democrat / Tallahassee, Florida*

DANISH KRINGLER

1 coffee cake

In Denmark the holiday bread is often pretzel shaped and delectably filled with almond paste.

6 tablespoons butter, softened
1½ cups all-purpose flour, divided
½ package active dry yeast
2 tablespoons warm water
¼ cup light cream or half-and-half
1 egg
2 tablespoons granulated sugar
¼ teaspoon salt

1 egg white, lightly beaten
Granulated sugar for topping
2 tablespoons sliced almonds

Almond Paste Filling:
½ cup almond paste
2 tablespoons butter
1 egg white
¼ cup shortbread or sugar cookie crumbs

Beat butter and 2 tablespoons flour until blended. With spatula, spread it into 8x4-inch rectangle on sheet of wax paper and chill. Sprinkle yeast into warm water in large mixing bowl and let stand until dissolved. Heat cream until warm, not hot, and add to yeast. Mix in egg, sugar and salt. Beat until smooth. Gradually add remaining flour and beat until smooth.

Turn out on lightly floured board and knead until smooth and satiny. Roll out into 8-inch square. Place chilled butter mixture in center of dough. Remove paper. Fold dough over chilled mixture from both sides, then fold in thirds. Roll out into 12x6-inch rectangle. Repeat folding and rolling twice. Wrap in wax paper and chill 30 minutes. Roll into 24x6-inch rectangle.

Almond Paste Filling: Beat almond paste, butter, egg white and crumbs until well mixed.

Spread Almond Paste Filling down center of dough. Fold dough from each side to cover it. Place on lightly greased baking sheet and shape into pretzel. Flatten lightly with rolling pin. Cover with towel and let rise at room temperature until doubled.

Preheat oven to 375°F. Brush top of kringler with egg white. Sprinkle with sugar and sliced almonds. Bake 20 to 25 minutes, or until golden brown.

Lou Pappas *The Peninsula Times Tribune* / Palo Alto, California

IRISH-AMERICAN TREACLE BREAD *1 loaf*

In Ireland, bread means soda bread. And there are probably as many vari-
ations as there were black iron pots hanging over turf fires in cottage
kitchens. The bread that baked in those pots was, basically, a mixture of
flour, salt, baking soda and buttermilk. Some cooks added a little sugar,
others added a little butter. A tablespoon or two of flakemeal (rolled oats)
varied the texture. Often, some of the white flour was replaced with
whole meal (whole wheat flour). Sometimes, to make a fancier loaf,
raisins, dried currants, nuts or caraway seeds were added. Chopped can-
died fruit or crystallized ginger made it a special occasion bread. Treacle
bread is a slightly sweet version of soda bread often baked for children.
The Irish use the word treacle for what we call molasses. The bread is
best sliced thin and served with butter. This recipe evolved from several
others. It's similar to some but identical to none.

3 cups sifted all-purpose flour	¾ teaspoon baking powder
1 teaspoon salt	1 cup whole wheat flour
1 tablespoon granulated sugar	½ cup molasses
1 scant teaspoon baking soda	1 cup (approx.) buttermilk, divided

Sift flour, salt, sugar, baking soda and baking powder in large
bowl. Thoroughly mix in whole wheat flour. Warm molasses
slightly. Combine with ½ cup buttermilk. Make a well in center
of flour mixture and stir in molasses-buttermilk mixture. Mix in
remaining buttermilk, adding more or less than ½ cup as necessary to make soft dough.

Turn out on floured board and knead a few times — only
enough to shape into ball. (Use a little additional flour on hands
and board if dough sticks.) Flatten to about 1½ inches in thickness. Place in greased and floured 8- or 9-inch round layer cake
pan (dough does not have to fill pan). Cut cross at least ⅜ inch
deep in top of dough, extending cross down sides. (This is more
than traditional decoration; it will help bread to rise and bake
evenly and will discourage cracking.) If desired, brush top with
additional buttermilk.

Preheat oven to 375°F. and bake bread 40 to 45 minutes, or
until bread is browned and pan sounds hollow when tapped on
bottom. Remove from pan and cool on rack. Slice thin, toast if
desired, and serve with butter.

Note: If you prefer not to sift all-purpose flour before sifting
with other dry ingredients, more buttermilk may be needed to
make soft dough.

Peggy Daum *The Milwaukee Journal / Milwaukee, Wisconsin*

AUNT RUTH'S CINNAMON ROLLS *100 small rolls*

These rolls are really good. My Aunt Ruth back in Indiana got the recipe from a friend years ago. I usually can count on a pan of them any time I go home.

2 packages active dry yeast
¼ cup warm water
2 cups milk, scalded
1 cup granulated sugar
2 teaspoons salt
1 cup (or more) margarine, divided
3 eggs, beaten

6 to 8 cups all-purpose flour
Cinnamon sugar (1 teaspoon cinnamon per cup granulated sugar)
Confectioners sugar icing (confectioners sugar plus enough water to moisten)

Mix yeast with warm water, stirring to dissolve; set aside. Scald milk in small saucepan and mix in granulated sugar, salt and ½ cup margarine until sugar is dissolved. Pour into large bowl and set aside to cool. When milk mixture is barely lukewarm, add yeast mixture and stir well. Add eggs and mix well. Add flour, a cup at a time, until dough is firm enough to turn onto well-floured board.

Knead until dough is smooth and satiny. Place kneaded dough in large, greased bowl and turn to grease top. Cover with clean towel and set aside in warm place to rise. When dough has almost doubled, punch down, cover again and let rise a second time.

Melt remaining margarine. Pinch off pieces of dough and roll into balls about the size of ping pong balls. Dip each ball into melted margarine and then into cinnamon sugar. (Don't skimp on margarine or sugar.) Place balls, not quite touching, in baking pans. You should end up with approximately 100 rolls. Allow to rise again, 10 to 15 minutes.

Preheat oven to 375°F. Bake 15 to 20 minutes, or until golden brown. While rolls are still warm, drizzle confectioners sugar icing over rolls.

Note: I use disposable foil pans, each holding 15 to 18 rolls. The rolls freeze beautifully after baking, and the foil pans are ideal for this.

These are good served cool, but they are even better warm. They can be reheated in preheated oven at 350°F. for about 5 minutes, or in a microwave oven on medium power for 2 minutes.

Karen K. Marshall *St. Louis Globe-Democrat* / St. Louis, Missouri

MOTHER'S CORN BREAD

6 to 8 servings

My mother made the world's best corn bread, the kind Southerners used to call egg bread. She never measured ingredients. For twenty years I tried to learn how to make it. I even gave her quantities of premeasured ingredients, then measured what was left over and figured how much she used. She started with buttermilk, stirring in leavening until it "sounded right." Then she added other ingredients. I never knew what she meant by "sounded right." And I never mastered her recipe. But after years of trial and error I came up with this recipe that my sisters say is as good as mother's.

3 tablespoons butter
1 cup cornmeal
½ cup all-purpose flour
2 teaspoons baking powder
½ teaspoon salt

1 tablespoon granulated sugar
2 eggs
1 cup milk

Melt butter in heavy iron skillet in oven while it is being preheated to 350°F. Combine cornmeal, flour, baking powder, salt and sugar in mixing bowl. Beat eggs; add milk and 2 tablespoons melted butter from skillet. Quickly stir milk mixture into cornmeal mixture. Pour batter into remaining butter in hot skillet. Bake 20 to 25 minutes. Serve hot with lots of butter.

Ann McDuffie The Tampa Tribune / Tampa, Florida

WHOLE WHEAT CRANBERRY BRAN BREAD

1 loaf

Years after the first harvest festival of 1621 at Plimoth Plantation, Priscilla Alden was asked what she cooked. It's said that she replied, "I don't rightly recall whether we had cranberries. I do love them and all, but my mind was on other things. I'm not even sure we had turkey." Today in New England, we can't imagine a Thanksgiving without cranberries. This bread is a delicious way to use them. It's dark and moist, like bran muffins.

1 cup all-purpose flour
2 cups whole wheat flour
½ cup all-bran or crushed bran cereal with raisins
¾ cup light brown sugar
1 teaspoon baking powder
1 teaspoon baking soda
1 cup chopped nuts

1 cup cranberries, chopped
¼ cup granulated sugar
1 egg
½ cup milk
½ cup orange juice
½ cup melted margarine or vegetable oil

Combine flours, bran cereal, brown sugar, baking powder, baking soda and nuts; mix well. Combine cranberries and granulated sugar. Stir sugared cranberries, egg, milk, orange juice and margarine into flour mixture all at once but only until mixed. Pour into greased 9x5x3-inch loaf pan. Preheat oven to 350°F. Bake in oven 60 to 70 minutes, or until firm in center. Cool in pan 10 minutes, remove to rack and cool on long side before slicing. Freezes well.

Note: One-half cup cranberry-orange relish can be substituted for sugared cranberries.

Donna Lee

The Providence Journal and Bulletin / Providence, Rhode Island

WHOLE WHEAT ZUCCHINI BREAD   *1 loaf*

This bread is less sweet than most quick breads. The zucchini adds color and an interesting texture.

1 cup sifted all-purpose flour	⅔ cup vegetable oil
1½ teaspoons baking powder	¼ cup honey
½ teaspoon baking soda	½ teaspoon lemon extract
½ teaspoon salt	1½ cups shredded zucchini
1 teaspoon ground cinnamon	½ cup chopped nuts
½ teaspoon ground allspice	¼ cup raisins
1 cup whole wheat flour	1 teaspoon sesame seeds (optional)
2 eggs	

Sift all-purpose flour, baking powder, baking soda, salt, cinnamon and allspice. Stir in whole wheat flour. Beat eggs, oil, honey and lemon extract with rotary beater until smooth and frothy. Stir in zucchini. Add flour mixture and stir well, but do not beat. Stir in nuts and raisins. Turn into greased 9x5x3-inch loaf pan. Sprinkle with sesame seeds. Bake in 325°F. oven 1 hour, or until toothpick inserted in center comes out clean.

Claire Barriger Free-lance writer / Ottawa, Ontario

SOUR CREAM YEAST ROLLS

72 bite-size rolls

When I have guests for dinner, I often serve these great sour cream yeast rolls. Leftovers, if any, freeze beautifully. Men love them.

1 package active dry yeast
¼ cup warm water
2 cups sour cream

2 tablespoons granulated sugar
¼ teaspoon baking soda
5½ cups biscuit mix, divided

Soften yeast in water. Let stand while combining sour cream, sugar and baking soda in large bowl. Add 2 cups biscuit mix, then yeast mixture. Mix well. Stir in 3 more cups biscuit mix. Turn dough onto board dusted with ½ cup biscuit mix. Knead to form smooth ball.

Shape dough into small rounds the size of a walnut. Place close together in buttered 9x13x2-inch pan. Let rise until doubled in bulk.

Preheat oven to 375°F. Bake rolls 15 minutes, or until done.

Note: Rolls can be made ahead of time and frozen. When ready to serve, thaw rolls and reheat in oven at 200°F.

Betty Straughan *The News Review* / Roseburg, Oregon

OUT-OF-THIS-WORLD ROLLS

2 to 2½ dozen rolls

This is a top favorite at our house.

2 packages active dry yeast
¼ cup warm water
3 eggs, well beaten
½ cup solid shortening
½ cup granulated sugar

1 cup warm water
2 teaspoons salt
4½ cups all-purpose flour, divided

Soften yeast in ¼ cup warm water. Combine eggs, shortening, sugar, softened yeast, remaining warm water, salt and 2½ cups flour. Beat until smooth. Add enough remaining flour to make soft dough. Cover and allow to rise until double. Punch down and place in refrigerator overnight. Three hours before baking, roll out as desired.

Variations: *Dinner Rolls*—Divide dough in half. Roll each half into rectangle ½ inch thick. Spread with butter. Roll up jelly-roll style and cut into 1-inch slices. Place in greased muffin tins, cut side down. Cover and allow to rise 2 to 3 hours.

Preheat oven to 400°F. Bake in oven for 12 to 15 minutes.

Orange Rolls—Combine ⅓ cup melted butter, ½ cup granulated sugar and grated zest of 1 orange. Spread on dough instead of butter. Continue preparation as for dinner rolls. Frost with confectioners sugar icing while hot. To make icing: combine 1 cup confectioners sugar and ¼ to ⅓ cup milk.

Garlic Parmesan Rolls—Pinch off small pieces of dough and roll between hands to make slender sticks. Place on greased baking sheet, brush with melted butter and sprinkle lightly with garlic salt and heavily with Parmesan cheese. Allow to rise and bake as for dinner rolls.

Donna Morgan   *Salt Lake Tribune* / Salt Lake City, Utah

SWOPE BREAD   *2 loaves*

This Swope Bread recipe was printed in a Tacoma, Washington, paper with the explanation that a local skier had picked up the recipe "in the Tyrol." My mother clipped it and discovered she had a family favorite. The bread tastes like far more than the limited number of ingredients. We printed it, and readers of European extraction declared it was indeed "just like something from the old country!"

4 cups unsifted graham or whole wheat flour
2 cups unsifted all-purpose flour
1 cup granulated sugar

2 teaspoons salt
1 quart buttermilk (or 3½ cups milk acidified with ½ cup vinegar)
2 teaspoons baking soda

Preheat oven to 375°F. Grease two 9x5x3-inch loaf pans.

Combine both flours, sugar and salt. Combine buttermilk and baking soda; stir into flour mixture. Turn into prepared loaf pans.

Place in oven. Turn down heat to 350°F. Bake 1 hour and 10 minutes, or until done in center when tested with toothpick. Remove from pans and cool on rack.

Janet Beighle French   *The Plain Dealer* / Cleveland, Ohio

HAWAIIAN BANANA BREAD

2 loaves

As far as I am concerned, this is absolutely the best banana bread recipe I have ever used. It has a much better texture and taste than any I have seen, and a food editor sees a million of them. My family does not consider it Christmas without banana bread for ourselves and some wrapped in foil to give to neighbors and friends. It freezes beautifully. But a warning . . . follow the directions exactly or you will not have this beautiful texture and taste.

2 cups granulated sugar
1 cup margarine
6 very ripe bananas, mashed
4 eggs, well beaten

2½ cups cake flour
1 teaspoon salt
2 teaspoons baking soda

Cream sugar and margarine. Add bananas and eggs. Sift flour, salt and baking soda three times. Blend flour mixture into banana mixture. Do not overmix. Turn batter into 2 greased 9x5x3-inch loaf pans.

Preheat oven to 350°F. Bake bread for 55 minutes, or until toothpick tests dry in center of loaf. Turn out immediately to cool on wire rack.

Betty Straughan *The News Review* / Roseburg, Oregon

OSAGE SQUAW BREAD

6 servings

4 cups all-purpose flour
2 teaspoons salt
1 tablespoon plus 1
  teaspoon baking powder

1 tablespoon solid shortening, melted
2 cups lukewarm milk
Fat or oil for deep frying

Sift flour, salt and baking powder into bowl. Stir in shortening and milk. Knead lightly to gather dough into ball. Roll out dough on lightly floured board. Cut into 2-inch squares.

Heat fat or oil in deep fryer to 370°F. Fry 2 or 3 at a time until golden on both sides. Drain on paper towels.

Note: Indians dip the bread in "sop," a mixture of corn syrup and bacon drippings.

Ivy Coffey *El Reno Tribune* / El Reno, Oklahoma

HOMEMADE SANDWICH BUNS

12 buns

Guests expect to taste the unusual from a food editor's table, and home kitchen-testing can involve anything from buffalo meat to shark, yellow Finnish potatoes to cactus. But once in a while, I enjoy serving everyday ordinary foods in novel ways. A big hit, for instance, at summer picnics is the deluxe ham sandwich. Heat a fully cooked ham in a covered grill with damp (hickory or apple) wood chips for that extra-special flavor. Then tuck thin slices of ham inside homemade sandwich buns. Slather with homemade herbed mayonnaise and add a little coarsely ground Pommery mustard, plus homemade pickle chips or sour little French cornichons. These buns are great for beginning bread-bakers because there's no worry about forming the perfect loaf.

3 tablespoons butter
1 small onion, minced
½ cup plain yogurt or
  sour cream
½ cup water
3 to 3½ cups all-purpose
  flour, divided
1 tablespoon toasted
  wheat germ

1 teaspoon granulated
  sugar
1 teaspoon salt
1 package active dry yeast
1 egg, at room temperature
1 cup shredded natural
  Swiss cheese

Melt butter and sauté onion in small saucepan until tender but not browned. Add yogurt and water; blend well and heat until very warm, nearly 120°F.

Meanwhile, blend ¾ cup flour, wheat germ, sugar, salt and dry yeast in large mixer bowl. Add warm liquids and blend quickly with spatula into dry ingredients. Mix at low speed with mixer to blend further, gradually increasing mixer speed. Beat 2 minutes at medium speed, scraping sides of bowl frequently. Add egg, ½ cup additional flour and shredded cheese. Beat at high speed 2 minutes; stir in enough additional flour (about 2 cups) by hand to make soft dough. Turn out and knead on lightly floured surface for 8 to 10 minutes, or until smooth and elastic. Place in clean, greased bowl and turn dough to grease top. Cover and let rise 1 hour, or until double in bulk.

Punch down dough and divide into 12 equal pieces. Smooth into ball shapes and space balls well apart on large, greased 15x10-inch baking sheet. Flatten each ball to make bun shapes. Cover loosely with plastic wrap and let rise 1 hour or more.

Preheat oven to 375°F.

Bake buns 12 to 15 minutes. Remove buns from sheet, cool slightly and split to fill as desired.

Joyce Rosencrans *The Cincinnati Post* / Cincinnati, Ohio

ICE BOX ENGLISH TEA MUFFINS

1 dozen muffins

This is an old family recipe we treasure.

¾ cup granulated sugar
½ cup butter
1 egg, beaten
½ teaspoon salt
¼ teaspoon ground cinnamon
2 teaspoons baking powder
2 cups all-purpose flour
1 cup milk

¾ cup raisins

Topping:

½ cup light brown sugar
1 teaspoon ground cinnamon
¼ cup chopped pecans

Preheat oven to 350°F. Cream sugar and butter. Add beaten egg; blend well. Combine salt, cinnamon, baking powder and flour and add alternately with milk to creamed mixture. Stir in raisins.

Topping: Thoroughly combine sugar, cinnamon and nuts.

Spoon batter into greased muffin cups and sprinkle with topping. Bake 20 minutes, or until done.

Note: If not using batter immediately, cover tightly and store in refrigerator until needed. Batter will keep 3 to 4 weeks.

Donna Morgan *Salt Lake Tribune* / Salt Lake City, Utah

PIZZA BREAD

2 loaves

This flavored bread is a welcome change from the ho-hum white loaf for sandwiches. It is an exceptional joy used for a grilled cheese sandwich and is really quite nice totally unadorned.

7 cups bread flour, divided
3 tablespoons granulated sugar
1 teaspoon salt
1 package active dry yeast

4 heaping tablespoons well-seasoned spaghetti sauce
2¼ cups tomato juice
2 tablespoons butter

Combine 3 cups flour, sugar, salt and yeast in large bowl. Combine spaghetti sauce, tomato juice and butter in small saucepan. Warm mixture to between 120° and 130°F. Add to flour mixture and beat with heavy wooden spoon or electric mixer about 3 minutes. (A heavy-duty mixer with dough hook or a food processor can also be used.)

Gradually add remaining flour until mixture is rather firm; you will have added about 3 more cups flour. Remove to floured surface and knead, adding more flour (about 1 cup) until dough is supple and no longer sticky. (If you are using a heavy-duty mixer or food processor, this step is not necessary.)

Generously butter large bowl and place dough in it, turning to coat all sides. Cover and allow to rise in warm, draft-free place until doubled, 1 to 2 hours.

Punch down dough and divide into 2 parts. Dough will be sticky. Shape into smooth balls; cover and let rest about 10 minutes. Shape into loaves and place in 2 well-buttered 9x5x3-inch loaf pans. Again cover and let rise until doubled, 45 to 60 minutes.

Preheat oven to 375°F. Bake loaves in oven 10 minutes. Reduce heat to 350° and bake 25 to 30 minutes. Bread should sound hollow when tapped with knuckles. Remove from pans and cool on wire racks.

Jeanne Cummins *Noblesville Daily Ledger* / Noblesville, Indiana

HERB BUTTER-SPREAD BREAD   *6 to 8 servings*

If Omar Khayyam had tasted Herb Butter-Spread Bread, his idea of paradise would never have been: a loaf of bread, a jug of wine and thou. The bread would have been enough.

1 loaf (16 ounces) white bread, unsliced
¾ cup unsalted butter, softened
½ teaspoon salt
½ teaspoon Worcestershire sauce
½ teaspoon whole-leaf dried thyme
½ teaspoon whole-leaf dried marjoram

With serrated-edge knife, cut off top, side and end crusts of bread. Do not cut away bottom crust. Cut bread, leaving bottom attached, in half lengthwise and into ¾-inch pieces crosswise.

Cream butter. Add salt and Worcestershire. Place thyme and marjoram leaves in palm of hand and crush lightly to release flavoring oils. Add herbs to butter and mix well. Spread all cut surfaces of bread inside and out with butter.

Place bread on rimmed baking sheet. (The butter will run as it heats.) Bake, uncovered, in 325°F. oven about 30 minutes, or until crisp. Serve hot.

Susan Manlin Katzman Free-lance writer / St. Louis, Missouri

WHOLE WHEAT BREAD, QUEBEC STYLE   *2 loaves*

Molasses was a popular sweetener in much of early Québec cooking. Imported from the West Indies, it flavored and colored breads, cakes, pies and cookies. Come springtime, when the maple sap was flowing, maple syrup was often substituted for molasses. A slice of this nutritious and flavorful bread needs no butter. It makes fine morning toast and freezes well.

1 teaspoon granulated sugar	1 tablespoon salt
½ cup lukewarm water (105° to 115°F.)	1 cup milk, scalded
	1 cup cold water
2 packages active dry yeast	5 cups whole wheat flour
⅓ cup solid shortening or lard, softened	2½ cups all-purpose flour
⅓ cup molasses (or ⅓ cup maple syrup plus ¼ cup light brown sugar)	

Dissolve sugar in lukewarm water in small bowl. Sprinkle yeast over water mixture and let stand 10 minutes without stirring.

Cream shortening in large bowl. Blend in molasses, salt and scalded milk. When shortening is melted, add cold water and blend in; then add yeast mixture. Add whole wheat flour, beating in well. Add enough all-purpose flour to make dough you can knead. Knead on floured surface, adding more flour as required, until dough is elastic in texture. Place in greased bowl, grease top of dough, cover with cloth and let rise in warm place until doubled in bulk.

Punch dough down, divide in two. Shape into two loaves and place in greased 9x5x3-inch loaf pans. Grease tops and cover with cloth. Let rise again until doubled in bulk. Bake in preheated 400°F. oven 25 minutes, or until browned and hollow when rapped sharply with knuckles.

Julian Armstrong *The Gazette / Montreal, Quebec*

Desserts

BIRTHDAY BAKED ALASKA
8 to 10 servings

Baked Alaska is our favorite family birthday cake. Rather than lighting candles, we flame the Alaska. The base is my husband's and daughters' favorite brownie. Baked Alaska should be made in steps, so that the ice cream layers have time to freeze thoroughly.

Fudge Sauce:
- 2 squares (2 ounces) semi-sweet chocolate
- 2 tablespoons margarine
- 1 cup granulated sugar
- 1 can (5 or 6 ounces) evaporated milk
- 1 teaspoon vanilla extract

Favorite Chocolate Brownies:
- ½ cup margarine, softened
- 1 cup granulated sugar
- 4 eggs
- 1 teaspoon vanilla extract
- 1 can (16 ounces) chocolate-flavored syrup
- 1 cup plus 1 tablespoon unbleached flour
- ½ teaspoon baking powder

Alaska:
- 1 quart coffee ice cream, divided
- ¾ cup coarsely chopped pecans, divided
- 5 egg whites, at room temperature
- ¼ teaspoon cream of tartar
- ⅔ cup granulated sugar
- Granulated sugar for browning meringue
- 1 tablespoon brandy or rum

Fudge Sauce: Melt chocolate and margarine over low heat; stir in sugar and evaporated milk. Cook over low heat until thick and blended, stirring constantly. Stir in vanilla; cool.

Chocolate Brownies: Preheat oven to 350°F. Beat margarine and sugar in food processor or mixer until fluffy. Beat in eggs, 2 at a time; mix well. Add vanilla and chocolate syrup; beat until blended. Add flour and baking powder; mix until just blended.

Pour batter into 2 greased and floured 9-inch round cake pans; spread evenly. (Only one round will be used for this recipe. Use other round for brownies, or freeze for future Baked Alaska.)

Bake in oven for 25 to 30 minutes, or until slight imprint remains when center is touched with finger. Do not overbake. Cool.

To Assemble Baked Alaska: Line deep, 1½-quart mixing bowl, 7 inches in diameter, with aluminum foil, allowing foil to extend over edge. Spoon ⅓ the ice cream into bowl; sprinkle with ⅓ the nuts; spread ⅓ the Fudge Sauce on top. Lightly cover with foil and freeze until firm. Repeat layers twice, freezing each time until firm. (This part can be done one or two days ahead.)

When ice cream layers are firm, beat egg whites with cream of tartar until frothy. Gradually beat in ⅔ cup sugar, beating until soft, shiny peaks form and sugar is completely dissolved.

Place 12-inch square of foil, parchment paper or heavy brown paper bag on sturdy baking sheet. Trim off any crisp edge of one brownie layer; place on foil or paper. Invert ice cream layers on brownie, using foil in bowl to ease ice cream from bowl. Quickly frost ice cream with prepared meringue, being sure to seal all edges with meringue. Place in freezer, uncovered, overnight. (If it is to be left in freezer longer, cover with foil.)

When ready to serve, preheat oven to 500°F. Sprinkle granulated sugar over meringue and bake 3 minutes, or until meringue is only lightly browned.

Gently heat brandy or rum in stainless steel measuring cup. Pour brandy over meringue after it is baked and light immediately. Serve flaming Alaska at once, as flame burns out quickly. Use sharp knife to cut dessert. (To ease slicing, dip knife in hot water.)

Note: The Fudge Brownies are delicious by themselves. If you make them alone, pour batter into a greased 15x10x1-inch jelly roll pan, spread evenly and bake in 350°F. oven 18 to 22 minutes. Makes 5 dozen brownies.

Donna Segal *Indianapolis Star* / Indianapolis, Indiana

NAKED APPLE PIE
6 servings

1 egg
½ cup all-purpose flour
1 teaspoon baking powder
½ cup light brown sugar
½ cup granulated sugar

1 teaspoon vanilla extract
Pinch salt
½ cup chopped pecans or walnuts
2 medium apples, pared and chopped

Beat egg. Sift flour and baking powder. Add flour mixture to egg with sugars, vanilla and salt. Add chopped nuts and apples. Spread batter in greased 9-inch pie pan. Bake in 350°F. oven 30 minutes.

Charlotte Hansen
The Jamestown Sun / Jamestown, North Dakota

STRAWBERRY-RASPBERRY SHORTCAKE *6 servings*

This is the best shortcake I know and the best biscuits ever. During the winter I often make just the biscuits and serve them hot for breakfast with whipped butter and white clover honey.

Shortcake:
- 2 cups all-purpose flour
- 4 teaspoons baking powder
- 3 teaspoons granulated sugar, divided
- ¼ teaspoon salt
- ½ cup butter or margarine
- ⅔ cup light cream or half-and-half
  Additional butter for assembling

Fruit:
- 1½ quarts fresh strawberries
  Granulated sugar to taste
- 1 package (10 ounces) frozen raspberries

- 1 to 2 cups heavy cream, whipped

Shortcake: Sift flour, baking powder, 2 teaspoons sugar and salt. Cut in butter until mixture resembles coarse meal. Stir in cream until dry ingredients are moistened and cling together. Roll or pat out into circle 1 inch thick. Cut into six 2½ - to 3-inch circles, shaping scraps to make the necessary number. Sprinkle surface of shortcake biscuits with remaining sugar. Bake on ungreased cookie sheet in 400°F. oven 15 to 18 minutes, or until golden brown. Shortcake biscuits should be served warm. They may be made ahead and reheated at serving time.

Fruit: *Strawberries*—Wash; reserve 6 of the best for garnish and hull remainder. Slice or leave whole as desired. Sugar as required. Refrigerate. *Raspberries*—Defrost and extract juices by pressing berries in strainer. Set juice aside in pitcher; discard pulp.

To assemble: Split and butter warm shortcake biscuits. Distribute half the strawberries over bottoms, cover with top halves and spoon on remaining strawberries. Top with whipped cream, garnish with whole strawberries and pour raspberry sauce over all. Pass extra raspberry sauce in pitcher.

Marilyn McDevitt Rubin
The Pittsburgh Press / Pittsburgh, Pennsylvania

PUMPKIN ANGEL SQUARES

Pumpkin Angel Squares might make you think of pumpkin pie. The unmistakable flavor of well-seasoned pumpkin is there. But it sits atop a buttery pecan crust and a layer of fluffy cream cheese. This do-ahead dessert makes a welcome alternative to autumn's favorite pie.

1 cup all-purpose flour
½ cup butter or margarine, softened
½ cup finely chopped pecans
1 package (8 ounces) cream cheese
¾ cup granulated sugar, divided
1 cup frozen whipped topping, thawed

1 envelope unflavored gelatin
¼ cup cold water
1 can (16 ounces) pumpkin
3 eggs, separated
½ cup light brown sugar
½ cup milk
1½ teaspoons pumpkin pie spice
½ teaspoon salt

Preheat oven to 375°F.

Mix flour, butter and pecans with pastry blender until crumbly. Pack into 9-inch square pan. Bake in oven 15 to 20 minutes, or until lightly browned. Cool.

Combine cream cheese, ½ cup granulated sugar and whipped topping with electric mixer. Spread on cooled crust and chill in refrigerator.

Soften gelatin in water. Combine gelatin mixture with pumpkin, egg yolks, brown sugar, milk, pumpkin pie spice and salt in large saucepan. Cook over moderate heat, stirring, until mixture begins to bubble. Cover and cool.

Beat egg whites until frothy. Slowly add remaining granulated sugar and continue beating until stiff and glossy. Fold into pumpkin mixture. Pour over cream cheese mixture. Chill until set. Cut into squares.

Sue Dawson *Columbus Dispatch / Columbus, Ohio*

PUDDING DELIGHT

8 servings

This is an ancient recipe, but one that I am continually asked for because it is no longer on the cereal box!

1 quart milk	1 cup granulated sugar
1 cup natural wheat and	Dash salt
barley cereal (Grape-Nuts)	1 teaspoon vanilla extract
4 eggs, beaten	Ground nutmeg

Warm milk and pour over cereal in bowl. Let stand 15 minutes. Add beaten eggs, sugar, salt and vanilla, mixing very well. Pour into 13x9x2-inch baking dish. Sprinkle nutmeg over top.

Place dish in larger pan with an inch or two of hot water in bottom pan. Bake in 350°F. oven 1 hour, or until custard is set. Test by inserting table knife in center. (It should come out clean when pudding is done.) If not, bake another 5 to 10 minutes. Recipe may be halved for smaller pudding.

Helen Wilber Richardson
The Providence Journal and Bulletin / Providence, Rhode Island

LEMON ZUCCHINI PIE

6 to 8 servings

Crust:

1½ cups all-purpose flour	1¼ cups granulated sugar, divided
1½ tablespoons granulated sugar	½ cup fresh lemon juice, divided
¾ teaspoon baking powder	1 tablespoon grated lemon rind, divided
Pinch salt	1 teaspoon caraway seeds
⅓ cup melted butter	½ cup butter, softened
⅓ cup water	5 egg yolks
2 egg yolks, slightly beaten	2 eggs

Filling:

2 tablespoons butter	2 tablespoons all-purpose flour
5 to 6 small zucchini, sliced ¼-inch thick	1½ tablespoons light rum

Crust: Combine flour, sugar, baking powder and salt. Stir in melted butter, water and 2 egg yolks to make soft dough. Chill for ease in handling. Roll dough to fit 10-inch fluted flan dish.

Filling: Melt 2 tablespoons butter in large, heavy skillet. Add zucchini, ¼ cup sugar, 3 tablespoons lemon juice, 1½ teaspoons lemon rind and caraway seeds. Sauté, stirring occasionally, 8 to 10 minutes or until liquid becomes syrupy and coats zucchini. Spoon zucchini evenly into flan shell. Blend softened butter and remaining sugar in blender until combined. Blend in egg yolks and eggs, one at a time. Stir in flour, then rum. Blend in remaining lemon juice and rind. Pour over zucchini in pie shell. Bake in 350°F. oven 50 to 60 minutes, or until pie is set in center. Cool slightly before serving.

Carol Haddix *Chicago Tribune*

ABBIE'S SUGAR COOKIES   *3 dozen cookies*

My Grandmother Abbott always had the dough for these cookies waiting in the freezer for me to cut into Santas, stars and Christmas trees. She didn't seem to mind that I got more of the red and green sugar sprinkles on the floor than on the cookies.

½ cup butter	1½ cups all-purpose flour
1 cup granulated sugar	2 teaspoons baking powder
2 eggs	Sugar, nuts, cherries for
1 teaspoon vanilla extract	decoration

Cream butter and add sugar gradually. Add eggs and vanilla; beat until light. Sift flour once before measuring, then sift again with baking powder. Add to butter mixture. Chill the dough.

Preheat oven to 400°F. Roll out dough very thin on floured surface and cut into shapes with cookie cutters. Place on cookie sheets and sprinkle with sugar or decorate with colored sugar sprinkles, nuts and cherries. Bake in oven 10 minutes, watching carefully so they do not burn.

Note: I usually freeze the dough until I'm ready to use it. Then I pull off just enough dough to roll out and cut about a dozen cookies and return the rest to the freezer. Left at room temperature, the dough is very sticky.

Jann Malone *Richmond Times-Dispatch / Richmond, Virginia*

MEXICAN PECAN CANDY

30 pieces of candy

This recipe is from my hometown — Eagle Pass, Texas, on the border between the United States and Mexico. Although not many people have heard of the town, its food is not to be ignored. This recipe produces the easiest and best Mexican pecan praline candy I have tried.

1 box (1 pound) light brown sugar
1 cup heavy cream

2 cups pecans, whole or broken
Pinch salt (optional)

Place sugar and heavy cream in heavy saucepan over moderate heat. Cook, stirring, until sugar is dissolved. Continue to cook, without stirring, to soft-ball stage, 238°F. (The mixture will boil up, then subside, and requires 10 minutes or more of additional cooking.) Remove from heat, add pecans and salt. Cool slightly. (To speed cooling, place pan in cool water.)

Beat with wooden spoon as for fudge. Mixture will begin to lose glossy appearance. Drop quickly by spoonfuls onto wax paper.

Note: Short beating will produce sugary or grainy candy like some New Orleans pralines. Beating to the exact point where gloss disappears will produce a creamy candy, but you will have to drop the spoonfuls very quickly.

Harriett Aldridge *Arkansas Gazette / Little Rock, Arkansas*

SWEDISH BOOZE CAKE

This is an old, old family favorite, which is actually deceiving — no booze! But, delicious it is and has been known to put members of the clan on a "high"!

1 package (16 ounces) raisins
3 cups water
2 cups granulated sugar
1 cup solid shortening
4 cups all-purpose flour
1 teaspoon baking soda
¼ teaspoon salt

½ teaspoon ground cinnamon
½ teaspoon ground nutmeg
½ teaspoon ground cloves
2 eggs
1 cup chopped nuts
1 teaspoon vanilla extract

Place raisins, water and sugar in saucepan; bring to boil. Reduce heat and simmer 20 minutes. Add shortening and stir until melted. Cool.

Preheat oven to 350°F. Sift flour, baking soda, salt, cinnamon, nutmeg and cloves in mixing bowl. Add raisin mixture, eggs, chopped nuts and vanilla. Blend well. Pour into greased and lightly floured 13x9x2-inch baking pan. Bake in oven 45 minutes, or until cake tests done.

Donna Morgan *Salt Lake Tribune* / Salt Lake City, Utah

PEPPERED STRAWBERRIES *6 to 8 servings*

On our honeymoon in Canada, my husband, Frank Judge, and I found a surprising entry on the dessert menu at Quebec's historic Château Frontenac: peppered stawberries. Peppered? Strawberries? This we had to try. We won't forget it, and we're glad we watched the waiter carefully as he prepared the berries at our table. When we returned home, Frank came up with this version. If you try it, we think you'll remember this dessert for a long time, too.

1 quart vanilla ice cream
2 tablespoons butter
¼ cup packed light brown
   sugar
1 orange, quartered
1 lemon, quartered
1 pint strawberries, washed,
   drained, hulled and halved

¼ teaspoon (or more) freshly
   ground black pepper to
   taste
¼ cup Benedictine
   Additional freshly ground
   pepper (optional)

Just before serving, divide ice cream among 6 to 8 dessert dishes. Set aside. (Or have another person dish up the ice cream while the strawberries are being prepared.)

Melt butter with sugar in skillet over medium-high heat, stirring constantly. Squeeze orange and lemon juice into pan. (It helps to put cheesecloth over each quarter to catch seeds.) Bring to gentle boil, stirring constantly, and cook until liquid is reduced slightly. Add strawberries. Sprinkle with pepper. Stir. Taste for pepper flavoring; correct seasoning, if necessary.

Warm Benedictine, if desired. Add to berry mixture and ignite with long match, or flame from tableside burner. When flames die out, spoon warm sauce over ice cream. If desired, add additional grindings of pepper to each dish.

Peggy Daum *The Milwaukee Journal* / Milwaukee, Wisconsin

GRANDMA'S BLUEBERRY BUTTER CAKE

10 to 12 servings

Nostalgia, for me, lies in an old suitcase full of unorganized recipes scribbled in my grandmother's handwriting. They are not always easy to decipher, but once prepared, they inevitably produce the tastiest gems I have ever eaten. One of her most delectable recipes is this one.

3 cups all-purpose flour, sifted
¼ teaspoon salt
3 teaspoons baking powder
⅔ cup butter
1 cup granulated sugar, divided
1 teaspoon vanilla extract
1 cup cold water
4 egg whites

Topping:
1 package (8 ounces) cream cheese
3 tablespoons milk
2 tablespoons granulated sugar
1 teaspoon vanilla extract
1 jar (4 ounces) apple jelly
1 pint fresh blueberries
1 cup heavy cream, whipped
2 tablespoons granulated sugar (optional)

Preheat oven to 350°F. Sift flour, salt and baking powder twice. Cream butter and ¾ cup sugar. Add vanilla to cold water. Alternately combine water and flour mixtures with butter mixture; mix well after each addition. Beat egg whites until stiff, then beat in remaining sugar. Fold egg whites into batter. Pour into well-greased 13x9x2-inch pan. Bake in oven 30 minutes, or until toothpick comes out clean. Prepare topping.

Topping: Beat cream cheese with milk, sugar and vanilla until of spreading consistency. Spread over cooled cake. Melt jelly in saucepan over low heat. When completely melted, remove from heat. Clean berries and add to jelly, tossing lightly until well coated. Be careful not to crush berries. Distribute evenly over cream cheese. Cover entire cake with whipped cream. Cream can be sweetened with granulated sugar if desired.

Kingsley Belle *The Chronicle* / Glens Falls, New York

CHOCOLATE CHIP CUPCAKES

16 cupcakes

This Chocolate Chip Cupcake recipe was published by the Nestlé company many years ago, and ever since has been one of my standbys. When the recipe was printed in the Post, during the editing process the ½ teaspoon baking soda became 1 teaspoon. A more significant error was the illustration — a drawing of a high, puffy cupcake, whereas they actually are small and dense — halfway between a cookie and a cake. Our phones lit up with calls from confused readers. When I decided to print the recipe again, I gave the recipe to four people for testing — two used ½ teaspoon baking soda and two used 1 teaspoon. Before the testing got underway, a local television station's newscast reporter related the incident on the air, saying the recipe caused toothaches and was a waste of $5.00 worth of ingredients. The reporter claimed the Post was apologizing. Our testing confirmed that there was little difference between the amounts of baking soda. However, I reprinted the original recipe, and the television reporter, this time, apologized. The cupcakes gained countless new fans.

Batter:
½ cup butter, softened
6 tablespoons granulated sugar
6 tablespoons light brown sugar
½ teaspoon vanilla extract
1 egg
1 cup plus 2 tablespoons all-purpose flour
½ teaspoon baking soda
½ teaspoon salt

Topping:
½ cup light brown sugar
1 egg
Pinch salt
1 cup (6 ounces) semisweet chocolate pieces
½ cup coarsely chopped walnuts
½ teaspoon vanilla extract

Preheat oven to 375°F.

Batter: Cream butter, sugars and vanilla. Beat in egg. Sift flour, baking soda and salt; stir into butter-sugar-egg mixture. Spoon by rounded tablespoonfuls into enough paper-lined muffin tins to make 16 cupcakes. Bake in oven 10 to 12 minutes. Remove from oven. While cupcakes are baking, prepare topping.

Topping: Beat brown sugar, egg and salt until thick. Stir in chocolate pieces, nuts and vanilla.

As soon as cupcakes are removed from oven, spoon 1 tablespoon topping over each and immediately return to oven; bake 15 minutes longer. Remove cupcakes from muffin tins at once.

Phyllis Richman *The Washington Post*

HOT FUDGE PUDDING

6 servings

This was always my favorite dessert as a child: It's my mother's recipe, and although it's easy to make, she always saved it for special occasions — it's very rich! The end result is also something of a miracle, considering how the recipe is put together. It's wonderful hot with whipped cream or with ice cream melting into it, but it's also great cold, the next day, as an indulgence.

1 cup all-purpose flour
2 teaspoons baking powder
6½ tablespoons cocoa powder, divided
¼ teaspoon salt
1¼ cups granulated sugar, divided

½ cup milk
2 tablespoons melted butter
1 teaspoon vanilla extract
1 cup chopped nuts (optional)
½ cup light brown sugar
1 cup cold water

Sift flour, baking powder, 1½ tablespoons cocoa, salt and ¾ cup granulated sugar. Stir in milk, melted butter and vanilla. Add nuts. Pour into well-buttered 9-inch square pan. Combine remaining sugars and cocoa. Sprinkle over batter. Pour water over all. Bake in 375°F. oven 45 minutes, or until done.

Kathy Lindsley *Rochester Times-Union* / Rochester, New York

MRS. HARVEY'S WHITE FRUITCAKE

One thing that has not changed in more than thirty years is the love of our readers for Mrs. Harvey's fruitcake recipe, which first appeared in The Tampa Tribune *in 1951. Requests for this recipe are so numerous that we publish the recipe annually.*

4 cups shelled pecans
¾ pound candied cherries
1 pound candied pineapple
1¾ cups all-purpose flour
1 cup butter
1 cup granulated sugar

5 large eggs
½ teaspoon baking powder
1 bottle (1 ounce) vanilla extract
1 bottle (1 ounce) lemon extract

Chop pecans, cherries and pineapple into medium-sized pieces; dredge with small amount of flour. Cream butter and sugar until light and fluffy. Add well-beaten eggs and blend well. Sift remaining flour and baking powder; fold into egg and butter mixture. Add vanilla and lemon extracts; mix well. Add fruits and nuts, blending well.

Grease 10-inch tube pan. Line with heavy brown paper and grease again. Pour batter into prepared pan. Place in cold oven and bake 3 hours at 250°F. Cool in pan on cake rack.

Note: Batter also may be baked in two 9x5x3-inch loaf pans for 2½ hours.

Mary Scourtes *The Tampa Tribune* / Tampa, Florida

EVERYDAY COOKIES
8 to 10 dozen cookies

"You should enter these in the Minnesota State Fair," I told a friend after tasting these sensational cookies. They're the best I'd ever had. Although she was quite ill at the time, she took some to the fair and won a ribbon.

1 cup butter or margarine	1 teaspoon cream of tartar
1 cup granulated sugar	1 teaspoon baking soda
1 cup light brown sugar	1 teaspoon salt
1 cup vegetable oil	1 cup crispy rice cereal
2 eggs	1 cup quick-cooking oats
1 teaspoon vanilla extract	1 cup shredded coconut
3½ cups all-purpose flour	½ cup chopped pecans

Preheat oven to 350°F. Cream butter, sugars and oil. Add eggs and vanilla; beat well so oil doesn't separate. Add flour mixed with cream of tartar, baking soda and salt. Stir in rice cereal, oats, coconut and nuts. Drop by teaspoonfuls onto ungreased cookie sheet; flatten slightly. Bake on lower shelf of oven 5 to 6 minutes.

Move to middle of oven and finish baking until lightly browned, about 5 minutes. Watch carefully so they don't become too brown. Remove from sheets and cool.

(If a pan of cookie dough is ready to put on the lower shelf of the oven when the one already in the oven is moved to middle shelf, baking will be speeded.)

Eleanor Ostman
St. Paul Pioneer Press and Dispatch / St. Paul, Minnesota

BOURBON BALLS

3 dozen Bourbon balls

Bourbon balls are a favorite holiday treat in Virginia. They are easy to make and they keep well in a tightly covered container. If they do dry out, just sprinkle them with a little more Bourbon.

2½ cups vanilla wafer crumbs
2 tablespoons cocoa powder
1 cup confectioners sugar
1 cup finely chopped pecans

2 tablespoons light corn syrup
½ to ¾ cup Bourbon
Additional confectioners sugar for rolling

Mix vanilla wafer crumbs, cocoa, confectioners sugar and pecans in large bowl. Add corn syrup and ½ cup Bourbon. If mixture seems dry, add more Bourbon.

Form into small balls and roll in confectioners sugar. Store in airtight container.

Note: Vanilla wafer crumbs are easily prepared in the blender or food processor. Or wrap cookies in plastic wrap or put them in a plastic bag; pulverize them with meat tenderizer or hammer.

Jann Malone *Richmond Times-Dispatch* / Richmond, Virginia

POPPY SEED TEA CAKE

This cake is wonderful for holidays such as Easter, when you don't want an especially sweet dessert. It is nice for serving with tea or coffee, and great for brown bag lunches.

⅓ cup poppy seeds
1 cup buttermilk
1 cup butter or margarine
1½ cups granulated sugar
4 eggs
2½ cups sifted all-purpose flour
2 teaspoons baking powder

1 teaspoon baking soda
½ teaspoon salt
1 teaspoon orange extract
Cinnamon sugar (2 tablespoons granulated sugar and 1 teaspoon ground cinnamon, thoroughly mixed)

Combine poppy seeds and buttermilk. Refrigerate overnight for full flavor.

Cream butter with sugar until light and fluffy. Add eggs, one at a time, beating after each addition. Sift flour, baking powder, baking soda and salt. Add orange extract to creamed mixture. Blend in flour mixture alternately with poppy seed mixture, beginning and ending with dry ingredients. Turn half the batter into greased and floured 10-inch Bundt or tube pan. Sprinkle cinnamon sugar on top. Add remaining batter. Bake in 350°F. oven 1 hour, or until cake tests done. Cool 10 minutes; remove from pan and finish cooling.

Mary Frances Phillips
San Jose Mercury and News / San Jose, California

PIONEER BREAD PUDDING
4 to 6 servings

This bread pudding recipe is just one of the drawing cards at Johnny's Cottage Restaurant in Sister Bay, Wisconsin. Some people have been known to eat it for breakfast, and orders of it go home to Chicago in carry outs. Four or five large pans of the pudding are sold every day.

2 cups day-old bread cubes
  (¼- to ½-inch pieces),
  crusts removed
2 cups milk
¼ cup granulated sugar
3 tablespoons butter
2 eggs
  Dash salt
½ teaspoon vanilla extract

Lemon Sauce:
1 cup granulated sugar
2 tablespoons cornstarch
⅛ teaspoon salt
2 cups water
1 tablespoon grated lemon
  peel
¼ cup butter
2 tablespoons lemon juice

Preheat oven to 350°F.

Place bread cubes in buttered 1-quart baking dish. Combine milk, sugar and butter in saucepan; heat until sugar is dissolved and butter melted. Beat eggs slightly, adding dash of salt. Stir into warm milk mixture and add vanilla. Pour over bread cubes.

Set baking dish in pan of hot water. Bake in oven 1 hour, or until knife comes out clean when inserted in center.

Serve hot or cold with plain cream, or serve hot with lemon sauce.

Lemon Sauce: Combine sugar, cornstarch and salt in saucepan. Stir in water and lemon peel. Boil one minute; remove from heat and stir in butter and lemon juice.

Dorothy Kincaid *Milwaukee Sentinel / Milwaukee, Wisconsin*

133

RICOTTA CASSATA

Every Easter, we looked forward to Ricotta Cassata, a deep-dish sweet ricotta pie, which was a specialty of my Sicilian grandmother. Some recipes call for the addition of golden raisins or tiny pieces of chocolate. Hers has only sugar and cinnamon as flavorings.

Crust:
- 1¼ cups all-purpose flour, sifted
- ½ teaspoon salt
- 1 tablespoon granulated sugar
- ⅓ cup solid shortening, chilled
- ¼ cup cold water

Filling:
- 3 eggs
- 1½ pounds ricotta cheese
- ¼ teaspoon salt
- ¼ cup light cream or half-and-half
- ½ cup granulated sugar
- 1 teaspoon ground cinnamon

Crust: Combine flour, salt and sugar in large bowl. Cut in shortening until mixture is crumbly. Sprinkle water, 1 tablespoon at a time, over mixture, mixing quickly with fork until pastry holds together.

Place dough on lightly floured surface; shape gently into ball and flatten. Lightly flour rolling pin and roll dough into large circle. Transfer pastry to 9- or 10-inch pie plate. Make filling.

Filling: Beat eggs in mixing bowl until light and frothy. Beat ricotta in large bowl until smooth; add eggs, salt and cream, beating until smooth.

Preheat oven to 375°F.

Pour mixture into pastry shell and sprinkle top with mixture of sugar and cinnamon. Bake in oven 10 minutes; reduce heat to 350° and bake 25 to 30 minutes, or until done.

Linda Giuca *The Hartford Courant / Hartford, Connecticut*

PECAN AND PEACH UPSIDE-DOWN CAKE

This upside-down cake is my hands-down favorite to take to a casual gathering. It's savory, rich, honey-sweet and delectable. The cake recipe originally came from James Beard's American Cooking. I adapted it for use in this recipe.

1½ cups butter,* divided
1⅓ cups all-purpose flour
  5 eggs
1⅓ cups granulated sugar
  1 teaspoon baking powder
  ¼ teaspoon salt
     *Do not use margarine.

½ teaspoon almond extract
1 cup light brown sugar
½ cup honey
1 can (30 ounces) peaches, drained and sliced
   Maraschino cherries
½ to 1 cup chopped pecans

Blend 1 cup butter with flour until well mixed. Beat in eggs, one at a time, then beat in granulated sugar, baking powder, salt and almond extract. Beat mixture until thoroughly combined. Set aside.

Preheat oven to 350°F.

Melt remaining butter in cast-iron frying pan or any other oven-proof skillet measuring at least 9 inches in diameter, but not more than 12 inches. Add brown sugar; mix well. Add honey and blend thoroughly. Remove from heat and arrange peach slices in decorative pattern, using cherries for accent and color. Sprinkle pecans in corners and over tops of peaches. Cover fruit with batter, spreading carefully with spatula to distribute evenly. Allow at least 1½ inches between batter and rim for expansion during baking. Bake in oven 30 minutes, or until toothpick inserted in center comes out clean.

Do not turn over at this time. The cake should be placed on rack and allowed to cool in order to avoid damaging tender cake. When cake is completely cool, invert skillet onto platter or cake dish. The cake is best stored, covered, at room temperature.

Joe Crea *Florida Times-Union* / Jacksonville, Florida

MRS. AMERICA CHOCOLATE CAKE

I received this recipe from a contestant in the Mrs. America Pageant in 1955. I'm not sure what state she represented or if she won the contest, but I do know this cake has been a winner every time it's been served. For all of our birthday celebrations, it's a "must."

3 squares (3 ounces) unsweetened chocolate
1 cup water
½ cup butter or margarine
1 teaspoon vanilla extract
2 cups granulated sugar, divided
3 large eggs, separated
2½ cups sifted cake flour
½ teaspoon salt
1 cup sour cream
1¼ teaspoons baking soda
1 teaspoon red food coloring (optional)
Cocoa for dusting pans

Chocolate Frosting:
¼ cup butter or margarine
2 squares (2 ounces) unsweetened chocolate
Dash salt
1 teaspoon vanilla extract
1 box (16 ounces) confectioners sugar, sifted
5 tablespoons (approx.) evaporated milk

Combine chocolate and water in small saucepan. Bring to boil and cook over low heat until chocolate is melted. Stir to blend. Remove from heat and set aside.

Cream butter, vanilla and 1½ cups sugar until light and fluffy. Add egg yolks and beat well. Sift flour and salt three times. Add to butter mixture alternately with sour cream. Blend well after each addition until smooth.

Sprinkle baking soda over chocolate and blend well. Add to creamed mixture and blend thoroughly. Add red coloring, if desired.

Whip egg whites, which have been warmed to room temperature in nonplastic bowl, until soft peaks are formed. Gradually add remaining sugar, a tablespoon at a time, and continue to beat until stiff, but still shiny, peaks are formed.

Add large spoonful meringue to cake batter and beat in. Add remaining meringue to batter and gently fold in with rubber spatula. Spoon batter evenly into 2 lightly greased and cocoa-dusted round 8- or 9-inch layer pans. Let set in pans 5 minutes before placing in oven. Preheat oven to 350°F.

Bake in oven 40 to 45 minutes, or until cake tests done when toothpick is inserted in middle. Remove from oven and cool in pans 5 minutes before removing to wire rack to cool completely. Frost when cold.

Frosting: Melt butter and chocolate in saucepan over very low heat or in top part of double boiler over hot, not simmering, water. Stir in salt and vanilla. Blend in sugar and enough milk to make smooth, spreading consistency, beating well after each addition.

Frost cake, using about ⅓ the frosting between layers and the rest on sides and top. Store cake in refrigerator until served.

Cy Meier
Thompson Newspapers of Upper Michigan / Calumet, Michigan

BRANDY ALEXANDER SOUFFLE   *8 to 10 servings*

2 envelopes unflavored gelatin
2 cups cold water, divided
1 cup granulated sugar, divided
4 eggs, separated

1 package (8 ounces) cream cheese, softened
3 tablespoons crème de cacao
3 tablespoons brandy
1 cup heavy cream, whipped
Ground nutmeg (optional)

Soften gelatin in 1 cup water in saucepan; stir over low heat until gelatin is dissolved. Add remaining water. Remove from heat; blend in ¾ cup sugar and beaten egg yolks. Return to heat and cook 2 to 3 minutes, or until slightly thickened. Gradually add softened cream cheese, mixing until well blended. Stir in crème de cacao and brandy. Chill until slightly thickened.

Beat egg whites until soft peaks form. Gradually add remaining ¼ cup sugar, beating until stiff peaks form. Fold egg whites and whipped cream into cream cheese mixture.

Wrap 3-inch collar of aluminum foil around top of 1½-quart soufflé dish; secure with tape. Pour mixture into dish; chill until firm. Remove foil collar before serving. Sprinkle with nutmeg, if desired.

Dotty Griffith   *The Dallas Morning News* / Dallas, Texas

ANN'S PASTRY

9-inch crust

This is the best pastry recipe I know. I got it from my friend Ann Kerr, a Tampa attorney and a good cook. We like to cook together and have used this pastry for pies, both fruit and custard; mushroom tarts; and sweet and nonsweet tartlets — it works with all of them.

6 tablespoons cold, unsalted butter, cut into small pieces

2 tablespoons solid shortening
1¼ cups all-purpose flour
2 tablespoons ice water

Cut butter and shortening into flour until mixture resembles coarse meal. Toss in water and mix until dough forms ball. Knead a few seconds. Refrigerate 1 hour before rolling out.

Ann McDuffie   *The Tampa Tribune* / Tampa, Florida

THE ULTIMATE RICE PUDDING

4 servings

This makes the best rice pudding for the least effort of any I've tried.

3 cups milk
¼ to ½ cup granulated sugar
2 cups cooked rice

2 to 3 tablespoons butter
1 teaspoon vanilla extract

Combine milk, sugar, rice and butter in saucepan. Simmer 20 to 30 minutes, or until thick. Remove from heat and stir in vanilla.

Note: You may use the lesser amount of sugar (¼ cup) and substitute half-and-half for the milk. In case a rice pudding binge leads you to dieting, try the recipe with ¼ cup granulated sugar substitute and skim milk or skim evaporated milk. It's still super.

Ann Criswell   *Houston Chronicle* / Houston, Texas

FRESH PINEAPPLE PIE

Fresh pineapple pie probably is one of the best-received recipes we've printed. The nut crust was a wonderful discovery and fits with a number of other pie recipes calling for a graham cracker crust.

1 large, fresh pineapple
½ cup granulated sugar
2 tablespoons cornstarch
1 teaspoon freshly grated lemon peel
⅛ teaspoon ground nutmeg
1½ cups water
3 drops yellow food coloring

Nut Crust:

⅔ cup toasted ground walnuts
¾ cup vanilla wafer crumbs
1 tablespoon granulated sugar
5 tablespoons butter, melted

Twist crown from pineapple. Cut pineapple into quarters. Remove fruit from shell. Core and cut pineapple into bite-size chunks.

Combine sugar, cornstarch, lemon peel and nutmeg in large saucepan. Stir in water and food coloring. Cook, stirring constantly, until sauce is clear and thickened. Remove from heat. Add pineapple chunks. Cool.

Nut Crust: *Toasted walnuts*—Preheat oven to 325°F. Grind walnuts; spread in shallow pan. Bake in oven 10 to 15 minutes, or until just roasted, turning occasionally to roast evenly. Advance heat to 400°.

Vanilla wafer crumbs—Add vanilla wafers, a few at a time, to blender and blend.

Combine walnuts, crumbs, sugar and melted butter. Press into bottom and up sides of 10-inch pie plate. Bake in oven 8 minutes. Cool.

Spoon fruit into cooled crust. Pour sauce evenly over fruit. Cover and chill overnight.

Joe Crea *Florida Times-Union / Jacksonville, Florida*

GINGERED PUMPKIN SLICES

6 servings

Fresh pumpkin has been rediscovered in the last few years for delights that extend far beyond pies. Next time you prepare fresh pumpkin for steaming, save a portion for this delicious accompaniment to grilled ham or sausage patties for Sunday brunch.

¼ to ⅓ small round pumpkin
  Lemon or lime juice
2 egg whites
½ teaspoon ground cinnamon
  Margarine or butter

½ cup granulated sugar
¼ teaspoon ground ginger
2 tablespoons finely chopped
  walnuts or almonds

Remove seeds and peel from pumpkin; cut into thin slices. Marinate for 1 hour in lemon or lime juice.

Beat egg whites until foamy; combine with ground cinnamon. Drain each pumpkin slice; dip into egg mixture and sauté in butter until lightly browned. Roll in sugar combined with ginger and nuts.

Sandal English *Arizona Daily Star* / Tucson, Arizona

ALMOND LEMON TORTE

This is my favorite Passover dessert.

8 eggs, separated
1½ cups granulated sugar
¼ cup sifted matzo meal
½ tablespoon lemon juice
  Grated rind of ½ lemon
¼ teaspoon salt
1 tablespoon cold water
½ cup ground pecans
½ cup ground almonds

Glaze (optional):

1 egg yolk
½ cup lemon juice
½ cup granulated sugar
  Grated rind of ½ lemon
1 teaspoon butter or pareve
  margarine

Beat egg yolks until light. Gradually add sugar and continue beating until eggs are lemon colored. Sift matzo meal and add to yolk mixture. Add lemon juice, lemon rind, salt and water. Fold in ground nuts.

Beat egg whites until stiff. Fold into yolk mixture.

Preheat oven to 325°F.

Grease 9-inch springform pan with butter or margarine and flour with matzo flour. Pour batter into prepared pan. Bake in oven 1 hour, or until toothpick comes out clean.

Serve as is, or with a glaze.

Glaze: While Almond Lemon Torte is still in oven, prepare glaze. Beat egg yolk, lemon juice, sugar and lemon rind. Place mixture in saucepan and bring to boil. Boil, stirring constantly, until mixture thickens slightly. Stir in butter.

Remove cake from oven and poke holes in top of cake at 1-inch intervals. When cake has cooled slightly, pour glaze over cake while still in pan. Let stand a few minutes so glaze sinks in, then remove cake from pan.

Joan Nathan Free-lance writer / Chevy Chase, Maryland

NUTMEG CAKE

2 cups light brown sugar
2 cups sifted all-purpose flour
½ cup margarine
½ cup finely chopped almonds, divided

1 cup sour cream
1 teaspoon baking soda
1 egg
1 teaspoon ground nutmeg

Preheat oven to 325°F.

Mix brown sugar, flour and margarine until fine and crumbly. Press one-fourth this mixture into well-greased 8- or 9-inch square pan. Sprinkle with half the almonds. Mix sour cream and baking soda; then mix in egg, remaining crumb mixture and nutmeg; blend well. Pour over mixture in pan. Sprinkle with remaining almonds. Bake in oven 40 to 50 minutes, or until done.

Kathleen Kelly *Wichita Eagle-Beacon* / Wichita, Kansas

VENTANA CHOCOLATE TORTE

This is adapted from a wonderful dessert served at Ventana, a resort over-looking the Pacific Ocean in Big Sur, California.

5 eggs
1 cup granulated sugar
1 cup melted unsalted butter
3 squares (3 ounces) semi-sweet chocolate
3 squares (3 ounces) un-sweetened chocolate
¼ cup sifted cornstarch
½ teaspoon vanilla extract
3 tablespoons orange liqueur

Glaze:
6½ squares (6½ ounces) semisweet chocolate
2 tablespoons unsalted butter
⅓ cup heavy cream

Ground almonds, pistachios or hazelnuts (optional)

Beat eggs and sugar in top of double boiler over hot water until mixture is very light and almost white in color. Remove from heat.

Melt butter and skim off foam. Return to heat and melt chocolates in butter.

Preheat oven to 325°F.

Beat sifted cornstarch slowly into egg mixture with electric mixer on low speed until thoroughly blended. Stir vanilla and orange liqueur into chocolate mixture, then add to egg mixture. Spoon into 10-inch springform pan which has been greased and floured. Bake in oven 20 to 25 minutes, or until torte pulls away from sides of pan. Knife inserted in center will not come out clean. Do not overbake. Cool in pan. Remove ring.

Glaze: Melt chocolate and butter with cream.

Spoon glaze over cooled torte. Refrigerate and chill completely.

If desired, decorate sides with ground almonds, pistachios or hazelnuts. Torte can be frozen before being decorated with nuts.

Marian Burros *The New York Times*

KEEPSAKE FRUITCAKE

My favorite recipe is a newcomer, certainly not the typical family heir-loom passed down through the generations. When the family gathered for Christmas at my grandparents' Missouri farm, the array of foods was magnificent. There were the scalloped potatoes, homemade yeast rolls, ham and turkey, eggnog, Grandma's Date Nut Roll, Mom's Chocolate Sheet Cake, Aunt Pearl's Banana Peanut Dessert and Aunt Muriel's Wal-nut Pumpkin Pie — but no fruitcake. They simply didn't like it. Through the years I made attempts at incorporating a fruitcake into the yearly festivities. The recipes used were for the familiar mixed candied fruit, dark batter combinations and the cakes were largely ignored, passed over for the more familiar treats. All of that changed a couple of years ago when I created this recipe, based on another called Old Mansion Fruit-cake. The combination of fruits, coconut, nuts and sherry in a light bat-ter seems to be just what the family ordered. It's now the most popular dessert served at our Christmas get-togethers.

1 pound candied cherries, halved
¾ pound candied pineapple, sliced
½ pound golden raisins
¾ cup cream sherry
1 cup flaked coconut, packed
2 cups chopped walnuts
¾ cup solid shortening

¾ cup butter or margarine
1½ cups granulated sugar
8 large eggs, well beaten
1 tablespoon vanilla extract
1 teaspoon almond extract
3 cups sifted all-purpose flour
1½ teaspoons baking powder
1 teaspoon salt

Measure and prepare cherries, pineapple and raisins; place in large bowl. Add sherry; mix well with fruits. Cover and let stand several hours or overnight at room temperature. Add coco-nut and nuts.

Cream shortening, butter and sugar until light and fluffy. Beat in eggs, vanilla and almond extracts. Resift flour with bak-ing powder and salt. Add flour mixture to creamed mixture along with fruit mixture. Mix batter with hands until well blended and fruit is thoroughly distributed throughout batter. (There will be about 4 quarts of batter.)

Pour batter into well-greased angel food cake pan. (Place cookie sheet on rack below to catch any drippings from pan.) Bake in 275°F. oven 3 to 4 hours, or until cake tests done. Re-move from oven and let stand 1 hour before removing cake from the pan.

Jan Townsend *The Sacramento Bee* / Sacramento, California

SAUCEPAN INDIANS

32 squares

This quick version of brownies bakes up beautifully in a jelly roll pan. I've adapted the recipe to use cocoa, which is less expensive than baking chocolate.

1 cup butter or margarine
¾ to 1 cup cocoa powder
2 cups granulated sugar
4 eggs
2 teaspoons vanilla extract

1⅓ cups all-purpose flour
1 teaspoon baking powder
1 teaspoon salt
1 cup chopped walnuts

Melt butter or margarine in large saucepan over low heat. Mix cocoa and sugar; stir into melted butter with wooden spoon. Continue stirring over low heat until ingredients are well blended. Beat in eggs one at a time, beating well after each addition; mix in vanilla.

Preheat oven to 350°F.

Combine flour, baking powder and salt. Add to cocoa mixture and beat to mix thoroughly. Stir in nuts. Spread in 15x10x1-inch jelly roll pan. Bake in oven for 30 minutes, or until top has dull crust and slight imprint remains when touched lightly. Do not overbake. Cool and cut into squares.

Kathleen Kelly *Wichita Eagle-Beacon / Wichita, Kansas*

ALMOND CHEESE PIE

This is without a doubt the best dessert I have ever tasted.

1½ cups chocolate wafer
    crumbs
1 cup chopped blanched
    almonds
1⅓ cups granulated sugar,
    divided
½ cup butter, melted
1 package (8 ounces) cream
    cheese

3 eggs, separated
1 tablespoon almond-
    flavored liqueur
1 cup heavy cream
    Toasted buttered almonds
    Additional almond-
    flavored liqueur

Make crust by mixing wafer crumbs, almonds, ⅓ cup sugar and butter. Press mixture into lightly greased 9-inch springform pan.

Beat cream cheese with remaining sugar in mixing bowl. Beat until fluffy; add egg yolks and liqueur. Set aside.

Whip cream. Whip egg whites in separate bowl until stiff. Fold whipped cream and beaten egg whites into cream cheese mixture. Pour into chocolate crust. Freeze.

When ready to serve, sprinkle top of pie with toasted and buttered almonds and pour a few tablespoons of almond-flavored liqueur over each slice.

Betty Caldwell *The Tennessean* / Nashville, Tennessee

PUMPKIN PIE CHEESECAKE

I'm a traditionalist when it comes to holiday fare, but this recipe for pumpkin pie has replaced the old-fashioned one I used to prepare.

1 can (16 ounces) pumpkin
⅔ cup light brown sugar
1 teaspoon ground cinnamon
1 teaspoon ground ginger
½ teaspoon ground nutmeg
½ teaspoon ground cloves
4 eggs, divided
1 cup evaporated milk

2 teaspoons vanilla extract, divided
1 deep dish (9- or 10-inch) unbaked pastry shell
1 package (8 ounces) cream cheese, softened
½ cup granulated sugar

Preheat oven to 350°F.

Combine pumpkin, brown sugar, cinnamon, ginger, nutmeg, cloves, 2 slightly beaten eggs, evaporated milk and 1 teaspoon vanilla in large mixing bowl. Pour into 10-inch pastry shell in deep-dish pie pan. Combine cream cheese, granulated sugar, remaining vanilla and 2 slightly beaten eggs in smaller mixing bowl; beat until smooth. Carefully pour cream cheese mixture over pumpkin filling. (You want the cream cheese mixture to stay on top.) Bake in oven 1 hour, or until knife inserted in center comes out clean. Chill before serving.

Note: The flavor improves overnight, so make it a day in advance, if possible.

Jane Baker *The Phoenix Gazette* / Phoenix, Arizona

HOLIDAY RAISIN CAKE

This recipe was shared by a reader who even sent a sample into the office for us to try. It was delicious, and all the staff members promptly adopted the recipe for personal use. It was one of our "year's favorite" recipes for 1979. I usually bake it only for the holidays, but it would be equally good at any time of year. This recipe is so simple that I usually mix it up with a wooden spoon right in the Dutch oven in which I have simmered the raisins, then transfer it to the baking pan.

1 pound raisins	1 teaspoon ground cloves
2 cups hot water	1 teaspoon ground allspice
1 cup cold water	1 teaspoon ground nutmeg
½ cup margarine (or part margarine, part butter)	2 teaspoons baking soda
	2 teaspoons hot water
2 cups dark brown sugar	4 cups all-purpose flour
1 egg, beaten	1 cup pecans, whole or chopped

Simmer raisins in 2 cups hot water in large (5-quart) Dutch oven or saucepan for 15 minutes. Remove from heat and add cold water.

Preheat oven to 350°F.

Stir in margarine, sugar, egg, cloves, allspice and nutmeg. Dissolve baking soda in 2 teaspoons hot water and stir into raisin mixture along with flour. Mix well. Fold in nuts. Pour mixture into well-greased 10-inch angel food cake or fluted tube pan. Bake in oven 1 hour, or until done.

Note: Some people may think this is a bread rather than a cake. Whatever you choose to call it, it is good just as it is. If a frosting is desired, simply sprinkle confectioners sugar on top.

This cake freezes well.

Barbara Gibbs Ostmann
St. Louis Post-Dispatch / St. Louis, Missouri

POACHED PEARS WITH RASPBERRIES AND CREAM

4 servings

When I was trying to decide on a light, pretty dessert to follow a Valentine's Day dinner, I thought of one of my favorite desserts — poached pears — and added raspberries for color.

2 cups water
½ cup dry white wine
1 cinnamon stick (2 inches)
1 vanilla bean (1 inch)
   Zest from ½ lemon

1¼ cups granulated sugar
   Juice of 1 lemon
   Cold water
4 ripe pears (Bosc or Anjou)
1 package (10 ounces) frozen raspberries
½ pint heavy cream

Combine water, wine, cinnamon, vanilla and zest in saucepan just large enough to hold pears submerged in syrup. Stir in sugar. Bring mixture to simmer over moderate heat, stirring to dissolve sugar; simmer 5 minutes. Remove from heat and set aside while preparing pears.

Add juice from one lemon to bowl of cold water. Peel pears and core from bottom to remove seeds. (Pears can be left whole or cut in half for poaching. Don't remove stems if you leave pears whole.) To prevent darkening, drop pears into lemon water as you work. Transfer pears to poaching liquid and heat until syrup is barely simmering. Keep syrup just at simmer for 8 to 10 minutes, or until pears are still firm but can be pierced easily with fork. Remove saucepan from heat, cover and let rest 20 minutes.

Thaw raspberries, drain well and reserve syrup. Whip cream until almost stiff; add raspberry juice to taste and continue whipping. Garnish pears with raspberries and whipped cream.

Note: Pears can be served warm or can be refrigerated overnight in the poaching liquid and served chilled.

Linda Giuca *The Hartford Courant* / Hartford, Connecticut

BUTTERSCOTCH BROWNIES

20 brownies

These rich, buttery brownies studded with chocolate pieces never last long, and they are super-easy to make. I got the recipe from my mother-in-law, who lives in the Adirondacks. She often has a pan of them waiting when we arrive, car-weary from New York City, to visit.

2 cups light brown sugar
1 cup margarine or solid
  shortening
4 eggs
1 teaspoon vanilla extract

½ teaspoon orange extract
  (optional)
2 scant cups all-purpose flour
1 to 2 cups semisweet
  chocolate pieces

Preheat oven to 350°F.

Cream sugar and margarine, then add eggs, one at a time, beating well after each addition. Add vanilla and orange extracts. Add flour and mix well. Stir in chocolate pieces. (Exact amount of chocolate depends on chocolate flavor desired.) Pour batter into greased 9x12x2-inch baking pan. Bake in oven 35 to 45 minutes, or until done. Cool before cutting.

Rosemary Black *The Record* / Hackensack, New Jersey

GERMAN APPLE PANCAKE

6 servings

½ cup plus 1 tablespoon
  all-purpose flour
½ teaspoon baking powder
¼ teaspoon salt
6 large eggs, separated
½ cup light brown sugar
½ cup granulated sugar

½ cup plus 1 tablespoon milk
2 teaspoons vanilla extract
¼ cup lemon juice
3 cups peeled, diced apples
¼ cup butter
1 teaspoon ground cinnamon
¼ teaspoon ground nutmeg

Combine flour, baking powder and salt in large bowl; set aside. Beat egg whites until foamy, then gradually beat in the sugars, reserving 2 tablespoons of each. Continue beating until whites are stiff. Beat yolks until thickened, then beat in milk and vanilla.

Pour lemon juice over apples. Stir egg yolk mixture into flour mixture. Continue beating until mixture is smooth. Fold in egg whites and apples.

Preheat oven to 375°F.

Melt butter in 12- or 14-inch skillet with oven-proof handle. Pour in pancake mixture, sprinkle with reserved sugars, cinnamon and nutmeg. Bake in oven for 15 minutes, or until set and lightly browned. Cut into wedges and serve immediately. Like a soufflé, this deflates rapidly as it cools.

Nancy Pappas The Louisville Times / Louisville, Kentucky

CHRISTMAS FRUIT BALLS

30 fruit balls

It wouldn't seem like Christmas at our house without these Christmas Fruit Balls. The recipe has been in the family so long I can't remember where it originated. Everyone in the family — including the toddlers — can help make them. There's no cooking. No refined sugar. Just grind the ingredients together (in food grinder or food processor) and roll with your hands.

1 cup golden seedless
  raisins
1 cup dates
1 cup dried apricots
1 cup chopped walnuts

1 teaspoon grated lemon
  rind
1 teaspoon grated
  orange rind
Confectioners sugar

Grind raisins, dates, apricots, walnuts and lemon and orange rinds in food grinder or food processor very fine. Mix well. Roll into bite-size balls. Roll in confectioners sugar. Store in covered jar in refrigerator for at least 2 weeks to mellow flavors. Before serving, you may want to coat again with confectioners sugar.

Woodene Merriman
Pittsburgh Post-Gazette / Pittsburgh, Pennsylvania

BUNDT CAKE

I first had this cake years ago at a benefit coffee at someone's home. One of the hostesses said her cook made it and promised to give me the recipe. It arrived on my doorstep tucked into a Bundt pan as a Christmas present. Although I've made many cakes, I keep coming back to this recipe year-in and year-out. It's also my family's favorite. My daughter makes it better than I do.

2 cups granulated sugar
2 cups all-purpose flour
1 cup margarine, softened
5 eggs, at room temperature

1 tablespoon combined flavorings (1 teaspoon each vanilla extract, almond or lemon extract, or other flavoring as desired)

Preheat oven to 325°F.

Grease Bundt pan generously (even the nonstick ones). Combine sugar, flour, margarine, eggs and flavorings in an electric mixer all at once and beat until smooth, about 10 minutes. Pour into prepared pan. Bake in oven 1 hour, or until cake is done.

Ann Criswell *Houston Chronicle / Houston, Texas*

Volume Two

FOOD EDITORS'
FAVORITES
C O O K B O O K

AMERICAN REGIONAL
and
LOCAL SPECIALTIES

A WORD OF THANKS

A cookbook such as this is made possible only by the enthusiastic cooperation of all members of an organization. With the help of contributors from around the country, this unique collection was compiled. We would like to thank the contributors for sharing their expertise on local lore and fare.

In addition, Karen Marshall, Diane Wiggins and Jane Moulton deserve a round of thanks for contributing considerable time and energy to the cookbook project.

We also would like to thank Virginia S. Marshall, Jerry Marshall and Rex Gibbs for their assistance.

And most of all, we would like to thank the readers of newspaper food sections around the country. Without them, we wouldn't know about the wonderful specialties contained in this collection.

Jane Baker
The Phoenix Gazette, Phoenix, Arizona

Barbara Gibbs Ostmann
St. Louis Post-Dispatch, St. Louis, Missouri
Chairpersons of the cookbook committee

Contents

Volume 2

Introduction   155

Appetizers   157

Soups, Stews and Salads   167

Main Courses   183

Side Dishes   237

Breads   247

Desserts   263

Index   301

INTRODUCTION

When putting together the recipes for our first cookbook,
Food Editors' Favorites, a collection of tried-and-true personal
recipes, we realized we had a double set of treasures. In addition
to the family favorites, we discovered a collection of regional and
local specialty foods from across the land.

In the beginning, we dubbed these specialties regional
junk food. Somehow, junk food didn't seem to be an
appropriate category for food editors. Besides, these foods
aren't junk. Many of them are fun, frivolous, amusing; others
are basic, hearty fare. But what makes them special is that
each is unique to its own region, often to its own city or
county. These are truly hometown favorites, in the sense that
many of them are so localized that they probably have never
been heard of outside their own small community.

Have you ever had Chicken Booyah from Wisconsin? Or
Toasted Ravioli from St. Louis? Benedictine from Louisville
or Devonshire Sandwiches from Pittsburgh? The list goes
on and on, making for enjoyable reading and even
more enjoyable eating.

We've also included some of the better known regional
specialties, such as Chicken-Fried Steak from Texas and
Hangtown Fry from California, because the book didn't seem
complete without them. But most of the recipes in this book
will be foods new to you, providing a mouth-watering look
into the culinary melting pot of American foods. In some
cases, ingredients may only be available locally. But the
recipe will at least provide food for thought.

We'd like to make it clear that these are recipes indigenous
to our areas; we make no claim that they are original. When
possible, we've given credit where credit is due. But in many
cases, the recipes simply evolved and it is difficult, if not
impossible, to say from where they came.

A collection as varied as this was made possible only through the network of food editors represented by the Newspaper Food Editors and Writers Association, Inc. (NFEWA). This professional organization was founded in 1974 to encourage communication among food editors and writers, to foster professional ethical standards, to share knowledge about foods and to promote a greater understanding among other journalists.

We hope you will enjoy exploring the culinary idiosyncracies of this country's cities and towns. It's a tasty experience.

BARBARA GIBBS OSTMANN
Past President, NFEWA
(1982-1984)

JANE BAKER
President, NFEWA
(1984-1986)

Appetizers

Nancy Pappas
The Louisville Times / Louisville, Kentucky

This recipe was originally from Miss Jennie Benedict, who ran a wonderful tea room in Louisville from 1900 until her death in 1928. She also catered posh parties. Eventually the recipe proved so popular it became available ready-made. Some restaurants now offer an "aberrant version"—cream cheese colored green.

BENEDICTINE

12 servings

1 medium cucumber, peeled, seeded and grated
2 packages (3 ounces each) cream cheese, softened
1 medium onion, grated
½ teaspoon salt
Dash hot pepper sauce
Enough mayonnaise to make of spreading consistency
2 drops green food coloring
Bread or crackers

Wring out grated cucumber pulp in clean cloth until quite dry.

Blend cream cheese, cucumber, onion, salt, hot pepper sauce, mayonnaise and food coloring thoroughly in a medium mixing bowl. Serve chilled on buttered white bread cut-outs, or toasted whole wheat or sprouted wheat bread, or with crackers.

Bernie O'Brien
Hollywood Sun-Tattler / Hollywood, Florida

Jane Fisher, widow of Carl Fisher, founder of Miami Beach, always served her famous onion sandwiches as hors d'oeuvres at her own cocktail parties. Mrs. Fisher said, "It takes three days to make them, but they're worth the work. They taste just like you're biting into an apple."

ONION SANDWICHES

Use flat white onions. Soak them in ice cubes in refrigerator overnight. Slice them the next day and soak slices in ice cubes overnight.

On the third day, cut soft, white sandwich bread into rounds using a small cookie cutter. Spread each round with mayonnaise. Drain onion slices and pat dry. Put slices between bread rounds. Wrap in waxed paper and refrigerate for 5 hours. Serve chilled.

Dorothy Sorenson

The Sacramento Bee / Sacramento, California

The Franciscan Padres brought almonds to California in the middle 1700s. It was found that ideal conditions for growing almonds prevailed in the great central valleys of Sacramento and San Joaquin. Today California is the only place in North America where almonds are grown commercially, and more than half the world's supply of these nuts is now produced here.

Sacramento is the home of the world's largest almond processing plant, hosting many tourist visitors each year. The many flavors of cocktail almonds, which can be tasted during the tour, are the inspiration for many holiday gifts.

FRENCH FRIED ALMONDS
2 cups

Vegetable oil
2 cups blanched whole almonds (see note)
Salt or seasoned salt

Heat oil in a deep-fryer to 360°F. Fry dry blanched almonds in oil until lightly browned, using a deep-fry basket or strainer for easy handling. Drain almonds on absorbent paper and sprinkle with salt while hot.

Note: To prepare blanched almonds, pour boiling water over shelled almonds and let stand just until brown skins can be easily slipped off (2 to 5 minutes). Allow nuts to dry thoroughly before using.

SMOKY COCKTAIL ALMONDS
1 cup

½ teaspoon liquid smoke   1 teaspoon vegetable oil
2 teaspoons water   Salt
1 cup natural (unblanched)
   almonds

Mix liquid smoke and water. Add almonds and toss to coat. Place in a shallow pan; cover and let stand overnight.

Add oil to almonds; toss almonds to coat. Roast in a 300°F oven about 25 minutes, stirring frequently. Sprinkle with salt while hot.

HUNGARIAN ALMONDS

2 cups

1½ tablespoons paprika
1 tablespoon all-purpose
   flour

2 teaspoons garlic salt
1 egg white
2 cups whole natural almonds

Combine paprika, flour and garlic salt in a small bowl; set aside.

Beat egg white until frothy. Add almonds; toss to coat. Drain on paper towels.

Toss almonds with paprika mixture to coat. Spread in a single layer in a greased shallow baking pan. Bake in a 300°F oven 15 to 20 minutes.

Kitty Crider
Austin American-Statesman / Austin, Texas

Whenever Texans want to jazz up a recipe, they add a can of tomatoes with green chilies. Pots of chili, casseroles, dips—every dish knows the zip that can come from this little ten-ounce can.

There are now other brands of tomatoes with green chilies on the market, but Texans have remained loyal to Ro-Tel, a home-state product that has distribution in half a dozen other states. (Incidentally, Ro-Tel tomatoes first came to fame during Lyndon B. Johnson's term as president. His now-famous Pedernales River Chili called for the product. From that time on, it received national recognition, which is quite an accomplishment for a hot little tomato from the small town of Elsa.)

Today the best-known use for these tomatoes is Cheese Dip, or Chile Con Queso, an embarrassingly simple two-ingredient operation that is standard fare for parties, ballgame watching and office occasions.

TEXAS CHEESE DIP

3 cups

1 pound pasteurized American cheese
1 can (10 ounces) tomatoes with green chilies, undrained
   Corn chips

Melt cheese in top of a double boiler, or in a microwave oven or slow cooker. Stir in undrained tomatoes and chilies; blend well, breaking up tomatoes. (For a thicker dip, add more cheese.) Serve warm with corn chips.

Note: Two variations are very popular. (1) Increase cheese to 2 pounds and add 1 pound cooked, crumbled pork sausage. (2) Add 1 pound cooked, crumbled pork sausage and 1 pound browned ground beef.

Barbara Gibbs Ostmann

St. Louis Post-Dispatch / St. Louis, Missouri

St. Louisans may take Toasted Ravioli for granted, but it is actually a strictly St. Louis phenomenon. Out-of-towners have never heard of Toasted Ravioli. There are several versions of the origin of the dish. Here's one from local newspaper files.

Mickey Garagiola, of Ruggeri's on the Hill (Italian community) in St. Louis, claims to have been present the night Toasted Ravioli was born. The event wasn't at Ruggeri's, but down the street at a long-gone restaurant called Oldani's, which was one of four Italian restaurants on the Hill in the late 1930s. Louie Oldani employed a German cook named Fritz who was, according to the story, "feeling a bit under the weather" and accidentally dropped a boiled ravioli into hot grease. When the dumpling came to the top, he dropped in a few more, then sent a plateful to the bar. The customers loved them and asked for another order. The Toasted Ravioli was born.

That first Toasted Ravioli was a distant cousin of today's beloved dish. It wasn't breaded or served with meat sauce. Oldani served them at the bar like potato chips or pretzels, according to Garagiola.

This up-to-date version of Toasted Ravioli comes from the Pasta House Company.

TOASTED RAVIOLI

Frozen ravioli, homemade or
  store-bought
Milk
Dry bread crumbs

Vegetable oil for deep-frying
Grated Parmesan cheese
Meat sauce, tomato sauce or
  butter sauce, for dipping

Remove ravioli from freezer. Do not brush off flour that was sprinkled over them before freezing. Pour milk in a small dish. Place bread crumbs in a small dish. Heat oil in a deep-fat fryer or pot to 375°F.

Dip frozen ravioli in milk. Then dip ravioli in bread crumbs. Deep-fry ravioli in hot oil until done, about 3 to 4 minutes, or until golden brown. The squares will sink at first, then rise to top of oil when done. Turn squares as they fry to promote even cooking. Remove from oil; drain well. Sprinkle at once with Parmesan cheese. Serve as is, or with a tomato sauce, meat sauce or butter sauce.

Note: Canned, brine-packed ravioli, well drained, can be used.

Janice Okun
Buffalo News / Buffalo, New York

Chicken wings are one of the foods for which Buffalo is famous. They are served in all bars and corner taverns, as well as in "fancy" restaurants and pizza joints.

Naturally, no restaurateur is about to divulge his recipe, so we set out to make our own—spying and tasting like mad. After many, many tries, we came up with a recipe with fourteen different ingredients. It was not bad and we printed it. The recipe was a fair success.

About two years later, a reader sent in the recipe that appears here with only two sauce ingredients: Louisiana hot sauce and butter. What do you know? An exact duplicate of restaurant chicken wings. Simplicity and perfection combined!

Incidentally, in Buffalo, chicken wings are always served with celery sticks and Blue Cheese Dressing. No one knows why, but it is part of the ritual. Use the dressing recipe given, or a commercial blue cheese dressing.

BUFFALO CHICKEN WINGS   *4 to 6 servings*

About 20 to 25 chicken
  wings
Vegetable oil for deep-frying
¼ cup butter or margarine
½ to 1 bottle (2½ ounces)
  Louisiana hot sauce, or to
  taste

Celery sticks
Blue Cheese Dressing (recipe
  follows)

Cut wings in half. Remove wing tips. Deep-fry wings, about half at a time, in hot oil until they are crisp and golden brown, about 10 minutes. (Do not use any batter or crumbs.) Drain wings well.

Melt butter in a saucepan. Add about ½ of the bottle of hot sauce; stir until well blended. (Using ½ bottle will give medium-hot chicken wings. If you like your wings hotter, add the whole bottle, or to taste. If you want them milder, add more butter.)

Place chicken wings in a large container with a cover. Pour sauce over wings; mix well. Serve warm, with celery sticks and Blue Cheese Dressing. Dip the wings and celery sticks in dressing as you eat. Provide plenty of napkins.

BLUE CHEESE DRESSING

2½ cups

2 tablespoons chopped onion
1 clove garlic, minced
¼ cup chopped fresh parsley
1 cup mayonnaise or salad
    dressing
½ cup dairy sour cream

1 tablespoon lemon juice
1 tablespoon white vinegar
¼ cup crumbled blue cheese
Salt, pepper and cayenne, to
    taste

Combine onion, garlic, parsley, mayonnaise, sour cream, lemon juice, vinegar and blue cheese in a medium mixing bowl. Season to taste with salt, pepper and cayenne. Chill for an hour or longer.

Serve as an accompaniment to Buffalo Chicken Wings.

Ruth Gray

St. Petersburg Times / St. Petersburg, Florida

Smoked fish, especially mullet and mackerel, are specialties of the Florida Gulf Coast. You can smoke your own fish or buy it. In my area, consumers can purchase smoked fish in restaurants to take home.

SMOKED FISH DIP

2 cups

¾ pound smoked mullet,
    mackerel or other fish
1 package (8 ounces) cream
    cheese, softened

2 tablespoons half-and-half or
    light cream
2 tablespoons lemon juice
¼ teaspoon garlic salt

Remove any skin or bones from fish. Chop fish fine to make about 1½ cups. Combine fish with cream cheese, half-and-half, lemon juice and garlic salt in a medium mixing bowl; mix well. Chill and serve with crackers or chips.

Note: This dip can be made with fish that is not smoked. Just add ½ teaspoon liquid smoke to cooked, flaked fish with the other ingredients.

When the subject of crayfish, or crawdads, comes up, most people think of New Orleans, where they are a popular menu item. However, the Sacramento-San Joaquin Delta region in California produces some 556,000 pounds of crayfish each year, many of which are exported to Sweden, where they are a prized delicacy.

Many Sacramento area fishermen set out crayfish traps and invite their friends to crayfish feeds. Restaurants along the river serve them for appetizers, lunches or for main dishes for dinner.

This simple method is the most popular way to cook them.

CRAYFISH
2 servings

Boiling water
Celery leaves and
  trimmings
2 tablespoons mixed
  pickling spices
1 can (12 ounces) beer

1 lemon, sliced
3 dozen crayfish
Curried Mayonnaise
  (recipe follows),
  or seafood cocktail sauce

Bring water to a boil in a deep kettle. Add celery, spices, beer and lemon. When mixture is boiling briskly, add crayfish and cook 4 to 5 minutes. When they turn red or float to the top, they are done.

Most of the meat is in the tail, but the head contains fat, which is delicious. Crack and eat crayfish with the fingers, dipping meat into Curried Mayonnaise or seafood cocktail sauce.

CURRIED MAYONNAISE
1 cup

1 egg
1 tablespoon red wine vinegar
½ teaspoon salt
½ teaspoon curry powder

½ teaspoon spicy mustard
Freshly ground pepper
1 cup vegetable oil

Place egg, vinegar, salt, curry powder, mustard and pepper in container of a food processor or electric blender. Process until blended. Slowly add oil, a few drops at a time, then faster until mixture is thick and smooth.

Sarah Fritschner

The Louisville Times / Louisville, Kentucky

Louisville is the home of many specialties, including the rolled oyster. This distinctive culinary invention resembles a croquette but is actually three or four oysters dipped in batter, rolled in white cornmeal and then deep-fried. Rolled oysters are eaten with the fingers at picnics, are served as "nibbles" at Louisville bars, or can be the main dish for a light supper.

As with most special dishes, the origin is a source of controversy. Al Kolb, an old-time restaurateur, insisted that his mother brought the recipe from New Orleans. Chefs at Mazzoni's restaurant tell a different story. According to them, back in the 1870s a Frenchman who ran a tavern on Third Street had some oysters left over. For lack of something better to do with them, he whipped up a flour-and-water batter and mixed the oysters in it. Because the oysters were so small, three or four were rolled together in cornmeal to make one great big croquette. Rolled oysters are still prepared this way at Mazzoni's.

This version is from Marion Flexner, a Louisville cookbook author.

LOUISVILLE ROLLED OYSTERS
6 servings

½ cup all-purpose flour
1 teaspoon baking powder
¼ teaspoon salt
1 egg, well beaten
¼ cup milk, or more as
    needed

18 medium oysters, drained
1 cup white cornmeal or
    cracker meal
Lard or solid shortening,
    for deep-frying
Dips of choice

Sift flour, baking powder and salt in a medium mixing bowl. Beat together egg and milk; add to flour mixture and mix well. Batter should be stiff, but if it is too stiff to coat the oysters, add additional milk. Beat until smooth. Put oysters in batter and stir to coat oysters well. Scoop up three oysters at a time and form them by hand into a croquette. Quickly roll croquette in cornmeal, covering it completely. Repeat with remaining oysters. After all croquettes have been formed, dip each again in batter and dust again with cornmeal. At this point, oysters can be refrigerated until time to fry them.

Heat lard to 375°F in a deep-fryer. Put 3 rolled oysters at a time in basket and lower into hot fat. The rolled oysters should cook on all sides; it may be necessary to turn them with a pancake turner. Cook through, about 3 to 4 minutes total cooking time. Drain on paper towels.

Serve rolled oysters hot, with a dipping sauce of choice. The most common choices are ketchup or tartar sauce.

Carol Brock

Daily News / New York, New York

Although very few Manhattanites will order a Bronx cocktail, and even fewer remember what a Staten Islander is, people around the country enjoy a Manhattan. Here's the authentic version.

MANHATTAN COCKTAIL

1 serving

1½ ounces blended whiskey
¾ ounce sweet vermouth
1 to 2 dashes angostura
    bitters

Ice
Maraschino cherry

    Put whiskey, vermouth and bitters in a cocktail shaker; add ice and stir. Strain into a cocktail glass. Add cherry and serve.

Nancy Pappas

The Louisville Times / Louisville, Kentucky

Our annual paroxysm of regional food jingoism occurs around Derby time. People call in and write for the same Derby specials each year. Two traditional Derby treats are Run for the Roses Pie (see page 135) and Mint Julep.

MINT JULEP

1 serving

2½ ounces (5 tablespoons)
    bourbon
2 teaspoons water
1 teaspoon confectioners
    sugar

4 sprigs fresh mint
Shaved ice

    Combine bourbon, water, sugar and mint sprigs in a frosted julep cup. Mix well. Fill with shaved ice and stir very gently.

Soups, Stews and Salads

Phyllis Hanes

The Christian Science Monitor / Boston, Massachusetts

The word chowder comes from the French "la chaudière," a huge copper pot in which French fishermen would share the catch at the return of the fleet. The tradition came to Canada with the French and then moved into New England, where the word became chowder.

The most famous chowders of this area today are the fish and clam chowders, with salt pork as essential an ingredient as the fish itself.

New Yorkers and people from Connecticut and Rhode Island add tomatoes to their fish chowder, and it is a fine dish, but this is never done in northern New England. Down Easters can become so annoyed at the idea of tomatoes in a clam or fish chowder that the Maine legislature once introduced a bill to outlaw forever the mixing of clams and tomatoes.

Since my father and both grandfathers were Down East fishermen, I consider our family recipe to be as authentic as you can get. According to some very old books describing chowders, herbs were sometimes added. However, in my family, no herbs, parsley or paprika are used.

MAINE FISH CHOWDER
6 to 8 servings

1 2-inch cube salt pork	3½ to 4 pounds haddock or
1 medium onion, chopped	cod, with bone
4 cups cubed or sliced	Water
potatoes	1 quart milk
1 tablespoon salt	Pepper, to taste

Cut salt pork into tiny cubes and cook in a large pot until light golden; remove with a slotted spoon and set aside.

Discard all but about 1 tablespoon of the fat. Add onion and cook over low to medium heat until soft.

Add potatoes and salt to the kettle. Place fish on top of potatoes, and add enough water to cover potatoes and steam fish. Bring to a boil and reduce heat to simmer for 10 to 15 minutes until both fish and potatoes are done. (Remove bone from fish, which can be done easily after fish has cooked.) When fish flakes easily into large pieces and potatoes are done, add milk and correct seasonings. Top with pork cubes. Serve with pickles and common or pilot crackers.

Note: Some New Englanders use half-and-half or half milk and half evaporated milk. Some add a tablespoon of butter before serving. Although some people use bacon instead of salt pork or use herbs or parsley, it is not typical.

Gail Perrin

The Boston Globe / Boston, Massachusetts

There are many versions of clam chowder. The main thing is that a TRUE New England clam chowder has no flour—just fried salt pork, milk, clams, salt, pepper and butter.

The following recipe does use some flour, and even allows for the addition of thyme, if desired. Although it may not be the most authentic version, it is perhaps the most realistic for today's tastes and ingredients. It is adapted from a recipe in our newspaper cookbook written by Margaret Deeds Murphy.

NEW ENGLAND CLAM CHOWDER   *1 quart*

4 tablespoons diced salt pork (see note)

1 medium onion, chopped

1 to 2 tablespoons all-purpose flour

2 cups strained clam juice

1 medium potato, peeled and diced

Pinch dried thyme (optional)

1 cup milk

1 cup chopped clams (see note)

Salt and freshly ground pepper, to taste

Butter

Pilot crackers

Slowly cook salt pork in a 1½-quart saucepan until pieces are crisp. Remove salt pork and reserve.

Add onion to drippings in saucepan and cook, stirring, until tender but not browned. Stir in flour, then add clam juice. Add potato and thyme. Bring to a boil, cover and simmer 15 minutes, or until potatoes are tender. Stir in milk and reheat, but do not let boil. Add clams and reheat, but do not let boil. Taste; add salt and pepper as needed.

Ladle clam chowder into bowls, top each with a pat of butter and sprinkle with reserved salt pork pieces. Serve with pilot crackers.

Note: Salt pork is the traditional ingredient for clam chowder, but many cooks today prefer bacon because it is more convenient. Substitute 4 slices bacon, diced, for salt pork, if desired. Leave bacon in saucepan and cook with other ingredients instead of sprinkling on top as for salt pork.

If you use fresh clams, strain juice through cheesecloth to remove sand and bits of shells. Wash clams well and chop in an electric blender or food processor.

Eleanor Ostman
St. Paul Pioneer Press and Dispatch / St. Paul, Minnesota

Minnesota, the country's leading producer of both truly "wild" and paddy-grown wild rice, also produces a banquet of recipes for the native grain. This soup recipe, borrowed from a Twin Cities hotel, has become a staple starter for company and holiday meals at our house.

MINNESOTA WILD RICE SOUP

12 servings

½ cup uncooked wild rice
1 large onion, diced
2 large fresh mushrooms, diced, or 1 can (4 ounces) sliced
    mushrooms, drained
½ cup butter
1 cup all-purpose flour
8 cups hot chicken broth
    Salt and pepper, to taste
1 cup half-and-half or light cream
2 tablespoons sherry or dry white wine

Add wild rice to 2 cups water in saucepan. Simmer for 45 minutes. Set aside.

Sauté onion and mushrooms in butter in a large pan about 3 minutes, or just until vegetables soften. Stir in flour, cooking and stirring until flour is mixed in, but do not let it begin to brown. Slowly add hot chicken broth, stirring until all of vegetable-flour mixture is well blended. Stir in cooked rice. Season with salt and pepper. Heat thoroughly. Stir in half-and-half. Add sherry and heat gently, but do not boil.

Note: Soup can be prepared to the point of adding half-and-half, set aside until needed, then reheated adding half-and-half and sherry.

Bev Bennett
Chicago Sun-Times / Chicago, Illinois

Every city has some fishy stories buried somewhere in its past. It's an essential part of a city's character. For example, in San Francisco, cioppino—a heady, herbed fish soup—is a readily identifiable element of the city's cuisine.

A city needs a fish soup to call its own, so I recently set out to compose one for Chicago, scaling all recipe possibilities. First, an assessment of what this culinary ode should be.

Chicago is a bold, gutsy city, and the soup should reflect that. No delicate cream base for Chicago. This is a city of tomatoes, onions and garlic. Chicago is also spicy, sometimes sweet, but with a bite.

It should salute our ethnic mix: Italians, Latinos, Irish, Polish and

Germans. It should include the natural bounty of the Midwest—corn, potatoes, tomatoes and grains. And, lest I forget, it should include the local catch.

I briefly considered alewives, but noticed that not even the seagulls would eat them. Not a fitting start for our city's fish soup. However, Lake Michigan does supply a wealth of Coho salmon and smelt. Smelt fishing is in fact an institution. It probably draws as many people to the lakefront as the bikini-filled Oak Street beach will on a good summer Sunday.

Then for added good measure, I included whitefish, available fresh in many supermarkets. While not immediately local, coming from Lake Superior waters, it's certainly a species Chicagoans are familiar with and enthused about.

Putting all those essentials together—onions, garlic, green pepper, celery and tomatoes with Irish potatoes, a can of Stroh's beer, Italian oregano, Mexican chili peppers, Illinois corn, Lake Michigan salmon and smelt and Lake Superior whitefish, I've created what I'd call a fine kettle of fish for Chicago.

CHICAGO FISH SOUP
4 main-course servings

1 medium onion, chopped
2 cloves garlic, finely minced
½ cup chopped green pepper
1 cup thinly sliced celery
3 tablespoons butter
1 can (29 ounces) tomatoes, coarsely chopped
1 cup diced potato
1 can or bottle (12 ounces) beer
1 teaspoon dried crushed basil
1 teaspoon dried crushed oregano
1 teaspoon salt
  Dash pepper
¼ teaspoon crushed dried red peppers
1 cup fresh corn kernels
½ pound salmon steaks, boned, flesh cut into cubes
¼ pound whitefish, cubed (or use ½ pound whitefish and omit smelt)
¼ pound smelt, boned and cubed

Sauté onion, garlic, green pepper and celery in butter in a large saucepot or Dutch oven until tender, about 15 minutes. Add tomatoes, potatoes and beer. Add basil, oregano, salt, pepper and red peppers. Simmer until potatoes are almost tender, about 15 minutes. Add corn and fish. Continue simmering about 10 minutes, or until fish is done.

Charlyne Varkonyi

Fort Lauderdale News & Sun Sentinel / Fort Lauderdale, Florida

Just as Pennsylvanians go to New York City for the weekend, we go to the Bahamas. When we can't get there, we hunger for a taste of island food.

Some of the most authentic island cooking is produced at the Bimini Sea Shack on State Road 84 in Fort Lauderdale. It's one of those places that you would never think of trying. It's in a rundown section where bikers on Harleys are part of the ambiance. Culinary clues are slim once you go inside. The tables and booths have no tablecloths, napkins are paper and the menu is written on a chalkboard, which is brought to your table and plopped on a chair.

Ironically, most diners don't drive here; they cruise in on their boats. Owner Hazel Day says many of the boat people take her food on trips. One couple ordered a quart of Conch Chowder and four loaves of Bimini Bread (see page 111) for their trip to Bimini in the Bahamas.

CONCH CHOWDER   *3 quarts*

½ pound bacon, finely chopped
1 large onion, chopped
2 cans (28 ounces each) tomatoes, cut up
1 can (46 ounces) tomato juice
3 cans (12 ounces each) whole kernel corn
5 pounds potatoes, peeled and diced
2 pounds conch (a type of seafood available in Florida and in good fish markets elsewhere)
2 cups cold water
1 teaspoon salt, or to taste
½ teaspoon pepper
½ teaspoon hot pepper sauce, or more, to taste

Fry bacon in a skillet. Add onion and cook until onion is tender. Remove bacon and onion from skillet with a slotted spoon and put in a 6-quart kettle. Add tomatoes with liquid, tomato juice, corn with liquid and potatoes. Cover and cook until potatoes are almost done, about 20 minutes.

Meanwhile, prepare conch. Slice into thin slices and pound on each side with a meat mallet or the back of a heavy spoon to help tenderize it. Then cut into small pieces.

Pour cold water into vegetable mixture to stop it from boiling. Add conch. Cook slowly at a simmer until conch is tender, about 25 minutes. Do not boil. Season with salt, pepper and hot pepper sauce.

Ann McDuffie

The Tampa Tribune / Tampa, Florida

An easy do-ahead dinner might feature Picadillo, sort of a Spanish or Cuban beef stew. Picadillo is good with a big green salad and a hearty red wine. Crusty bread, too, of course.

PICADILLO   *6 servings*

2 pounds ground beef (chuck or rump)
  Olive oil
1 medium onion, chopped
½ medium green pepper, chopped
1 large ripe tomato, peeled, seeded and chopped, or
    2 to 3 tomatoes if preferred
1 clove garlic, minced
1 bay leaf
½ teaspoon dried crushed oregano
1 bottle (3 ounces) capers, drained (optional)
8 pimiento-stuffed green olives, sliced into rounds
1 tablespoon red wine vinegar
3 to 4 tablespoons tomato sauce
¼ cup Burgundy wine
2 to 3 drops hot pepper sauce
  Handful of raisins
  Dash ground nutmeg
½ cup water if needed
  Salt to taste
½ teaspoon light brown sugar if needed

Brown ground beef in a spoonful of olive oil in a large skillet or Dutch oven until red disappears. Add onion, green pepper, tomato, garlic, bay leaf, oregano and capers. Stir and cook, covered, about 30 minutes.

Add olives, vinegar, tomato sauce, wine, hot pepper sauce, raisins and nutmeg. Stir well. Cook, uncovered, about 5 minutes.

Add water, salt and brown sugar, if needed. (Dish is not supposed to be sweet.) Cover and cook over low heat about 30 minutes, until most of liquid is absorbed.

Serve over long-grain white rice with ripe, fried plaintains, if available.

Note: It is easy to multiply Picadillo for a crowd. Or, if more people show up than you expect, you can easily stretch this dish as the Cubans do by stirring in a couple of potatoes, cubed and fried in oil.

The capers can be omitted, if desired, but I like them. Some of my Cuban friends also stir in a handful of walnut halves.

Jane Benet
San Francisco Chronicle / San Francisco, California

Cioppino is a San Francisco favorite. It is a fish stew of sorts and, as with the bouillabaisse of southern France, it relies pretty much on whatever fresh fish and shellfish are available. Serve it with plenty of hot, buttered French bread, glasses of a good dry white wine and a tossed green salad, if desired. It's messy to eat, so be sure to provide plenty of napkins.

CIOPPINO
6 to 10 servings

1 cup fine olive oil
2 large onions
1 large bunch parsley, stems removed
2 large or 3 medium cloves garlic
2 cans (29 ounces each) solid-pack tomatoes
2 cans (6 ounces each) tomato sauce
2 whole bay leaves
½ teaspoon dried oregano
¼ teaspoon dried basil
   Salt and coarsely ground black pepper, to taste
2 cups dry white wine
1 pound prawns, cooked, shelled, deveined
2 pounds uncooked sea trout, bass, rock cod or other firm fish, skinned and boned, cut in bite-size pieces
3 or 4 cooked Dungeness crabs

    Heat oil slowly in a large, deep, heavy kettle. Chop onion, parsley and garlic together until fine. Sauté in oil until lightly browned. Add tomatoes, tomato sauce, bay leaves, oregano and basil; add salt and pepper to taste. Simmer gently, covered, for 1 hour. Add wine, prawns and fish. Cook 20 minutes, stirring occasionally. Crack crab claws, leaving meat in shells; remove remaining meat from crabs. Put crab meat and cracked claws in kettle; correct seasoning and cook another 10 minutes to heat through. Serve in soup plates.

Ann McDuffie
The Tampa Tribune / Tampa, Florida

Potaje de Garbanzos, or Spanish Bean Soup, is very popular here in Spanish restaurants. The soup is served on the streets of Ybor City, Tampa's Latin Quarter, during the Gasparilla Festival Week in February. Tourists love it. It's also tinted green for St. Patrick's Day! And even though I hate tinted foods, I get a kick out of green garbanzo soup.
   This recipe is from Clara Garcia, wife of the second-generation owner of Las Novedades Restaurant, which no longer exists in Ybor City. She also

authored the cookbook, Clarita's Cocina *(Clara's Kitchen). This is her personal recipe, one her restaurateur husband liked.*

POTAJE DE GARBANZOS

6 generous servings

1 pound dried garbanzos (chick peas)
Water
Salt
½ pound smoked bacon
1 ham bone (½ pound)
½ pound lean beef (flank)
2 chorizos (Spanish sausages), or 4 to 5 inches kielbasa
1 small whole onion
½ green pepper
1 whole ripe tomato
1 bay leaf
Pinch saffron
3 medium potatoes, peeled and cubed

Wash beans in cold water. Discard imperfect ones. Cover with salted water at least 3 inches above beans. Soak overnight. The next morning, drain and rinse beans thoroughly. Set beans aside.

Place bacon, ham bone, beef, chorizos, onion, green pepper, tomato and bay leaf in a 3- to 4-quart saucepan or soup pot. Cover with water 2 inches above ingredients. Bring to a rapid boil; skim several times. Lower heat to moderate, cover, and place saffron on the cover to toast. Cook about 30 minutes

Add beans and bring to a boil again. Cover and reduce heat to moderate; cook another 30 minutes. Crumble toasted saffron and add. Stir gently once. Cover and cook another 30 minutes, or until beans are tender and not overcooked.

By this time, meats should be tender. Remove meats to heated platter and reserve. Discard ham bone and remainder of onion, green pepper, tomato and bay leaf.

Add potatoes to beans and correct salt seasoning. Cover and cook over moderate heat until potatoes are done, about 30 minutes.

Cut beef into small portions. Slice chorizos into thin rings. Cube the cooked bacon. Return meats to soup kettle. Heat thoroughly and serve hot.

Note: Tampans make a full lunch on this soup with salad and hot Cuban bread with butter. Others could substitute crusty Italian or French bread for the Cuban bread. I have served it as a main dish at night with a "galumptuous" flan (custard with burnt sugar topping) for dessert, a meal my husband loved.

Carol Hanson

The Post-Crescent / Appleton, Wisconsin

One of my fond memories of growing up in Green Bay, Wisconsin, and spending summers at a cottage along the Bay shore of Lake Michigan is the special weekends when the men in the family decided to cook a huge kettle of booyah. It would bubble all day long over an open fire, sending a tantalizing aroma over the area and bringing the children in the family to the kettle often, anxious for the men to begin serving it in huge white bowls.

On summer Sundays in later years, we frequented Belgian taverns, where the thick soup was cooked in outdoor summer kitchens. Ladled into the familiar pristine bowls, the soup was enjoyed around picnic tables and eaten with crackers and mugs of cool beer.

The recipe came from a friend of my mother; she has brewed many a pot to feed an army of friends, who seem to be always present at the cottage in northern Wisconsin.

CHICKEN BOOYAH
4 gallons

5 pounds stewing chicken, cut up	4 cups diced carrots
1½ pounds beef stew meat	2½ cups diced onions
¼ pound lean pork, cubed	3 cups diced celery
½ pound dried navy beans, soaked overnight	½ lemon, peeled and cut into pieces
½ pound split green peas	8 cups diced potatoes
2 cups canned whole tomatoes	4 cups shredded cabbage
	4 tablespoons butter
	Salt and pepper, to taste

Place cut-up chicken, beef stew meat and pork in a large soup kettle. Cover with cold water. Slowly bring to a boil. Skim. Simmer 1 hour.

Add drained navy beans, green peas, tomatoes, carrots, onions, celery and lemon. Cook about 3 hours, or until chicken is very tender.

Add potatoes, cabbage, butter, salt and pepper. Simmer 30 minutes.

Note: During cooking, it will be necessary to add cold water to keep meats and vegetables covered and to ensure a soup that is not too thick.

Evelyn Wavpotich

The Island Packet / Hilton Head Island, South Carolina

Peanut soup is a Southern specialty. This version is from Dotty Cason, who studied at the Cordon Bleu in Paris but likes cooking the Southern way, too.

CREAMY PEANUT SOUP

10 to 12 servings

¼ cup butter or margarine
1 medium onion, chopped
2 ribs celery, chopped into small pieces
3 tablespoons all-purpose flour
8 cups canned or homemade chicken broth

2 cups creamy peanut butter
1¾ to 2 cups light cream or half-and-half
⅓ cup chopped peanuts (unsalted), for garnish
Paprika, for garnish

Melt butter in a large pan. When butter is bubbly, stir in onion and celery; cook until clear but not browned. Add flour and stir until well mixed. Pour in chicken broth; blend well, stirring constantly, and bring to a boil. Turn down heat and add peanut butter, stirring until blended.

Put soup through a sieve. Add cream slowly to the strained soup and stir for a few minutes to blend.

Pour soup into small bowls (it's very rich); garnish with chopped peanuts and dash of paprika for color.

Betsy Balsley

Los Angeles Times / Los Angeles, California

The Cobb Salad has been a Los Angeles tradition ever since it was created by the Original Hollywood Brown Derby restaurant. With the advent of the food processor, it's easier to prepare at home. This main-course salad is marvelous for luncheon parties. The unassembled salad is usually presented at the table and then tossed, because it is most attractive before tossing.

THE ORIGINAL HOLLYWOOD BROWN DERBY COBB SALAD

6 servings

½ head iceberg lettuce
½ bunch watercress
1 small bunch curly endive
½ head romaine lettuce
2 tablespoons minced chives
2 medium tomatoes, peeled, seeded and diced
1 whole chicken breast, cooked, boned, skinned and diced

6 slices bacon, cooked and diced
1 avocado, peeled and diced
3 hard-cooked eggs, peeled and diced
⅓ cup Roquefort cheese, crumbled
French Dressing (recipe follows)

Chop lettuce, watercress, endive and romaine in very fine pieces using a knife or a food processor. Mix chopped ingredients together in one large wide bowl, or in individual wide shallow bowls. Add chives. Arrange tomatoes, chicken, bacon, avocado and eggs in narrow strips or wedges across top of greens. Sprinkle with cheese. Chill.

At serving time, toss with ½ cup French Dressing. Pass remaining dressing.

FRENCH DRESSING

1½ cups

¼ cup water
¼ cup red wine vinegar
¼ teaspoon granulated sugar
1½ teaspoons lemon juice
½ teaspoon salt
½ teaspoon black pepper

½ teaspoon Worcestershire sauce
¾ teaspoon dry mustard
½ clove garlic, minced
¼ cup olive oil
¾ cup vegetable oil

Combine water, vinegar, sugar, lemon juice, salt, pepper, Worcestershire sauce, mustard, garlic and oils in a container with lid. Shake well before using.

Jann Malone

Richmond Times-Dispatch / Richmond, Virginia

If ever a dish were misnamed, this is it, because the eggs are just a garnish for a glorious crab and shrimp salad with a spicy vinaigrette dressing. The Pontchartrain part of the name is right—the dish comes from New Orleans, which is next to Lake Pontchartrain.

Kolb's, a German restaurant in New Orleans, serves this salad to customers who are savvy enough to know what they're ordering. I devised this recipe from my recollections of how the salad tasted.

EGGS PONTCHARTRAIN   *2 servings*

Lettuce
1 pound crab meat
½ pound shrimp, cooked and
   peeled
2 hard-cooked eggs, peeled
2 tomatoes

Dressing:
1 clove garlic
½ teaspoon salt
½ teaspoon pepper
½ teaspoon granulated sugar
1 tablespoon Creole mustard
   (see note)
3 tablespoons red wine
   vinegar
½ cup vegetable oil

Line two plates with lettuce. Put half of crab meat in the center of each plate. Arrange shrimp around crab meat. Slice eggs into thin circles and place egg slices on top of crab meat. Slice tomatoes and arrange tomato slices around the outside of the plates.

Prepare dressing by crushing garlic in a small bowl. Add salt, pepper, sugar and mustard; stir to make a paste. Blend in vinegar. Slowly whisk in oil. Pour dressing over the salad. Serve immediately.

Note: Creole mustard is a brown, spicy mustard available in the specialty food section of most supermarkets. Dijon mustard is a fine substitute.

Jane Baker
The Phoenix Gazette / Phoenix, Arizona

Jicama is a not-so-pretty root vegetable whose popularity has spread from Mexico to the Southwest. It is available in Phoenix supermarkets from November to July. Despite its outward appearance, jicama is quite tasty— something of a cross between a potato, an apple and a water chestnut. It's low in calories (only forty-five calories per medium jicama) and low in sodium. Sticks of jicama rolled in chili powder often are sold by street vendors in Mexico. I like to use jicama in this salad.

JICAMA SALAD

6 servings

1 medium jicama, peeled and cut into strips
1 small red onion, cut into rings
1 cucumber, sliced
3 large seedless oranges, peeled and cut into sections

⅓ cup lime juice
¼ cup vegetable oil
½ to 1 teaspoon chili powder
1 clove garlic, chopped

Prepare jicama strips, onion rings, cucumber slices and orange sections; arrange on individual plates, or toss together in a salad bowl.

Combine lime juice, oil, chili powder and garlic in a small container; mix well. The amount of chili powder varies according to how spicy you like your food. Drizzle dressing over salad.

Karen K. Marshall
St. Louis Globe-Democrat / St. Louis, Missouri

This Italian salad was originally served at Rich and Charlie's Pasta House, a local restaurant. It is now served at all the Pasta House Company restaurants and has become more or less classic fare for St. Louisans, whether dining out or at home.

ITALIAN SALAD

6 servings

1 head iceberg lettuce, shredded
⅓ head romaine lettuce, shredded
1 pimiento, chopped
1 jar (6 ounces) artichoke hearts, drained

¾ cup olive oil
¼ cup vinegar
¼ cup grated Parmesan cheese
Salt and pepper, to taste
Additional grated Parmesan cheese, for garnish

Combine iceberg and romaine lettuces in a salad bowl. Add pimiento and artichoke hearts. Toss well.

Combine oil, vinegar and ¼ cup Parmesan cheese in a shaker; mix well. Coat salad greens generously with the dressing. Add salt and pepper to taste.

Serve generous portions on individual plates; garnish with additional Parmesan cheese.

Peggy Daum
The Milwaukee Journal / Milwaukee, Wisconsin

In many restaurants in the Milwaukee area, spinach salad with hot bacon dressing is a specialty. The idea originated with the city's German population, but the recipe has spread far beyond German homes and restaurants.

Sometimes the dressing is used with a mixture of spinach and lettuce. And in summertime, when home cooks pour the dressing over tender leaf lettuce from the garden, the combination is known as wilted lettuce.

Proportions for the dressing vary with the chef or cook. At some restaurants, the dressing is thickened. This version comes from Jim Hahm, who grows lots of lettuce in his side-yard garden.

SPINACH SALAD WITH HOT BACON DRESSING
4 to 6 servings

2 bunches (about 1 pound) untrimmed fresh spinach
6 slices bacon, diced
¼ cup white vinegar
¼ cup granulated sugar

Wash spinach and remove stems. Drain and spin or wrap in toweling to dry.

Fry diced bacon in a skillet over medium-high heat until crisp. Remove from heat and pour off half the grease (or more if desired), leaving ¼ cup or less in pan. Stir in vinegar and sugar.

Tear spinach into bite-size pieces and place in a heat-proof salad bowl.

Bring dressing mixture to a boil over high heat. Pour over salad and toss. Serve immediately. (It is important to serve and eat this salad quickly because the bacon fat congeals as it cools.)

Peggy Daum

The Milwaukee Journal / Milwaukee, Wisconsin

This warm salad is so much a part of Milwaukee that it seems to be on the table at every family gathering, church supper, club potluck, company picnic—you name it. It's also found at deli counters and on restaurant salad bars.

I was eleven or so before I knew that any other kind of potato salad existed. That's when I saw an egg-and-mayonnaise version at a Girl Scout potluck supper and said, "What funny potato salad!"

Unfortunately, I was speaking to the Scout whose mother had prepared it.

I've learned to like a number of potato salads since, but German Potato Salad is still my favorite.

GERMAN POTATO SALAD
8 to 10 servings

3 pounds small red potatoes
1 bunch green onions,
    chopped (tops included)
6 slices bacon, diced
3 tablespoons all-purpose flour
½ cup granulated sugar

1½ teaspoons salt, or to taste
¼ teaspoon pepper
1 cup cider vinegar
1 cup water
1 tablespoon chopped fresh
    parsley (optional)

Wash potatoes but do not peel. Place in a kettle with water to cover. Cover and boil over medium heat just until tender, about 20 minutes. Do not overcook; potatoes should not be mushy. Drain and cool slightly for easier handling. Peel potatoes and cut in thin slices. Place in a large bowl. Add onions to potatoes. Cover and set aside.

Fry diced bacon in a skillet over medium heat until crisp. Remove from heat. Remove bacon with a slotted spoon and drain on paper towels, reserving drippings in skillet. Add bacon to potatoes.

Combine flour, sugar, salt and pepper in a small bowl. Add to bacon drippings in skillet and stir over medium heat to form a smooth paste. Stir in vinegar and water. Bring to a boil and boil 2 to 3 minutes, stirring constantly.

Pour hot sauce over potatoes, onions and bacon. Mix gently. If desired, sprinkle with parsley before serving.

Main Courses

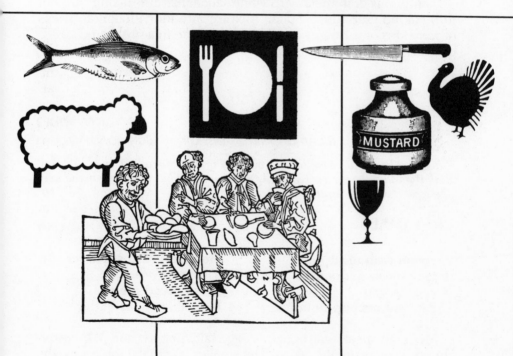

Jann Malone

Richmond Times-Dispatch / Richmond, Virginia

This recipe is a favorite with Virginia cooks. The seasonings are subdued, so the subtle crab flavor will still come through.

CRAB IMPERIAL

4 servings

3 tablespoons butter
3 tablespoons all-purpose flour
1 cup milk
1 teaspoon dry mustard

1 teaspoon Worcestershire sauce
2 tablespoons mayonnaise
1 pound crab meat

Make a white sauce by slowly melting butter over low heat in a medium saucepan. Add flour and stir with a whisk for 3 to 4 minutes (this eliminates the taste of raw flour). Slowly add milk; simmer and stir with a wire whisk until sauce has thickened and is smooth.

Combine dry mustard, Worcestershire sauce and mayonnaise in a small bowl; mix well. Add mayonnaise mixture to white sauce.

Gently mix crab meat with white sauce mixture, taking care not to break up crab meat. Spoon mixture into individual crab shells or ramekins or a 1-quart casserole dish. Bake in a preheated 350°F oven 20 minutes, or until bubbly.

Jann Malone

Richmond Times-Dispatch / Richmond, Virginia

When she heard me complaining about too much breading in crab cakes, Ruth Ramsay gave me her recipe. As you can see, it has very little bread in it. She uses claw crab meat.

CRAB CAKES

2 to 4 servings

1 pound crab meat
1 tablespoon mayonnaise
1 egg, beaten
Salt and pepper, to taste

Worcestershire sauce, to taste
Fresh bread crumbs
4 to 6 tablespoons butter

Mix crab meat, mayonnaise, egg, salt, pepper and Worcestershire sauce; form into cakes. (The smaller you make the cakes, the better they hold together.) Dip both sides of each cake in bread crumbs.

Melt butter in a skillet. Cook crab cakes in butter over moderate heat until heated through and lightly browned.

Jane Benet
San Francisco Chronicle / San Francisco, California

Hangtown Fry comes from the Gold Country in California's Sierra foothills, but it is served in old San Francisco restaurants still.

There are several stories about the origin of the dish, and this one seems most plausible:

A gold miner, a Forty-Niner, came to town (town being today's Placerville, which was then, for fairly obvious reasons, called Hangtown) with a sack of gold nuggets. He walked into the first restaurant he saw and demanded that the cook prepare the most expensive thing he had in the house, spilling the nuggets onto the counter to prove he could pay.

Since oysters had to travel all the way from the East Coast in barrels in those days, and since eggs were scarcer than hens' teeth in the Sierra foothill town, those two items were the most expensive ones on hand, so the cook dished them up in the original Hangtown Fry.

HANGTOWN FRY

4 servings

9 eggs, divided
Salt and pepper, to taste
8 medium-size oysters
Bread crumbs
Butter

4 link sausages
4 lamb kidneys
4 slices bacon
Parsley

Beat 1 egg in a shallow bowl with a little salt and pepper. Dip oysters in beaten egg, then in bread crumbs; sauté in butter until plump and golden. Remove and drain on paper towels.

Put link sausages in a small heavy pan and add a few drops of water. Cover and cook slowly until browned. Set aside.

Split lamb kidneys in half, remove membranes, then place on a rack with the bacon and broil, turning once, until bacon is crisp and kidneys are done to your liking. Set aside.

Beat remaining 8 eggs with salt and pepper to taste. Melt some butter in a medium pan and pour one-fourth of egg mixture into it when it is hot. Arrange 2 oysters, 1 sausage, 2 kidney halves and 1 slice of bacon in the egg in pan. Cook as you would any omelet, but don't roll it; then finish the last-minute cooking under the broiler. Serve immediately, garnished with fresh parsley, or keep warm in a low oven while you cook the other three omelets.

Fran H. Zupan

The Columbia Record / Columbia, South Carolina

According to Eva Anderson, a staff writer, this is an old Charleston recipe that has been handed down through the generations.

SCALLOPED OYSTERS   *4 to 6 servings*

½ cup butter or margarine,
  melted
1 cup crushed salted soda
  crackers
½ cup dry bread crumbs
1 pint fresh shucked oysters
  (reserve liquid)

Salt
Paprika
6 tablespoons light or heavy
  cream, or more, as
  needed
2 tablespoons butter or
  margarine

Combine melted butter, crushed crackers and bread crumbs. Place half of crumb mixture in a greased 8-inch square pan. Cover with oysters, being careful to remove any shells. Sprinkle lightly with salt and paprika. Top with remaining crumb mixture.

Combine oyster liquid with cream to make ½ cup. Pour over crumbs. Dot with butter. Bake in a preheated 400°F oven 25 to 30 minutes, or until top is nicely browned.

Jane Benet

San Francisco Chronicle / San Francisco, California

Oyster loaf is an old, old San Francisco favorite. The dish used to be served in restaurants all over the city but is much harder to come by now, so we most often make our own. It may be made with a standard long loaf of bread, but traditionally it is prepared using a round loaf.

OYSTER LOAF   6 to 8 servings

1 fresh round loaf sourdough French bread
½ cup butter, or more
24 medium-size oysters

Fine dry bread crumbs
Salt and pepper
Fresh lemon juice
Chopped fresh parsley

Cut off top of loaf of bread about two-thirds of the way up. Scoop out center of loaf and top, leaving a 1-inch crust all around. (Either dry the scooped-out bread in the oven and make it into fine crumbs, or reserve it for another use.) Melt butter in a skillet and use to paint inside of loaf (and top) generously. Toast loaf lightly in a 400°F oven 5 to 10 minutes.

Add more butter to that you've melted, if necessary, for frying oysters. Drain oysters, then coat lightly with fine dry bread crumbs, adding salt and pepper to taste. Cook oysters in butter in a skillet just until golden and plump.

Now, layer fried oysters into buttered loaf, sprinkling lightly with fresh lemon juice and chopped fresh parsley as you go. Place top back on loaf, paint outside with butter, place on a baking sheet and pop into a 400°F oven 8 to 10 minutes.

Serve with thin slices of dill pickle (or French cornichons) and any favorite dunking sauce for oysters—or plain.

Note: To serve and eat Oyster Loaf, it really is best to break the loaf into chunks, being sure each diner gets his or her share of the plump oysters. Then eat it out of hand—or use forks, if you're fussy.

Editor's note: Oyster Loaf is also a New Orleans favorite. You'll find it in many bars and small restaurants there.

Evelyn Wavpotich
The Island Packet / Hilton Head Island, South Carolina

South Carolina Governor Dick Riley's wife, Ann, enjoys cooking, but, understandably, doesn't have much time to spend in the kitchen. And, of course, she doesn't have to when they're at the Governor's Mansion. She created this tasty regional dish.

COLONIAL OYSTER AND HAM PIE
4 generous servings

1 pint fresh oysters
½ cup butter
½ cup all-purpose flour
½ cup white wine
½ cup milk

1 medium onion, chopped
2 teaspoons butter
1½ cups diced, cooked ham
2 cups canned or frozen
    green peas

Drain fresh oysters and reserve ½ cup oyster liquor. Melt the ½ cup butter in a saucepan; stir in flour. Add reserved oyster liquor, white wine and milk. Cook until thick. Remove from heat. Cook onion until soft in 2 teaspoons butter; add to liquid mixture along with drained oysters, ham and peas. Turn mixture into a 2-quart casserole dish. Bake in a preheated 400°F oven 15 minutes.

Helen Wilber Richardson

The Providence Journal-Bulletin / Providence, Rhode Island

These are an extremely popular item at shore restaurants in Rhode Island.

RHODE ISLAND CLAM CAKES   *6 servings*

¼ cup liquid from clams
1 egg, well beaten
1 cup all-purpose flour
1 teaspoon baking powder
½ teaspoon salt

1 cup chopped quahogs (large, hard-shelled clams; see note)
Vegetable oil for frying

Combine clam liquid, beaten egg, flour, baking powder and salt in a medium mixing bowl. Mix well, then stir in chopped clams and mix well again.

Heat 3 or 4 inches of oil in heavy pan. Drop batter by teaspoonful into oil. Fry until golden brown, 4 to 6 minutes.

Note: For those without access to quahogs, substitute two cans (7 ounces each) minced clams. Drain very well, reserving ¼ cup liquid, as called for in ingredients.

Barbara Durbin
The Oregonian / Portland, Oregon

When you say "fish" in the Northwest, the first one to come to mind is salmon. It should be cooked only until flaky but still moist, not until it's dry.

The West Coast Fisheries Development Foundation sponsored a grilled seafood contest in Portland in 1983. This stuffed salmon recipe, entered by Deborah McGuire of Lake Oswego, placed third.

GRILLED RICE-STUFFED SALMON
6 servings

½ cup diced onion
½ cup diced celery
½ cup diced green pepper
4 cloves garlic, or garlic
   powder, to taste
3 tablespoons butter
1 cup sliced fresh mushrooms
2 cups cooked rice

½ cup sliced olives
½ cup chopped fresh parsley
3 tablespoons fresh basil, or
   dried basil, to taste
1 salmon (6 to 8 pounds),
   head removed
1 lemon, thinly sliced

Sauté onion, celery, green pepper and garlic in butter in a skillet for 3 minutes. Add mushrooms. Add sautéed vegetables to rice; add olives, parsley and basil.

Place salmon on heavy-duty aluminum foil. Stuff salmon with lemon slices and rice mixture. (Any remaining rice may also be wrapped in foil and grilled.) Wrap securely. Grill over medium coals 30 minutes to 1 hour.

Charlotte Hansen
The Jamestown Sun / Jamestown, North Dakota

This Norwegian favorite is popular among ethnic groups in North Dakota.

LUTEFISK

Lutefisk
Salted water

Salt, to taste
Butter

Remove any bones or skin on lutefisk. Cut fish into serving pieces. Soak overnight in salted water. Take directly out of water (do not rinse) and place on aluminum foil. Season with salt and butter, then wrap in foil. Bake in a 350°F oven 30 minutes.

Serve lutefisk with melted butter and boiled potatoes, if desired.

Note: Lutefisk is codfish that has been dried, then soaked first in water, then in lye or chemicals, then again in water. After this, it is cooked.

Carol Haddix

Chicago Tribune / Chicago, Illinois

The following dish was said to have originated in De Jonghe's, a traditional Chicago restaurant at the turn of the century which is now defunct. The dish, however, lives on in many other Chicago restaurants and across the country.

SHRIMP DE JONGHE

8 to 10 servings

1 small onion, sliced
2 celery tops
6 peppercorns
1 bay leaf
1¾ teaspoons salt, divided
4 pounds medium shrimp in the shell
1 cup butter, melted, divided

¼ cup dry sherry
3 cups fine fresh bread crumbs
¼ cup minced parsley
1 clove garlic, crushed
½ teaspoon paprika
Dash cayenne

Heat 3 quarts water, onion, celery, peppercorns, bay leaf and 1 teaspoon salt to boiling in a large saucepot. Add shrimp; cover and return to a boil. Drain shrimp and peel. Toss shrimp in a large bowl with ½ cup melted butter and sherry; set aside.

Combine bread crumbs and remaining ½ cup melted butter. Stir in parsley, remaining ¾ teaspoon salt, garlic, paprika and cayenne.

Spoon half of shrimp mixture into a 2-quart casserole. Sprinkle with half of bread crumb mixture. Top with remaining shrimp mixture and remaining bread crumb mixture. Bake in a 350°F oven 45 to 55 minutes, until crumbs are lightly browned and shrimp is tender.

Pat Baldridge

Morning Advocate and State-Times / Baton Rouge, Louisiana

Etouffée means smothered. Shrimp or Crawfish Etouffée is not only a South Louisiana favorite, but it also is a quick dish, made from scratch in just a few minutes.

SHRIMP OR CRAWFISH ETOUFFEE   *4 to 6 servings*

½ cup butter or margarine
1½ tablespoons all-purpose flour
¾ cup chopped celery
¾ cup chopped green pepper
¾ cup chopped onion
1 pound peeled, uncooked shrimp, or 1 pound uncooked
     crawfish tails
   Salt, black pepper and cayenne, to taste
¼ cup chopped green onion tops
¼ cup chopped fresh parsley
   Hot cooked rice

Melt butter in a large skillet. Add flour and lightly brown it. Add celery, green pepper and onion; cook until tender, stirring occasionally. Add shrimp or crawfish tails. Cover and cook 15 minutes on low heat, stirring occasionally. Add salt, pepper and cayenne to taste. Add onion tops and parsley. Simmer a few minutes, covered, to blend seasonings. Serve over rice.

Note: For extra gravy, add ¼ cup vermouth, white wine or chicken broth with onion tops and parsley. Stir well.

Louise Dodd
The Courier Herald / Dublin, Georgia

We were served this recipe at an old inn on Cumberland Island, off the coast of Georgia. The inn was formerly the home of Andrew Carnegie and was run by his grandchildren. The hostess willingly shared it, and I have enjoyed serving this dish many times at parties. It's very simple, but oh, such a delicious main course on a hot Georgia night.

CUMBERLAND ISLAND SHRIMP   *8 to 10 servings*

5 pounds shrimp
½ teaspoon garlic powder
5 to 10 whole cloves
3 cups cooked rice
2 ribs celery, cut into small pieces
1 onion, grated (save juices from grating)
1 green pepper, finely chopped
1 cup mayonnaise
  Curry powder, to taste
  Lettuce, tomatoes, sliced cucumbers, for garnish (optional)

Cook shrimp very quickly (for only a few minutes) in water to cover, in a large kettle, with garlic powder and cloves. Drain, peel and chop or break into pieces. Reserve a few whole shrimp to use for garnish, if desired.

Combine chopped shrimp, rice, celery, onion and onion juices, green pepper, mayonnaise and curry powder in a bowl. Toss lightly. This may be served as is, or may be placed in a lightly oiled fish mold and then turned out on a platter.

This is attractive when garnished simply with lettuce, tomatoes, sliced cucumbers and a few reserved whole shrimp.

Evelyn Wavpotich
The Island Packet / Hilton Head Island, South Carolina

This is a recipe that is so simple and quick, so flexible for stretching, and so ideal for any occasion that it belongs in everyone's file.

At our last family reunion, my husband took down our largest pot from a high shelf, filled it with water, and within half an hour we feasted on the three main ingredients. As former Northerners, we latched on to this Carolina recipe really fast.

LOW-COUNTRY BOIL

2 **tablespoons crab and shrimp boil** (seasoning mixture available in most supermarkets)
   Hot (or mild) Polish-type sausage, cut into 1-inch pieces
   Corn on the cob, broken in half (allow one ear per person)
   Raw, unpeeled shrimp (allow ½ pound per person)

Fill a large pot with enough water to cover ingredients. Add crab and shrimp boil. When water comes to a boil, add sausage and corn. Boil 10 minutes. Add shrimp. Boil 2 to 3 minutes, until shrimp turns pink. (Long cooking toughens shrimp.) Remove and drain sausage, corn and shrimp.

Note: Shrimp is served unpeeled, and everyone peels his own. This adds to the fun. Of course, the host or hostess can attend to this chore, if preferred, for a neater party. Be sure to have melted butter available for the corn and a sauce (usually a mixture of ketchup and horseradish) for dipping the shrimp. Cole slaw and beer complete the menu.

Peggy Daum

The Milwaukee Journal / Milwaukee, Wisconsin

The Scandinavian fishermen who came to Door County—the "thumb" of Wisconsin that juts into Lake Michigan—are credited with starting the custom of the fish boil. For them, the fish boil was a necessity, a way to cook part of the day's catch for supper.

Today, for the tourists who flock to Door County in the summertime, the fish boil is a popular attraction, a spectacular show—and a tasty supper. It's staged by many of the restaurants and hotels that dot the vacationland.

Fish, potatoes and, usually, onions are boiled in a large kettle of salted water over a wood fire. When they're ready for eating, the boilmaster adds kerosene to the fire. The flames shoot up, the show is dramatic and the pot boils over, carrying off the fish fat that has accumulated on the water.

The boiled dinner is completed, traditionally, with cole slaw, rye bread and cherry pie—made from Door County's tart cherry crop, of course.

A home-size version of a fish boil can be done in any very large kettle, but one with a removable basket is helpful.

The following recipe is adapted from one worked out for home cooks by Phillip and Rosemary Voight, owners of the Viking Restaurant in Ellison Bay, which claims to have Door County's oldest and largest fish boil.

DOOR COUNTY FISH BOIL   *8 servings*

16 small onions
16 small red potatoes
½ pound non-iodized salt,
   divided

16 chunks whitefish (7 to 8
   pounds)
8 lemon wedges, for garnish
¾ cup melted butter

Peel onions. Wash potatoes and slice a small piece off ends, but do not peel.

Bring 2 gallons water to a boil in a large kettle. Add ¼ pound of the salt and bring to a boil again. Add potatoes and boil, uncovered, 16 minutes. Add onions and boil, uncovered, 4 minutes longer.

If insert basket is available, place fish in basket. Add fish and remaining ¼ pound salt. Boil, uncovered, 10 minutes longer.

Remove from heat. Skim off any fish oil that accumulated during cooking. Drain into a colander. Place fish and vegetables on a serving platter or individual plates; garnish with lemon wedges. Serve with melted butter.

Note: A large quantity of salt is traditional in this recipe. The amount may be reduced, if desired.

Diane Wiggins
St. Louis Globe-Democrat / St. Louis, Missouri

Although I work in St. Louis, I live in a rural area near Belleville, Illinois, across the Mississippi River. Belleville and the smaller surrounding towns have a tradition of Friday fish fries that I have not found in other areas, even as near as St. Louis. The tradition probably stems from the Catholic practice of abstaining from meat during the Fridays of Lent. Gradually, the serving of fish as an alternative entrée became extended to every Friday.

On Friday nights, many taverns, schools, churches and community groups, such as VFWs, sponsor fish fries that are open to the public. A few private entrepreneurs operate small family-run weekend fish stands that do a landslide business, especially during warm weather, when you can eat on picnic tables in outdoor beer gardens attached to the stands. Carryouts are popular.

The food is generally good, reasonable in price and served on heavy paper plates. A cold beer is the standard accompaniment, with sodas for the kids. The menu is limited, generally, to deep-fried squares of cod served on white or rye bread, with tartar sauce, cole slaw and French fries. A few places also offer catfish, jack salmon and, if you want to get fancy, shrimp. Cut-ups, chunks of fish deep-fried and accompanied by bread, are available by the plate or the pound. Non-fish lovers can get a hamburger or, sometimes, pizza.

Here is a recipe for fried fish the way my mother, Dorothy Raab, makes it. She uses the bluegill or bass she and my father catch in local lakes. The fish are filleted into boneless pieces that are dipped in batter and deep-fried.

BEER-BATTERED FISH

4 servings

1 cup buttermilk baking mix
1 cup beer (your favorite brand)
   Garlic salt, salt and pepper, to taste
2 to 3 pounds of fillets (the catch of the day, cleaned and filleted)
   Vegetable oil for frying

Combine baking mix, beer, garlic salt, salt and pepper in a bowl. Dip cleaned fish fillets in batter. Fry in hot oil in a deep-fryer or skillet until golden brown. Drain on absorbent towels. Serve hot.

Marian Burros

The New York Times / New York, New York

This recipe for Maryland stuffed ham is from a story I did in a magazine. A woman named Alice Shorter, who lives in southern Maryland, showed me how to do it.

Traditionally, a country ham is used in this recipe, but we found that regular ham works very well. Because this ham should be cooled in the broth in which it has been cooked, you may wish to prepare the ham the day before it is to be served.

SOUTHERN MARYLAND STUFFED HAM   *15 servings*

2 large, green cabbages (about 3 pounds each), cored and finely chopped
1½ pounds kale, finely chopped
3 medium onions, finely chopped
4 ribs celery, finely chopped
½ teaspoon cayenne
½ teaspoon pepper
1 teaspoon dry mustard
1 precooked bone-in ham (about 10 pounds)

For stuffing: Place cabbage, kale, onions, celery, cayenne, pepper and mustard in a large stockpot; add water to within 1 inch of the top of vegetables and, stirring occasionally, bring to a boil over moderate heat. Turn off heat, cover the pot and let vegetables rest for 10 minutes in the hot water. Pour vegetables into a colander set over a bowl to catch the broth. Reserve broth; cool vegetables to room temperature.

To stuff ham: Cut an "X" measuring 1 inch square and 2 inches deep on underside of ham. Fill "X" with vegetable stuffing until no more will fit. Continue cutting "X's" about ½- to 1-inch apart all over ham, stuffing them as they are cut. Center ham on a 4-foot-long piece of double-thickness cheesecloth and place any remaining stuffing on top of ham. Wrap cheesecloth around ham and tie ends together to hold stuffing in place.

To cook ham: Return ham to the stockpot along with reserved broth; add enough water to cover ham. Place lid on pot and bring liquid to a boil over high heat. Reduce heat to low and continue to cook ham for 2 hours, adding water as needed to keep ham covered. Remove pot from heat and allow ham to cool for an hour in the cooking broth. Then transfer ham to a large colander or a rack to drain for about 1 hour. Remove and discard cheesecloth and place any extra vegetable stuffing on top of ham in a serving dish. To serve, slice ham and accompany with vegetable stuffing.

Bernie Arnold

Nashville Banner / Nashville, Tennessee

We're sure this recipe would work just as well with country hams from other parts of the United States. It's just that we've never cooked hams from West Virginia, North Dakota, Georgia, etc., etc.

HOW TO COOK A TENNESSEE COUNTRY HAM

In the morning, scrub **ham** with a stiff brush; soak all day in cold water. In the evening, lift out and put on stove in a large container with a good top. Pour hot water in container until ham is covered. Add to water:

1 cup pickle juice, or ½ cup cider vinegar
1 red (hot) pepper, seeds removed

1 lemon, quartered
1 onion, cut in half
2 bay leaves

Put top on tight and turn stove on high. When a rolling boil is reached, cook for 1 hour. Cut off stove and cover lid with thick newspapers (preferably the *Nashville Banner*).

Cover all with a woolen blanket and tie around sides to keep heat in. Let stay on the "cut off" stove until morning.

When ham is cool enough to handle, lift out bone, skin the rind and lightly pierce the fat side. Rub in **2 teaspoons prepared mustard**. Pat on **brown sugar** and **bread crumbs**. Pour **½ cup sherry** over top of ham. Stick with **whole cloves**.

Brown in oven. Watch carefully so as not to burn. Let cool *overnight* before slicing thin. (The last step is very important.)

Elaine Corn

The Courier-Journal / Louisville, Kentucky

Country Ham is a classic in Kentucky. The term "red-eye" supposedly comes from the little red circles or "eyes" of grease that form in the gravy on the plate.

COUNTRY HAM AND RED-EYE GRAVY   *8 to 10 servings*

Vegetable oil
8 slices (¼-inch thickness) raw
   country ham

¾ cup black coffee
1 teaspoon granulated sugar

Heat a few drops of oil in a large skillet until skillet is medium hot. Lay ham slices in skillet. Cook on one side for 8 minutes over medium-high heat. Turn slices and fry 8 minutes more. Pour coffee into skillet with ham slices. Sprinkle with sugar and stir. Cover and let simmer over very low heat for 5 to 10 minutes. Serve ham and red-eye gravy together.

Sandra Day

The Times-Picayune/States-Item / New Orleans, Louisiana

This is a traditional Monday dish in New Orleans. It started out as a way to use the ham bone left over after Sunday dinner. The beans could be put on the back of the stove to cook all day, since Monday was wash day. All of the cafeterias still have this for luncheon plates on Monday.

RED BEANS AND RICE   *4 to 6 servings*

1 pound dried red beans or
   kidney beans
1 quart hot water
1 large ham bone with meat
1 large onion, chopped
½ cup chopped green onion
2 cloves garlic, pressed

1 bay leaf
½ teaspoon cayenne
1½ teaspoons salt
1 pound smoked sausage, cut
   into 1-inch pieces
Hot cooked rice

Sort beans and rinse well; cover with tap water and soak overnight. Drain beans and place in a large heavy pot; add hot water, ham bone, onion, green onion, garlic, bay leaf, cayenne and salt. Bring mixture to a boil; cover and reduce heat. Simmer beans 2 hours, or until tender, adding more water if necessary to keep from sticking; stir often.

Add sausage to beans and simmer, uncovered, about 15 minutes longer, or until a thick gravy forms; stir occasionally. Serve over rice.

Joyce Rosencrans
The Cincinnati Post / Cincinnati, Ohio

Scrapple (a Pennsylvania Dutch specialty) and its next of kin, Goetta, are exactly the same thing, except that while Scrapple is thickened with cornmeal, Goetta is thickened with pin (also called cross-cut) oats. Goetta, fried like cornmeal mush, is found on Cincinnati restaurant breakfast menus.

These dishes have a long history that goes back to midwinter butchering time on farms. Scrappy bits of fresh pork were simmered in water with seasonings until the meat would easily come off the bones. After the meat was removed from the bones, it was finely chopped or put through a food grinder. Then the mixture of meat and broth was brought to boiling and thickened with cornmeal or pin oats and poured into pans to chill.

It was kept in a cold place for a couple of weeks or longer before it was sliced and cooked on a griddle or skillet until golden brown and crusty. Drenched with maple syrup, it made (and still does) a dish fit for the gods. Don't forget—Scrapple and Goetta are as good at lunch or supper as for breakfast.

Goetta is similar to chili in that everyone has his or her own version. This version comes from Fern Storer, former food editor.

GOETTA
5 to 6 servings (18 slices)

1 pound high-grade pork sausage
1 quart water
1¼ cups pin (cross-cut) oats, uncooked
1 bay leaf
1 small onion, chopped
1 small sage leaf, or to taste
   Salt and pepper, to taste
¼ cup flour
1 teaspoon salt
½ teaspoon paprika
¼ teaspoon pepper
   Butter or margarine, for cooking
   Butter and maple syrup

Combine sausage and water in a medium saucepan. (Use a pan that is heavy and has a tight-fitting lid.) Mash sausage with a potato masher. Stir in oats; add bay leaf and chopped onion. Bring to a boil, then reduce heat so mixture simmers gently. Cook, covered, stirring every 10 or 15 minutes to make sure mixture doesn't stick. Use a straight-end spatula, pancake turner or similar device for stirring. After about 2 hours of cooking, add one small sage leaf, rubbed fine, and salt and pepper as needed. (This depends on the seasoning in the sausage.) Cook about 15 minutes longer.

Near end of cooking time, spoon off any fat that accumulates on surface. Then pour cooked mixture into a 9x5x3-inch loaf pan which has been rinsed with cold water. This will fill loaf pan about halfway. Cover and refrigerate.

To use, cut into ½-inch slices. Mix flour with salt, paprika and pepper. Coat slices with seasoned flour. Sauté slowly in butter in a skillet or on a griddle, until golden on both sides. Allow about 15 minutes cooking time. Serve with butter and maple syrup.

Note: This recipe was purposely given in small size. Double if you wish, keeping the proportions the same. Cooking time will be about the same.

Variation: *To make Scrapple,* proceed using same measurements except use cornmeal instead of pin oats. Stir cornmeal into cold liquid, rather than waiting for liquid to boil. Cook and stir until cornmeal thickens the mixture. (Cornmeal thickens more quickly than pin oats.) After the mixture has thickened, cover pan and set over a pan of boiling water to cook, stirring occasionally, about 1 hour.

Tasso is a smoked, highly seasoned strip of pork, usually taken from along the back of the hog. It's a product of the Cajun boucherie. Cajuns use it to season beans and such dishes as jambalaya, gumbo, etc. It takes well to long cooking.

WHITE BEANS AND TASSO

6 to 8 servings

1 pound dried white beans
 (navy or Great Northern)
½ to 1 pound tasso, cut in
 ½-inch cubes
2 large onions, chopped
2 cloves garlic, minced
1 tablespoon salt
1 teaspoon black pepper
 Cayenne, to taste

1 tablespoon Worcestershire
 sauce
¼ teaspoon dried oregano,
 crumbled
¼ teaspoon dried thyme,
 crumbled
1 bunch green onions,
 chopped
1 cup chopped fresh parsley
 Hot cooked rice

Cover beans with 2 quarts water and soak overnight. (Or, for quicker preparation, put beans in 2 quarts boiling water; remove from heat and allow to stand 1 hour.)

Bring beans and soaking water to a boil; reduce heat to low. Simmer 45 minutes. Add tasso and continue to simmer 1 hour. Add onions, garlic, salt, pepper, cayenne and Worcestershire sauce. Continue simmering for 1 more hour.

Remove from heat and allow to cool 30 minutes. Bring again to a boil. Add oregano, thyme, green onions and parsley. Reduce heat and simmer 30 minutes. Additional water can be added if needed (there should be a little "gravy"). Serve over rice.

About sixty miles south of St. Louis lies the charming, historic town of Ste. Genevieve. This picturesque town, on the banks of the Mississippi River, is Missouri's oldest existing town and the second-oldest town west of the Mississippi. It was settled by the French and still retains its French heritage. However, the German influence is stronger today than the French, and the culinary heritage of the town reflects the French, German and other cultural backgrounds.

Outstanding among the German dishes is a local specialty called leberknaefly, or liver dumplings. There are probably as many versions of this dish as there are cooks in Ste. Genevieve, but this one is representative.

LEBERKNAEFLY
6 to 10 servings

1 pound liver (calf, beef or pork)
½ cup ground pork
1 medium onion, finely chopped
3 cups all-purpose flour
3 eggs
1 tablespoon finely chopped parsley
½ teaspoon dried basil, or ½ teaspoon ground allspice
Salt and pepper, to taste
About 1 cup milk
Salted water
1 tablespoon fat

Grind liver; mix with ground pork and onion. Mix in flour, then add eggs, parsley, basil, salt and pepper. Add enough milk to make a stiff dough.

Transfer some of dough to a flat platter. Use a knife, dipped in hot water, to cut and drop tiny pieces of dough into boiling salted water to which fat has been added to keep dumplings from sticking together. When dumplings rise to the surface, they are ready to be skimmed off and drained.

Serve dumplings hot. Dumplings can be fried lightly in sausage drippings or served with a light gravy.

Note: The dough can be frozen for a short time.

Carol Hanson

The Post-Crescent / Appleton, Wisconsin

Cousin Jack Pasties are a treat my family seeks each time we return to Michigan's Upper Peninsula, where we lived for fifteen years. And we do return often!

We became well acquainted with pasties during those years—learning to eat them, steaming hot and covered with ketchup, just as the natives do. We carried them in our picnic basket, served them for lunch, savored them at casual parties.

This is a treasured recipe, given to me by a friend's mother who was considered by many to be one of the best pasty makers. She was Welsh, and a native of that area. Her recipe uses the traditional lard in the crust, with a sprinkle of suet topping the filling to ensure a moist interior.

COUSIN JACK PASTIES

5 servings

Dough:
- 3 cups all-purpose flour
- 1 tablespoon salt
- 1 cup lard
- 1 cup cold water

Filling:
- 3¾ cups cubed potatoes, divided
- 15 ounces flank steak, cubed, divided
- 5 ounces pork, cubed, divided
- 5 teaspoons suet, divided
- 5 tablespoons diced onion, divided
- Salt and pepper, to taste

For dough: Sift flour and salt into a mixing bowl; sift again. Cut in lard until mixture is the size of small peas; add cold water, a little at a time. Toss until mixture holds together, handling as little as possible. Cut into 5 portions. Roll each portion on a floured board until 9 inches across.

To fill: Place ¾ cup potatoes, 3 ounces flank steak, 1 ounce pork, 1 teaspoon suet, 1 tablespoon onion, salt and pepper on each portion of dough. Fold dough in half over filling, pinching edges to seal. Slit top. Repeat for other pasties. Place on a greased baking sheet. Bake in a 400°F oven 1 hour, or until nicely browned.

The Times-Picayune/States-Item / New Orleans, Louisiana

Gumbo is a classic dish in New Orleans. Just about every restaurant offers a version. This recipe uses ingredients that are available everywhere. Seafood gumbos are the most popular in New Orleans, but the ingredients are not so readily available in other parts of the country.

CHICKEN AND SAUSAGE GUMBO

8 servings

1 fryer (3 to 3½ pounds), cut up
½ cup bacon drippings or vegetable oil
½ cup all-purpose flour
2 onions, chopped
2 ribs celery, chopped
1 green pepper, chopped
6 to 8 cloves garlic, minced
1 to 1½ pounds smoked sausage, cut into ½-inch slices
2 quarts hot water or chicken stock
1 tablespoon salt
1 teaspoon black pepper
¼ teaspoon cayenne
½ cup chopped green onion tops
¼ cup finely chopped fresh parsley
2½ to 3 tablespoons gumbo filé (ground sassafras leaves)
Hot cooked rice

Brown chicken pieces in hot bacon drippings in a large, heavy pot. Remove chicken from pot and set aside. Make a roux by gradually adding flour to hot drippings, stirring constantly over medium heat until roux turns the color of a dirty copper penny, about 10 to 15 minutes. Do not let roux burn or gumbo will be ruined.

When roux reaches the right color, immediately stir in onion, celery, green pepper, garlic and sausage. Cook, stirring constantly, until vegetables are tender, or about 5 minutes. Add hot water, salt, pepper, cayenne and browned chicken pieces, stirring well to blend seasonings. Bring mixture to a boil; reduce heat and simmer 45 minutes to 1 hour, or until chicken is tender; stir occasionally. Stir in green onion and parsley; cook 5 minutes longer.

Remove gumbo from heat. Stir in filé and let stand 5 minutes to thicken. (Do not boil mixture after adding filé or it will become stringy.) Serve gumbo over rice with additional filé, if desired.

Note: Almost any kind of meat, poultry or seafood can be used in this recipe. You might want to try ham, shrimp, crab meat, oysters, pork, turkey or any game. For okra gumbo, add 2 cups fresh or frozen sliced okra with the sausage and omit filé.

Kitty Crider

Austin American-Statesman / Austin, Texas

The world's largest ranch, King Ranch, covers 900,000 acres in South Texas and extends into eight counties. The folks there don't eat beef at every meal; sometimes they have this casserole, which has become a favorite with homemakers and caterers because it's easy to extend. It has become the traditional Lone Star State standby for potluck suppers.

KING RANCH CHICKEN CASSEROLE
8 to 10 servings

 1 chicken (2½ to 3 pounds)
12 corn tortillas, torn, or 16 taco shells, broken
 1 can (10¾ ounces) condensed cream of mushroom soup, undiluted
 1 can (10¾ ounces) condensed cream of chicken soup, undiluted
 1 large onion, chopped
 1 can (10 ounces) tomatoes with green chilies, undrained
 1 to 2 cups grated Cheddar cheese

Stew chicken in water in a large saucepot until tender. Reserve 1 cup chicken broth. Bone chicken, cutting meat into bite-size pieces.

Grease a 9x13x2-inch baking dish. Place torn tortillas or broken taco shells in bottom of dish. Layer chicken pieces on top. Combine soups, onion, tomatoes and reserved 1 cup chicken broth in saucepan; cook over medium heat until hot. Pour soup mixture over chicken. Top with grated cheese. Bake in a 350°F oven 50 to 60 minutes, or until bubbly hot.

Jean Thwaite

The Atlanta Journal-Constitution, / Altanta, Georgia

No one really seems to know the origin of this dish. Some say it was brought back from India to England by a British Navy officer. Others say it was a favorite in the English countryside and was originally Country Capon. The story Georgians like best is that it was created by an inventive Columbus cook for Franklin Delano Roosevelt when he was at the little White House in Warm Springs.

Still another version appears in "Georgia Heritage," published by the Colonial Dames. Mrs. Sewell Brumby of Athens writes that, some sixty-five years ago, her mother ordered a cookbook by Alexandre Fillipini, chef of Delmonico's for many years. Her mother changed this one dish radically, and it became a party favorite, taken all over the world by Army friends. Her mother's butler-chef ended up as chef at the White House and introduced it to Roosevelt. So take your pick.

Some versions call for using a hen, cooking it and pulling the meat off the bones. Others use cut-up fryers. The most recent ones use chicken breasts. The one constant seems to be that to be authentic, the recipe must call for currants and slivered toasted almonds. No raisins and pecans allowed.

CHICKEN COUNTRY CAPTAIN   *12 servings*

12 chicken breasts
    Flour and salt, for dredging chicken
2 generous tablespoons lard
2 onions, sliced fine
2 green peppers, sliced
2 cloves garlic, crushed
2 cans (16 ounces each) whole tomatoes, broken up
½ teaspoon white pepper
½ teaspoon dried thyme
1 to 2 teaspoons curry powder, or to taste
    Salt, to taste
3 heaping tablespoons currants soaked in 1 tablespoon white or
    red wine
    Cooked fluffy white rice (to serve 12)
¼ pound almonds, blanched, slivered and toasted
1 teaspoon chopped fresh parsley

Coat chicken pieces with flour and a little salt. Heat lard in a skillet. Fry chicken gently until brown. Remove chicken from skillet; put into a large casserole and keep warm.

Gently wilt onion and green pepper along with garlic in the same skillet. Add tomatoes, white pepper, thyme and curry powder; mix well. Check for salt, pepper and acidity. (Some canned tomatoes are more acidic than others and may need a little sugar.)

Pour the tomato sauce over chicken in casserole. Deglaze pan and add liquid to chicken. Cover tightly and cook on stovetop until chicken is very tender.

Put currants in a little wine and warm to plump. Place chicken breasts on a warmed platter. Make a ring of rice around chicken. Add currants to tomato sauce and pour sauce over rice and chicken. Scatter almonds over rice. Sprinkle with parsley.

Note: Curries are much better if made a day ahead; the seasonings blend into the meat much better. Rice can be cooked a day ahead, sealed in foil and reheated with the Country Captain.

Jann Malone

Richmond Times-Dispatch / Richmond, Virginia

I don't think I ever ate half a chicken in one sitting until I tasted the barbecued chicken at the 1982 Delmarva Chicken Festival—the chicken had a wonderful flavor that didn't stop at the skin but went all the way through the meat.

The secret is in the barbecue sauce—it turns out to be one that's been used on the Eastern Shore for some time. This version comes from Roy Beauchamp of Chesapeake Foods.

DELMARVA BARBECUED CHICKEN   *4 generous servings*

1 teaspoon salt
1 teaspoon pepper
2 teaspoons poultry seasoning
1 cup cider vinegar

½ cup vegetable oil
1 egg, well beaten
2 chickens, each split in half

Combine salt, pepper and poultry seasoning in a small bowl. Add vinegar, oil and egg; mix well.

When coals are ready, put chicken on the grill and baste with sauce. Keep mixing sauce as chicken cooks, because sauce tends to separate. Cook chicken slowly over medium coals 1½ to 2½ hours, or until juices run clear. Cooking time will depend on size of chicken. Baste chicken frequently with sauce, and turn chicken frequently.

Note: To serve 8, cut each half in two with poultry shears or a sharp knife.

Los Angeles Herald Examiner / Los Angeles, California

The hottest fast-food item in Los Angeles is El Pollo Loco. Pass any of its nineteen locations anytime and watch lines of people waiting to order this Mexican-style char-broiled bird. Even the price is right. For under $6, you get a whole chicken, a container of fresh, spicy salsa and ten hot tortillas...enough for four people...but so good two can polish it off easily.

El Pollo Loco, or crazy chicken, was born eight years ago in Guasava, Mexico. Juan Francisco Ochao—Pancho to his friends—and his brother, Jaime, opened a roadside stand, broiling chicken for passersby. The first day, they sold fifty chickens and were on their way.

A year later, Jaime opened a restaurant specializing in the same fare, and it was equally successful. Today the family owns some ninety take-out eateries in Mexico.

In 1980, the Ochaos reasoned their chicken would be just as welcome to Mexicans elsewhere, and opened El Pollo Loco in the heart of the Hispanic community in Los Angeles.

El Pollo Loco's success spawned imitators. Now there's El Pollo Tonto (stupid chicken), Pollo Blanco (white chicken), Pollo de Oro (golden chicken), Pollo Gordo (fat chicken) and more.

El Pollo Loco's exact recipe is, of course, a secret, but rumor has it that the chicken is first marinated in something with fruit juices for twenty-four hours. When done, the skin is golden, and there are a few tinges of yellow on the meat, which means that it is either treated with food coloring (doubtful), turmeric or Mexican asafran, remotely related to saffron.

After experimenting with a good many "crazy chickens," Bess Greenstone, who writes regularly for the food section, came up with this recipe for "crazy chicken in your own kitchen."

EL POLLO LOCO DE TU COCINA   *4 servings*

3 quarts water
1 onion, coarsely chopped
2 carrots, coarsely
    chopped
3 to 4 sprigs fresh cilantro
2 teaspoons asafran or
    turmeric

1 tablespoon kosher salt
1 chicken (3½ to 4 pounds),
    quartered
Salsa
Hot tortillas

Combine water, onion, carrots, cilantro, asafran and salt in a large saucepot or Dutch oven. Bring to a boil and cook for 10 minutes. Add chicken. When liquids return to a boil, cook for 5 minutes. Turn off the heat and cover pot. Allow chicken to cool in the broth.

Remove chicken to a platter. Reduce broth to half by rapid boiling. Place chicken on grill over hot coals and cook until done. Baste with broth and turn frequently. Serve with salsa and tortillas.

Marge Hanley
Indianapolis News / Indianapolis, Indiana

The Iron Skillet restaurant in Indianapolis is part of the city's culinary heritage. It's known for its Hoosier fried chicken dinners, complete with whipped potatoes, cream gravy, green beans seasoned with ham and onion, and buttered corn.

THE IRON SKILLET'S HOOSIER FRIED CHICKEN

3 to 4 servings per chicken

Chicken fryers (2½ to 3 pounds each)
Salt

All-purpose flour
Lard for frying

Clean, cut and salt chicken pieces the day before frying. Cover and refrigerate.

When ready to fry, coat pieces with flour, shaking off excess. Heat lard, about 1 inch deep in large skillet. Add chicken pieces to hot lard, being sure chicken is not added too quickly, as it may reduce lard temperature. Turn chicken and brown on both sides. Reduce heat so lard is about 275°F. Continue frying and turning chicken pieces until crisp and well done, about 25 to 35 minutes, depending upon size of pieces. Drain and serve immediately.

Mary Frances Phillips
San Jose Mercury News / San Jose, California

This is healthy California cooking at its finest. A good friend, Jim, showed me how to make this dish. Complete the California meal with rice pilaf (rice, chicken stock and sautéed onion), fresh zucchini or string beans, and a platter of fresh strawberries, cantaloupe slices and kiwi halves.

CALIFORNIA BAKED CHICKEN

2 to 4 servings

1 frying chicken (3 to 3½ pounds)
3 to 5 large cloves garlic

Melted butter for basting
Herbs (optional)

Rinse and dry chicken, removing gizzard, heart, etc. Place chicken in single-chicken-size granite roaster. Insert garlic cloves in cavity; tie legs together with butcher's string. Baste with melted butter. Sprinkle with herbs, if desired. Cover with lid. Bake in a 500°F (this is correct) oven for 30 minutes. Reduce temperature to 350°F and bake 1 hour more.

Place chicken on a platter, cut down through breast with a case knife and remove bones.

Ann Criswell
Houston Chronicle / Houston, Texas

Chicken-Fried Steak is one of the most traditional Texas foods, linked to both our Old West and our Southern heritage. To prepare them for the cowboys, range cooks would tenderize tough beefsteaks with a cleaver, season them with salt and pepper, dust them with flour and fry them in sizzling fat.

In West Texas, Chicken-Fried Steak is typically served with a skillet gravy made from drippings and water, with a little flour for thickening. In East Texas and some other areas, a batter like fried chicken batter is used, and the steaks are served with cream gravy made from pan drippings or butter, flour and milk. Don't skimp on the gravy!

TEXAS CHICKEN-FRIED STEAK
4 to 6 servings

2 pounds round steak
2 eggs
½ cup milk
1 cup all-purpose flour

1 teaspoon salt
¼ teaspoon pepper
Vegetable oil for frying
Cream Gravy (recipe follows)

Cut steak in serving pieces and pound flat with a tenderizer mallet. Beat eggs with milk. Mix flour with salt and pepper. Dip steak in egg mixture, then in seasoned flour. Fry in ½ inch of hot oil in a large skillet until brown on both sides. Serve with gravy.

CREAM GRAVY
1 cup

1 tablespoon butter or
  drippings
1 to 2 tablespoons all-purpose
  flour

1 cup milk or half-and-half,
  warmed
Salt and pepper

If using butter, melt in skillet. Stir in flour. Remove from heat; whisk in milk. Return to heat and stir until thickened. Season to taste with salt and pepper. (I like a healthy sprinkling of pepper.)

Carol Brock
Daily News / New York, New York

Not only is New York the nation's melting pot; it is its cooking pot as well, providing recipes for menus across the land. Many dishes enjoy a short period of popularity and then fade away. But some outlive the fabled restaurants and hotels that made them famous, adding to New York's reputation as a cradle of culinary invention.

The legacy of Delmonico's is a case in point. Although the restaurant died along with the age of opulence that spawned it, many of its dishes are still served throughout America. Delmonico's was one of several earlier-day eateries that helped to establish New York's way with steak, and the Delmonico Steak is, obviously, named for the restaurant.

DELMONICO STEAK

2 servings

2 Delmonico steaks (about 1¼ pounds each), cut from rib eye
    roast
  Salt
  Melted butter or olive oil

Maître d'Hotel Butter:
 4 tablespoons butter, softened
 1 tablespoon minced parsley
 ¼ teaspoon salt
  Pepper
 ½ teaspoon lemon juice

Start heating the broiler 10 minutes ahead of time. Sprinkle steak with salt and brush with melted butter. For a 1½-inch thick steak, broil 9 minutes per side for rare, 10 minutes for medium, 12 to 13 minutes for well done.

For Maître d'Hotel Butter: While steak is broiling, blend softened butter with parsley, salt, a speck of pepper and lemon juice. Serve butter in individual containers alongside steaks.

Ann Criswell
Houston Chronicle / Houston, Texas

Fajitas (fah-heet-us), marinated skirt steak cut into pieces and served in a warm flour tortilla, is a popular specialty in northern Mexico that's catching on in Texas and the Southwest like wildfire.

The meat is usually labeled skirt steak in the supermarket and is a thin, flat piece of beef somewhat resembling flank steak. It is actually a supportive organ that comes from the inside of the rib cage.

The meat is marinated several hours or overnight, then drained and quickly grilled over coals, chopped into small pieces, then rolled up and served in a warm flour tortilla. Usually a variety of sauces accompanies fajitas—Guacamole, Salsa Verde (a mild green chili sauce), Salsa Roja (a hotter red sauce) or Salsa Cruda, a mixture of fresh chopped tomatoes, white onion, a little cilantro (fresh coriander) and a dash of salt and pepper (mashed or chopped jalapeño peppers are optional).

Like brisket, skirt steak has a layer of fat that should be trimmed. Any membrane also should be peeled off so the meat won't be too chewy. The steak should be thin; if it is more than ¾-inch thick at the thickest portion, cut it in half lengthwise so that it will cook quickly. The rule for cooking is hot fire, short cooking time.

Various marinades are used. Some cooks just use bottled barbecue sauce, but a mixture of beer, a little oil, garlic and chopped vegetables is more typical. This marinade comes from one of our photographers, Carlos Antonio Rios.

FAJITAS   *1 quart marinade*

4 **cups soy sauce** (the heavy dark imported kind is too strong)
1 **cup packed light brown sugar**
1 **teaspoon garlic powder**
1 **teaspoon onion powder**
8 **tablespoons fresh lemon juice**
4 **teaspoons ground ginger**
1 **skirt steak (about ¾-inch thickness) for every 3 persons**
  Warm flour tortillas

Combine soy sauce, brown sugar, garlic powder, onion powder, lemon juice and ginger in a jar; shake to mix well and dissolve sugar. Let marinade stand in sealed jar overnight. Pour marinade over beef and let marinate 2 hours or overnight in refrigerator in sealed container.

Remove fajitas from marinade and grill over very hot coals a short time, about 10 minutes per steak if meat is ¾-inch thick. Brush meat with marinade two or three times while cooking.

Refrigerate extra marinade in tightly sealed jar for future use.

Chop meat with a cleaver and wrap in warm flour tortillas to serve.

Billie Bledsoe

San Antonio Express-News / San Antonio, Texas

Texas pit barbecue requires three essential ingredients: a good solid (5- to 10-pound) piece of beef, brisket by choice, well marbled with fat; a slow-burning or smoldering fire using mesquite or oak; and a "pit." The pit is made either from stone or from a 55-gallon drum. The meat is not grilled over the coals, but rather smoked for four to eight hours in the draft of the hot fumes and smoke from the fire.

Some people say that good barbecue can only be achieved south of the Red River. That's where mesquite and live oak are most plentiful; these produce the slow heat and savory smoke flavor that make first-rate barbecue.

Everyone has his own special barbecue sauce for marinating, basting and pouring over the sliced meat. There is a basic recipe to which your own "secret" ingredients can be added.

The use of the sauce, however it is prepared, varies from person to person and locale to locale. It may be used to marinate the beef overnight, as a baster during the cooking process, and/or as a gravy served with the meat.

Slow cooking away from direct heat will produce delicious barbecue beef that is well done through and through, and soft, tender and juicy.

Barbecue is traditionally eaten with potato salad, onions, pickles and a slice of bread or saltine crackers.

BASIC BARBECUE SAUCE
FOR TEXAS PIT BARBECUE

¾ to 1 cup

1 medium onion, chopped
1 clove garlic, minced
2 tablespoons butter or
    margarine
½ cup ketchup
¼ cup water
2 tablespoons vinegar

1 tablespoon light brown sugar
1 teaspoon prepared mustard
    Salt and pepper, to taste
½ teaspoon hot pepper sauce
    (optional)
1 lemon or orange, sliced
    (optional)

Cook onion and garlic in butter in a medium saucepan until tender. Add ketchup, water, vinegar, brown sugar, mustard, salt, pepper and hot pepper sauce. Bring to a boil. Remove from heat and let stand for flavors to mingle.

A sliced lemon or orange can be added, or a bit of the juice of either.

Note: "Secret" ingredients include beer, wine, bourbon, bay leaves, chili powder, tomatoes, vegetable oil or fat.

Billie Bledsoe
San Antonio Express-News / San Antonio, Texas

This is one of the most famous barbecue recipes in Texas—and the origin, of course, is obvious. President Lyndon B. Johnson gets all the credit for this one.

LBJ BARBECUE SAUCE
2½ cups

1 cup ketchup
½ cup cider vinegar
1 teaspoon granulated sugar
1 teaspoon chili powder
½ teaspoon salt
1½ cups water
3 ribs celery, chopped
3 bay leaves

1 clove garlic, minced
2 tablespoons chopped onion
4 tablespoons Worcestershire sauce
1 teaspoon paprika
Dash black pepper
4 tablespoons butter

Combine ketchup, vinegar, sugar, chili powder, salt, water, celery, bay leaves, garlic, onion, Worcestershire sauce, paprika, pepper and butter in a medium saucepan. Bring mixture to a boil. Simmer 15 minutes. Remove from heat and strain.

Ivy Coffey

The El Reno Daily Tribune / El Reno, Oklahoma

This is a modern adaption of an old Chickasaw Indian recipe which was originally made with venison.

CHICKASAW BAKED STEAK

6 servings

2 pounds rump steak (½-inch thickness), cut in 6 pieces, pounded
Salt and pepper, to taste
All-purpose flour, for dredging
Butter or vegetable oil, for frying
1 large onion, chopped fine
1 large green pepper, chopped
½ cup chopped celery
½ cup sherry
½ cup tomato sauce or tomato juice
½ teaspoon paprika
1 cup water

Season steak with salt and pepper. Dip pieces in flour and fry in butter or oil for 1 minute on each side. Transfer steaks to a pan suitable for baking.

Sauté onion, green pepper and celery in same skillet. Add sherry, tomato sauce, paprika and water. Pour over steaks in baking dish. Bake, uncovered, in a 375°F oven 30 minutes. Turn steaks over and bake another 30 minutes.

Dotty Griffith

The Dallas Morning News / Dallas, Texas

This isn't a World Championship chili recipe. It would have to be doctored to reach those gastronomic heights. But it's real. It is based on the formula used by famed chuck wagon cook Richard Bolt from the 175,000-acre 4-Sixes Ranch in West Texas, one of the largest ranches to outfit a chuck wagon.

TEXAS CHUCK WAGON CHILI   6 to 8 servings

    3 pounds beef chuck roast, cut into small stew-size chunks
        (including fat)
    6 tablespoons chili powder
    3 tablespoons ground oregano
    6 cloves garlic, minced
    3 tablespoons ground cumin (cominos)
    1 tablespoon cayenne (less if you don't like it really hot)
 1½ to 2 quarts water
    ⅓ cup masa harina or cornmeal

Using some of the fat, render fat for browning rest of meat. Brown meat in a cast-iron Dutch oven. Add chili powder, oregano, garlic, cumin and cayenne. Stir to coat meat. Add water and stir. Bring liquid to a boil and simmer, covered, for 1 to 1½ hours. Make a thick paste of masa or cornmeal and add to chili stew. Stir to prevent lumping. Remove lid and simmer 30 to 45 minutes longer (more if you like) to thicken and reduce stew to desired consistency.

Note: You may need to tone down the seasonings to suit more tender, non-Texas palates. An Ohio food editor tamed it down to 3 tablespoons chili powder, 2 teaspoons ground cumin, 1½ teaspoons ground oregano and 1 teaspoon cayenne, to start.

Billie Bledsoe

San Antonio Express-News / San Antonio, Texas

San Antonio is famous for its annual Fiesta which features the many ethnic recipes which are part of the city's culture. Literally hundreds of thousands of these anticuchos are sold every year.

ANTICUCHOS

2 to 4 servings

¾ cup red wine vinegar
2¼ cups water
2 to 3 serrano peppers
Salt
Whole black peppercorns
½ to 1 teaspoon garlic salt, or
2 to 3 cloves garlic

Big pinch dried oregano
Big pinch ground cumin
(cominos)
1 to 2 pounds cubed meat
(beef or pork)
Bacon grease

Put vinegar, water, peppers, salt, peppercorns, garlic salt, oregano and cumin in container of an electric blender; blend well. Pour over cubed meat in a nonmetallic bowl; marinade should cover meat. Let marinate in refrigerator at least several hours; overnight is preferable.

Remove cubes of meat from marinade, saving marinade. Skewer meat. Add bacon grease to reserved marinade and use as a basting sauce. Cook meat over hot coals until done. (The bacon grease adds additional flavor and makes the meat smoke during cooking.)

Toni Griffin

The Tribune / San Diego, California

Chili Relleno Casserole is a good example of Southern California cooking. It is good with char-broiled steak, or alone with Spanish rice and a salad.

CHILI RELLENO CASSEROLE
6 *servings*

6 green chilies (fresh, roasted and peeled; or canned)

6 ounces Monterey Jack cheese, cut in strips

4 eggs

⅓ cup milk

½ cup all-purpose flour

½ teaspoon baking powder

1 cup shredded longhorn cheese

1 can (8 ounces) tomato sauce, seasoned with herbs of choice

Pitted ripe olives, chopped, for garnish

Stuff chilies with Monterey Jack cheese strips (or use a mixture of Monterey Jack and longhorn, if preferred). Arrange stuffed chilies side by side in a greased shallow baking dish.

Beat eggs with an electric mixer until thick and foamy. Add milk, flour and baking powder. Beat until as smooth as possible (batter will be a little lumpy). Pour batter over chilies, making sure that all the chilies are moist. Sprinkle with longhorn cheese.

Bake, uncovered, in a 375°F oven 25 minutes, or until casserole is puffed and appears set. Just before casserole is ready, heat seasoned tomato sauce to serve in a gravy boat. Garnish hot casserole with chopped olives.

Note: This can be assembled ahead of time and refrigerated. When ready to serve, bake in a 375°F oven 35 minutes.

Mary Frances Phillips

San Jose Mercury News / San Jose, California

For typical California fare, serve this hot tamale pie with a green salad, sourdough bread or baking powder biscuits, red wine and a fresh fruit platter.

HOT TAMALE PIE

6 to 8 *servings*

Cornmeal Crust:
1 cup yellow cornmeal
1 cup water
2 cups boiling water
1 teaspoon salt
2 tablespoons butter or
   margarine

Filling:
1 pound lean ground beef
1 large onion, minced
2 tablespoons vegetable oil
2 tablespoons all-purpose flour

2 cans (8 ounces each) tomato
   sauce
⅓ cup Burgundy or claret wine
2 teaspoons chili powder, or
   more, to taste
½ teaspoon cumin seeds
   (optional)
   Salt, garlic salt and pepper,
   to taste
1 cup whole ripe pitted black
   olives
1 can (16 ounces) whole kernel
   corn, drained
½ cup grated natural Cheddar
   cheese

For crust: Combine cornmeal with 1 cup water in top of a double boiler; mix until smooth. Gradually stir in 2 cups boiling water; add salt. Stir constantly over direct heat until mixture thickens. Add butter. Cover and cook over boiling water for 20 minutes, stirring occasionally. Line a well-greased 2-quart baking dish with mixture, smoothing it evenly over surface of dish with your fingers or the back of a spoon. This is easier to do when mixture is slightly cool. Next, prepare filling.

For filling: Sauté beef and onion in oil until meat is no longer red, stirring with a fork so meat is broken into small bits. Blend in flour; add tomato sauce and wine. Cook, stirring constantly, until mixture boils and thickens. Simmer 5 minutes or so. Add chili powder, cumin seed, salt, garlic salt, pepper, olives and corn.

Pour filling into cornmeal crust. Sprinkle with grated cheese. Bake in a 350°F oven 45 minutes.

Joyce Rosencrans

The Cincinnati Post / Cincinnati, Ohio

Many recipes for Cincinnati Chili are called Empress Chili. Empress is a local chili parlor chain begun by a Greek family. That chain, and its competitors, add cinnamon and make the beef fine textured by simmering it in water. The real recipe is secret, so many versions float around.

In a Cincinnati chili parlor, you must know the lingo. Chili is always ladled over spaghetti, with shredded cheese on top, and oyster crackers on the side. That's "three-way chili." "Four-way chili" has chopped onion. "Five-way chili" has kidney beans, too.

CINCINNATI CHILI   6 *servings (1½ quarts)*

2 pounds ground beef
2 medium onions, chopped
1 quart water
1 can (16 ounces) tomatoes
1½ teaspoons vinegar
1 teaspoon Worcestershire sauce
1 tablespoon chili powder
2 teaspoons ground cumin (cominos)
1½ teaspoons ground allspice
1½ teaspoons salt
1 teaspoon cayenne

1 teaspoon ground cinnamon
½ teaspoon garlic powder
2 bay leaves
6 servings hot, cooked spaghetti
1½ cups shredded Cheddar cheese
1 carton (11 or 12 ounces) oyster crackers
1 cup chopped onion (optional)
1 can (16 ounces) kidney beans, heated (optional)

Combine ground beef, onions and water in a saucepan. Simmer until beef turns brown. Add tomatoes with liquid, vinegar, Worcestershire sauce, chili powder, cumin, allspice, salt, cayenne, cinnamon, garlic powder and bay leaves. Cover; simmer 3 hours.

The fat will float. If there is time, chill chili and lift off fat layer. Or spoon off fat.

To serve basic "three-way chili," serve chili on spaghetti and top with cheese. Pass oyster crackers. For "four-way chili," add chopped onion. For "five-way chili," spoon heated kidney beans on top.

Mary Alice Powell

The Blade / Toledo, Ohio

For years, downtown Toledo boasted a chili parlor, really a greasy spoon, but everyone raved about the Chili Mac. We came up with this recipe the night a pressman hosted a former chili-parlor cook to an over-consumption of beer and he began to utter the secret ingredients.

CHILI MAC, TOLEDO STYLE   *8 servings*

1 tablespoon solid shortening
1¼ cups cubed or ground suet
1¼ cups water, divided
2¼ pounds coarse ground beef, divided
1 onion (about 2¼ inches), chopped
4 or 5 cloves garlic, finely chopped
3½ teaspoons hot chili powder
1 teaspoon crushed dried red peppers
¾ teaspoon cumin seeds

¼ teaspoon black pepper
1 teaspoon ground sage
¼ teaspoon cayenne
1 teaspoon salt
½ teaspoon monosodium glutamate (MSG)
Cooked pinto beans (no chili seasoning)
Cooked spaghetti
Grated Parmesan cheese
Additional crushed dried red peppers (optional)

Place shortening, suet, small amount of water (about ¼ cup) and a little of the ground beef in a large pan. Cover and cook on medium heat until suet softens. Then add remaining beef and brown. Add onion, garlic, the remaining water, chili powder, dried peppers, cumin seed, black pepper, sage, cayenne, salt and MSG. Simmer on low heat, uncovered, until sauce becomes orange and oily and no longer watery, about 1 hour. Sauce must be stirred frequently.

To serve, nestle cooked beans in cooked spaghetti and spoon meat sauce over all. Sprinkle generously with Parmesan cheese. If desired, serve with additional crushed dried red peppers.

Billie Bledsoe

San Antonio Express-News / San Antonio, Texas

Like the Alamo, this is a feature of Texas EVERYONE knows. What is more, every Texan has THE best recipe for it, and probably one or two ancestors who knew the guy who invented it. It is a strictly Texan dish; you won't find it south of the border.

Chili meat is most often mature, muscular beef (neck or shoulder); sometimes goat, venison or rabbit. The important thing is that it should be solid enough to withstand long cooking. The meat is usually in small cubes, but there are those who use it chopped, shredded and even ground. Some add onions; some add tomato; any of the chili peppers is eligible, and other spices—from bay leaf to paprika—may be added. It may be served with or without beans. These variations make each new "bowl of red" an adventure.

Try this version for a start.

CHILI CON CARNE
8 to 10 servings

3 pounds cubed beef
2 tablespoons vegetable oil or lard, for cooking
4 cups water
⅓ teaspoon cayenne
2 tablespoons ground cumin (cominos)

5 tablespoons chili powder
2 teaspoons salt
4 cloves garlic, pressed
3 teaspoons dried oregano
2 tablespoons paprika
1 can (6 ounces) tomato paste
Sugar, to taste

Cook meat in oil in a large skillet or Dutch oven until gray in color. Add water and simmer for 30 minutes. Add cayenne, cumin, chili powder, salt, garlic, oregano, paprika and tomato paste. Simmer at least 2 hours, until meat is tender. A pinch of sugar helps to bind the flavors and mellow them. (If mixture seems too thin, pour off some and mix with flour to thicken, then return to pot and stir.)

Serve steaming hot in a bowl, with minced onion on top, if you like, and crackers or tortillas.

Carol Haddix

Chicago Tribune / Chicago, Illinois

The following two pizzas are unique to Chicago. The first is the original deep-dish Chicago pizza, with a cornmeal-based crust and sausage and cheese filling baked in a two-inch deep pizza pan.

The second pizza is fast gaining Chicago converts over the deep-dish. It is the stuffed pizza—the filling is lodged between two layers of dough and then topped with a fresh tomato sauce.

CHICAGO DEEP-DISH PIZZA   *6 servings*

Crust:
- 1 cup water
- ¼ cup solid shortening
- 1½ tablespoons granulated sugar
- 2¼ teaspoons salt
- 1½ packages active dry yeast
- ½ cup lukewarm water
- ¾ cup yellow cornmeal
- 3 to 3½ cups all-purpose flour
- Vegetable oil

Filling:
- 1 can (28 ounces) Italian-style tomatoes
- 1 small onion, chopped
- 1 small green pepper, chopped
- 1 clove garlic, minced
- ¾ teaspoon dried oregano
- ½ teaspoon fennel seeds
- ½ teaspoon salt
- ¼ teaspoon pepper
- 2 tablespoons vegetable oil
- 1 can (4 ounces) sliced mushrooms, drained
- 1 pound mild Italian sausage
- 1 package (10 ounces) mozzarella cheese, thinly sliced
- ½ cup grated Parmesan cheese

For crust: Heat 1 cup water, shortening, sugar and salt until shortening melts; cool to lukewarm. Soften yeast in ½ cup lukewarm water. Combine yeast and shortening mixtures in a large bowl. Add cornmeal. Add 2 cups of the flour; beat well. Stir in enough additional flour to make a soft dough. Turn onto a lightly floured board; knead until smooth and elastic, working in more flour as needed. Brush a round, 12-inch pizza pan (at least 2 inches deep) with oil. Press dough evenly over bottom and up sides of pan. Bake in a preheated 425°F oven 5 minutes.

For filling: Drain tomatoes in colander; chop tomatoes and return to colander; set aside to drain. Sauté onion, green pepper, garlic, oregano, fennel seeds, salt and pepper in oil until onion and green pepper are tender. Stir in well-drained tomatoes and mushrooms; cook lightly, then remove from heat.

Remove sausage from casing; crumble into pizza crust (sausage need not be cooked beforehand). Arrange mozzarella slices over sausage. Top with tomato mixture; sprinkle with Parmesan cheese. Bake in a 425°F oven 45 minutes, or until crust is golden brown. Let stand 5 minutes before serving.

CHICAGO STUFFED SPINACH PIZZA

6 servings

Dough:
1 tablespoon granulated
  sugar
2 packages active dry yeast
2 cups very warm water
  (105°F to 115°F)
⅓ cup vegetable oil
4 to 6 cups all-purpose flour

Sauce:
2 tablespoons olive oil
1 clove garlic, minced
1 can (28 ounces) crushed
  tomatoes with added
  puree
2 teaspoons dried oregano
1½ teaspoons dried basil
½ teaspoon salt
½ teaspoon freshly ground
  pepper

Filling:
3 packages (10 ounces each)
  frozen chopped spinach,
  thawed, well drained
2½ cups shredded mozzarella
  cheese
½ cup freshly grated
  Parmesan cheese
½ cup freshly grated Romano
  cheese
¼ teaspoon salt
¼ teaspoon freshly ground
  black pepper
1 teaspoon dried basil
2 cloves garlic, minced
2 tablespoons olive oil
2 cups sliced mushrooms
  (optional)

For dough: Dissolve sugar and yeast in water in a large bowl; let stand until bubbly. Stir in oil. Stir in 4 cups of the flour until smooth; stir in remaining flour as needed until stiff dough forms. Knead on lightly floured surface until smooth and elastic. Put in greased bowl; turn to coat top. Let rise, covered, in a warm place for 1 hour, or until double in bulk.

For sauce: Heat olive oil in a large saucepan. Add garlic; sauté 2 minutes. Stir in tomatoes, oregano, basil, salt and pepper. Simmer 30 minutes, or until very thick.

For filling: Mix spinach, mozzarella, Parmesan, Romano, salt, pepper, basil, garlic, olive oil and mushrooms in a large bowl.

Punch dough down. Let rest 10 minutes. Roll two-thirds of dough into a 16-inch circle. Fit into 12-inch diameter, deep-dish pizza pan; let sides of dough overhang.

Put spinach filling into center of dough; smooth evenly over surface. Roll remaining one-third of dough on lightly floured surface to a 12-inch circle. Put over filling; crimp edges; cut excess dough at edges so dough is level with top crust. Pour tomato sauce over dough to cover. Bake in a preheated 450°F oven 30 to 40 minutes, or until dough is golden.

Jane Baker
The Phoenix Gazette / Phoenix, Arizona

The Southwest has many foods that are dubbed "Mexican" when they really are American-Mexican creations. One example is chimichangas (pronounced chee-mee-chan-gas). Arizonans like to think they are their own invention, but you now can find them on many Mexican restaurant menus in the United States. The Mexicans, of course, have never heard of "chimis."

A chimichanga is a flour tortilla filled with a meat or bean mixture and deep-fried. The tortillas become flaky, like pastry dough, when they are fried.

CHIMICHANGAS

6 servings
(12 chimichangas)

2½ cups Shredded Beef Filling
(recipe follows)
12 flour tortillas (7 inches in
diameter)
Vegetable oil or solid
shortening, for frying

Shredded lettuce
1½ cups shredded Cheddar
cheese
Dairy sour cream or
guacamole (optional)

Spoon 3 tablespoons meat filling down the center of 1 tortilla. Fold sides of tortilla over filling and roll it up. Secure with a toothpick, if necessary. Assemble only 2 or 3 at a time, because the tortilla will absorb liquid from the sauce.

Deep-fry in hot oil (about 350°F) in a deep-fryer 1 to 2 minutes, or until golden brown. Lift from fat with a slotted spoon. Drain well. Keep in a warm oven and finish cooking the rest.

Serve on a bed of shredded lettuce; top with cheese and, if desired, sour cream or guacamole.

SHREDDED BEEF FILLING

2½ cups

1 medium onion, chopped
1½ tablespoons vegetable oil
2 cups finely chopped or
shredded cooked lean beef
(leftovers from a pot roast
are good)

1 can (4 ounces) chopped green
chilies
1 teaspoon ground cumin
(optional)
1 cup canned or homemade
enchilada sauce

Sauté onion in hot oil in a skillet. Blend in beef, chilies, cumin and enchilada sauce. Simmer 10 minutes, stirring occasionally. Use to fill Chimichangas.

Note: This beef filling also can be used for tacos, enchiladas or tamales.

SMOTHERED BURRITOS

Smothered Burritos are unique to Denver, at least as far as visiting Mexican food experts tell us. A Smothered Burrito is a seasoned beef or beef and bean burrito covered with a green or red chili gravy. Sam Arnold, local expert on chilies, gave me his favorite recipe.

Spread warm refried beans on a flour tortilla. Sprinkle with chicharonnes (you can substitute crisp bacon bits), chopped green onions and green chili gravy (recipe follows). (Sam likes his chili gravy inside the burrito.) Roll up tortilla, enclosing filling. Cook in a microwave oven or under a broiler to warm through.

If you want the burrito smothered, just hold the gravy until after you have rolled up the tortilla, then liberally cover burrito with gravy.

Make green chili gravy by adding pureed, peeled and roasted Anaheim chilies to a roux of flour and butter. Season with oregano and salt to taste. Use to make burrito described above.

Serve Smothered Burritos garnished with shredded lettuce, shredded cheese and chopped tomato.

Note: Some chili-fanciers add diced pork to the chili gravy for a more filling meal.

BREAKFAST BURRITOS

Sam also has a favorite recipe for Breakfast Burritos from Santa Fe, New Mexico.

Spread crisp hashed brown potatoes and 3 to 4 pieces of crisp bacon, crumbled, on a flour tortilla. Roll up. Top with grated Monterey Jack cheese and green or red chili puree. If desired, add a fried egg sunny-side up. Put in the oven long enough to melt cheese. Serve immediately.

TOASTED CHILIES AND CHEESE

This is another Sante Fe breakfast item from Sam.

Toast a green chili under the broiler until skin is puffed and well browned. Rotate chili to brown (char) all sides. Peel, but do not seed. Put chili on a plate and top with a pat of butter and a slice of Havarti cheese. Cook in a microwave oven or under a broiler until cheese melts. Serve with crisp French bread and, if desired, scrambled eggs.

Jane Baker
The Phoenix Gazette / Phoenix, Arizona

Admittedly, the Tuba City (Arizona) Truck Stop Cafe is not on the way to anywhere. It's north of Flagstaff, on the western edge of the Navajo nation. But this cafe makes the best Navajo Tacos. Many native Americans are well known for their fry bread—particularly the Navajos. This taco, which uses fry bread as a base, is unusual—and very tasty. If your journeys don't take you to Tuba City, here's my rendition of the cafe's recipe.

NAVAJO TACOS
6 large servings

6 dinner-plate-size pieces fry bread (recipe follows)
3 cups chili with beans (homemade or canned), heated
1 cup chopped onion
1½ cups chopped fresh tomatoes

3 large green chilies, seeded, deveined and chopped
2 cups shredded lettuce
1½ cups grated Cheddar cheese
Salsa or hot pepper sauce (optional)

Place each warm fry bread on a large plate. For each taco, layer a portion of warm chili, onion, tomato, chilies and lettuce on fry bread. Top with a portion of cheese. Serve immediately with salsa or hot pepper sauce, if desired.

NAVAJO FRY BREAD

4 cups all-purpose flour
1 tablespoon baking powder
1 teaspoon salt
2 tablespoons nonfat dry milk
   powder

1¼ to 1½ cups warm water
1 to 2 cups solid shortening
   or lard, for frying

Combine flour, baking powder, salt and dry milk powder in a large mixing bowl. Gradually stir in warm water. Mix until dough forms a ball and comes clean from edge of bowl. You may need to add a little additional water.

Knead dough with your hands until well mixed and dough is elastic. Divide dough into 6 large pieces and roll into balls. Using palms of your hands, pat out dough into circles that are about ½-inch thick.

Melt shortening in a large skillet. You will need about ¾ inch of melted fat. Heat to 500°F. Slip a rounded, flat piece of dough into the hot fat—it will start to rise to the top. When the underside is brown, turn over and brown the other side. Drain on paper towels. Repeat with remaining dough. Use to make Navajo Tacos.

Note: If you just want to make fry bread—it's a great snack sprinkled with confectioners sugar or drizzled with honey—divide dough into small portions to make 2-inch balls. This recipe will make 8 to 10 smaller portions.

Marilynn Marter

The Philadelphia Inquirer / Philadelphia, Pennsylvania

PHILADELPHIA CHEESE-STEAK

"Philadelphia's greatest gifts to our society are as follows:
"Seventeenth Century: Religious freedom
"Eighteenth Century: Political independence
"Nineteenth Century: Culture
"Twentieth Century: The cheese-steak."

Thus began an ode to the Philadelphia Cheese-Steak by Bill Collins, a staff writer. According to loyal cheese-steak fans, the sandwich, in all its greasy glory, is the greatest gastronomical advance since cooking oil.

Begun more than fifty years ago at a small sandwich stand in South Philadelphia, the basic cheese-steak is composed of thinly sliced beef (usually rib eye or eye of round), mild American cheese (or gooey Cheez Whiz) and Italian bread (either a torpedo-shaped roll or a half of a long, thin loaf). The meat is fried on a griddle with oil. If real cheese is used, it is melted over the nearly done meat. The meat is placed on the bread, then topped with fried onion slivers and sauce—sweet, spicy or bland (or just plain ketchup). Sometimes a cheese-steak is topped with mustard, fried mushroom slices, or sweet or hot peppers.

For the sake of outsiders, here is an explanation of cheese-steakese: "One with" is a cheese-steak with fried onions. "One cheese" is a plain cheese-steak. "One" is a steak sandwich without adornment.

There is even an art to eating a cheese-steak. One must execute a perfect cheese-steak bend from the waist to avoid spilling food on one's clothes.

Legend has it that this culinary delicacy began back in 1930 or 1932. Business was so bad at Pat Olivieri's South Philadelphia hot dog stand that when a cab driver saw Pat preparing some grilled beef on a roll for dinner for himself, the cabbie suggested that the resulting concoction would sell better than Pat's hot dogs. Soon thereafter, Pat perfected the first cheese-steak. Because the invention wasn't patented, the question of who actually made the first cheese-steak may never be answered. But to Philadelphians, "Pat's King of Steaks" at Ninth and Passyunk is the birthplace of the city's special sandwich. Numerous other eateries now offer the same treat, or various versions thereof.

The Hot Brown takes its name from the hotel in whose kitchen it originated. The Brown Hotel opened in 1923, and it is believed that the first Hot Brown was served shortly thereafter. Although the Brown Hotel is now closed, its name lives on in its sandwich, which is served in restaurants all around the city.

As the story goes, a chef at the Brown Hotel in the 1920s came up with an idea to use leftover turkey. He put the turkey on toast points and covered it with a cheese sauce. It was dubbed a Hot Brown. Today, there are many versions of the recipe. This one is the Brown's original, from the files of The Courier-Journal's *late food editor, Cissy Gregg.*

LOUISVILLE HOT BROWN
4 servings

4 tablespoons butter
1 small onion, chopped
4 tablespoons all-purpose flour
2 cups milk
½ teaspoon salt
¼ teaspoon white pepper
¼ cup shredded Cheddar
  cheese

¼ cup grated Parmesan cheese
8 slices trimmed toast
  Cooked chicken or turkey
    breast, sliced
  Crisp-fried bacon, crumbled
  Mushroom slices, sautéed

Melt butter in a saucepan. Sauté onion in butter until transparent. Add flour; mix well. Stir in milk, salt and pepper; whisk until smooth. Cook over medium heat until sauce thickens, stirring occasionally. Add Cheddar cheese and Parmesan cheese; continue heating until cheeses are melted and blended with sauce. Remove sauce from heat.

Put 1 slice of toast in each of four oven-proof individual serving dishes. Top each piece of toast with slices of chicken or turkey. Cut remaining toast slices diagonally and place 2 triangles alongside each sandwich. Ladle cheese sauce equally over all four sandwiches. Place dishes under broiler until sauce begins to bubble, about 2 minutes. Garnish with crumbled bacon and sautéed mushroom slices. Serve immediately.

Diane Wiggins

St. Louis Globe-Democrat / St. Louis, Missouri

At a recent professional meeting, talk turned, as always, to food. When the subject of local specialties came up, we were introduced to a new one, courtesy of Bob Gonko of the State Journal-Register *in Springfield, Illinois.*

THE SPRINGFIELD HORSESHOE

"It's one of Springfield's major contributions to the world. Undoubtedly, it's the city's foremost contribution to the food world. Strangely, nobody's been able to explain why it isn't found in very many places outside the greater Springfield area.

"What I'm talking about is Springfield's sandwich of distinction: the Horseshoe," said Gonko.

"The men said to have created the Horseshoe at the old Leland Hotel in 1928 are Steve Tomko, retired but still living in Springfield, and Joseph Schweska, who died a number of years ago.

"The two collaborated in writing the recipe at the Leland. Tomko wouldn't give out the proportions. But even if he would, he couldn't, because he claims he never measures anything.

"The sandwich is made by laying two pieces of toast on a preheated steak sizzle platter, then placing on the toast any sort of meat, eggs, poultry, seafood or any combination of meats. Although there usually is no vegetable, a tomato or other desired vegetable can be placed on top of the first layer.

"Then comes the 'star of the show'—the creamy, slightly spicy cheese sauce. A good quantity of French fries then circles the platter, which is topped by a dash or two of paprika.

"Among the different Horseshoe sandwiches served in Springfield are ham and egg, all egg, hamburger, ham and chicken, chicken (all white meat), all ham, bacon, shrimp, turkey and corned beef.

"The sauce is the thing, as all accomplished Horseshoe chefs will tell you. Above everything else, the sharp English Cheddar cheese that Tomko and other chefs use is the basis of the sauce.

"The name *Horseshoe* was derived from the shape of the cut of ham used on the original sandwich at the Leland. Tomko and the other cooks there started with ham and then decided the sauce tasted good with every kind of meat. The French fries represent the nails of the shoe, and the sizzle platter represents a hot anvil."

During his research on the Horseshoe, Gonko found concensus among chefs that the sauce was the key. Most recommended the classic Welsh Rabbit or Rarebit sauce; others recommended a basic cream sauce with Cheddar cheese added. This sauce recipe appeared in the Christmas 1939 issue of the *Illinois State Journal*. In an article featuring favorite recipes from the chefs at the Leland Hotel, there was this recipe for Joe Schweska's version.

WELSH RAREBIT SAUCE

8 cups

¾ cup butter
¾ cup all-purpose flour
½ teaspoon salt
⅛ teaspoon cayenne
¼ teaspoon dry mustard
1 tablespoon Worcestershire sauce
1 quart milk, scalded
1 pound sharp Cheddar or Old English sharp process American cheese, grated
2 cups (1 pint) beer

Melt butter in top of a double boiler over direct heat. Add flour, salt, cayenne, dry mustard and Worcestershire sauce; whisk until smooth. Cook over direct heat until bubbly. Slowly stir in scalded milk; cook until mixture thickens. Place over hot water and stir in cheese until smooth. Stir in beer just before serving.

Carol Haddix
Chicago Tribune / Chicago, Illinois

A famous Chicago treat is the hot dog. Chicago dogs are not like other city dogs, though. Here's how to make hot dogs our way.

CHICAGO HOT DOGS

1 serving

1 Vienna frankfurter, boiled
1 poppy seed hot dog bun
  Ballpark (prepared) mustard
  Ketchup
  Sweet pickle relish (preferably dyed bright green with food coloring)
  Chopped onions
  Chopped tomatoes
  Whole small hot green peppers (the hotter the better)

Put hot dog in bun and layer each ingredient in the order given. Then try to get one end in your mouth. It's a feat to eat!

Pittsburghers have been eating the original Devonshire Sandwich, and some of its many variations, since 1934. That was the year it was "invented" in an elite supper club called The Stratford. Frank Blandi, owner of the Park Schenley restaurant now, owned The Stratford, and remembers how it happened:

"My chef, Pasquale Pirotti, was from Buffalo, New York. He made a chicken dish with a cream sauce, but it was flat." That would never do. "I'm Italian, and I don't like anything flat."

So Cheddar cheese was added to the cream sauce, some other changes were made, and the Devonshire was born. Blandi called it the Devonshire, incidentally, because of the English motif of the club. Devonshire Street was nearby.

The sandwich was an almost instant success. The restaurant had to keep making the sauce in five-gallon batches to keep up with the demand. Chefs who worked for Blandi over the years learned how to make the sandwich, taught others how to make it, and now it's served throughout the city in many variations. Crab, chicken, shrimp, tomato and asparagus often turn up in a Devonshire, depending on who's making it. But this recipe, Blandi says, is the original.

THE ORIGINAL DEVONSHIRE SANDWICH   *6 sandwiches*

6 slices toast, crust trimmed
  off
18 slices bacon, cooked crisp
30 thin slices cooked turkey
  breast

Cheese Sauce (recipe follows)
Melted butter
Grated Parmesan cheese
  mixed with a little paprika

For each serving, use a flat, individual-serving size, oven-proof casserole dish. Put 1 slice toast in each dish; top toast with 3 slices bacon. Add 5 slices turkey. Cover each sandwich with ⅙ of the Cheese Sauce. Drizzle with butter, then sprinkle with Parmesan cheese-paprika mixture. Bake in a preheated 450°F oven for 10 to 15 minutes, or until golden brown.

CHEESE SAUCE

5 *cups*

6 tablespoons butter
1 cup all-purpose flour
2 cups chicken broth
2 cups hot milk

¼ pound Cheddar cheese,
   grated
1 teaspoon salt

Melt butter in a large saucepan; add flour, stirring constantly. Add chicken broth and then hot milk, stirring constantly. Add cheese and salt. Bring sauce to a boil, then reduce heat and cook slowly for 20 minutes, stirring constantly. Cool to lukewarm. Beat with a wire whisk until smooth before using to make Devonshire Sandwiches.

Note: Makes enough for 6 Devonshire Sandwiches.

Christine Arpe Gang
The Commercial Appeal / Memphis, Tennessee

MEMPHIS BARBECUE

In Memphis, if a person says he wants to have a barbecue for lunch, he means a chopped barbecue pork sandwich. It is always served on a hamburger bun and is topped with cole slaw and barbecue sauce. If you don't want the slaw on the sandwich, you must always tell the person making the sandwich to hold the slaw. The pork shoulder—which barbecues slowly for 14 to 16 hours—is chopped to order as each sandwich is made. Sauces are available in hot or mild varieties. If you want mostly the interior, light, juicy meat, you ask for a white sandwich. If you like the crusty exterior, ask for it brown. If you like both, order it mixed.

Clara Eschmann
The Macon Telegraph and News / Macon, Georgia

Picnics in the deep South are always held in oak groves near a body of water to help cool the scene. Naturally, sports of all sorts are enjoyed by the guests—softball, horse shoes, swimming, races and hiding for the young children.

I've become nostalgic about this and gone back in my mind to the church picnics we had at Myrtle Springs, near my home in Americus, Georgia. The main event was when the dinner bell rang and all came to the sheltered area for the big spread of food. Following a blessing (it always seemed much too long to me as a child, because I certainly peeked at the luscious spread of food), everyone would converge upon the laden table.

A typical menu would include fried chicken, barbecue, sliced ham, homemade biscuits, deviled eggs, homemade pickles and relishes, potato salad surrounded by thick slices of vine-ripened tomatoes, pimiento-cheese sandwiches and potato chips. Caramel and chocolate layer cakes and lemon cheesecake were always there, and sometimes a Lane cake or a devil's food one, too. Pies included peach, blackberry, pecan or berries in season.

I well remember filling my plate with cakes and pies and having my mother tell me I'd have to share them with the whole family and eat some "substantial food." What a jolt!

Iced tea was served the "grown-ups," and the children had lemonade. (I'm sure, after all these years, that soft drinks have far outpaced the lemonade.)

PIMIENTO-CHEESE SANDWICHES   *12 sandwiches*

1 pound New York sharp
   cheese
1 jar (4 ounces) pimientos
   Cayenne, to taste
1 teaspoon Worcestershire
   sauce

Dash hot pepper sauce
Coarsely ground black
   pepper, to taste
Mayonnaise
24 slices bread (white or whole
   wheat)

Grate cheese on small side of a hand grater in a large mixing bowl. Drain liquid from pimientos; mash with a fork and add to cheese in bowl. Add cayenne, Worcestershire sauce, hot pepper sauce and black pepper to taste. Add enough mayonnaise (about 3 tablespoons) to reach desired consistency and mix thoroughly. Use hands or a big, wide fork to mix. Mixture will become firmer as it sets in refrigerator.

Trim edges of bread. Spread each slice of bread with mayonnaise on one side. Put cheese filling on 12 slices of bread, then put the other 12 mayonnaise-coated bread slices on top. Slice sandwiches diagonally or into strips. Be sure to put lots of filling into sandwiches.

Side Dishes

The recipe for Boston Baked Beans was submitted, naturally, by both food editors from the Boston area. Gail Perrin of The Boston Globe *noted that Vermonters insist on using maple syrup instead of molasses in their baked beans. Because these baked beans are typical of all of New England, not just Boston, we'll call them New England Baked Beans.*

NEW ENGLAND BAKED BEANS
12 servings

2 cups dried pea beans
½ pound salt pork with rind
½ teaspoon salt
1 tablespoon dark molasses

1½ tablespoons granulated sugar
1 teaspoon dry mustard
3 cups hot water
3 small onions

Pick over and wash beans. Cover with cold water and soak overnight in a large saucepot or Dutch oven.

In the morning, drain beans, cover with fresh water, heat slowly, and simmer until skins burst. (You can test by taking a few beans on the tip of a spoon and blowing on them. When cooked, skins will burst.) Drain.

Scald pork. Cut off a piece and put in bottom of bean pot. Slice remaining piece to the rind at ½-inch intervals, making cuts about 1-inch deep. Pour beans into pot, filling only three-fourths full, and bury pork in beans, leaving rind exposed.

Mix together salt, molasses, sugar, mustard and hot water in a bowl; pour over beans. Bury onions in top of bean pot. If beans are not completely covered with liquid, add more boiling water. Cover beanpot and bake in a 275°F oven 6 to 8 hours. Uncover during last hour to let rind get brown and crisp. Look at beans every hour or so to see if water is needed and add to keep it level with top.

Billie Bledsoe

San Antonio Express-News / San Antonio, Texas

The lowly dried bean was the cowboy's staple, so much so that mealtime often was called "bean-time." The frijole (free-holy)—kidney, red or pinto beans—will keep almost forever. No amount of cooking can really harm it, although about five hours usually does it right.

A small dish of ranch-style beans, served in their own spicy cooking liquid, was traditionally the first thing set on the table in many Texas inns. It still is, in a few.

FRIJOLES A LA CHARRA
8 servings

2 small ham hocks
4 cans (15 ounces each) pinto
 beans
 Juice from 1 bulb garlic, or
 to taste
⅔ teaspoon cumin seeds
1 small green pepper, finely
 chopped

2 or 3 sprigs cilantro (Chinese
 parsley), minced
1 medium onion, finely
 chopped
1 can (16 ounces) tomatoes
1 tablespoon chili powder
 Pinch salt

Cook ham hocks in a large saucepot with as little water as possible, until meat is tender. Allow hocks to cool slightly; remove meat from bones. Drain beans in colander; rinse in cold water and drain well. Put beans in saucepot with ham and cooking liquid. Add garlic juice, cumin seeds, green pepper, cilantro, onion, tomatoes with liquid, chili powder and salt. Cook over medium heat until beans are hot and flavors are blended.

Serve with cooking liquid in small pottery bowls. Old-timers say these beans taste better eaten with a spoon.

Christine Arpe Gang

The Commercial Appeal / Memphis, Tennessee

Fried Dill Pickles were made famous by the former Hollywood Cafe, which was just south of Memphis in Hollywood, Mississippi. The restaurant was best known for its pickles and frogs' legs. All of the food was mighty greasy, but people seemed to love it.

FRIED DILL PICKLES
4 to 6 servings

3 to 4 large dill pickles, whole
½ cup all-purpose flour
¼ cup beer
1 tablespoon cayenne
1 tablespoon paprika

1 tablespoon black pepper
1 teaspoon salt
2 teaspoons garlic salt
3 dashes hot pepper sauce
Vegetable oil for frying

Cut dill pickles into slices of ¼-inch thickness. Combine flour, beer, cayenne, paprika, pepper, salt, garlic salt and hot pepper sauce in a medium mixing bowl. Dip pickle slices into batter. Heat oil to 375°F in a large, deep saucepan. Fry pickles until they float to the surface, about 4 minutes.

Mary Alice Powell

The Blade / Toledo, Ohio

This recipe is a Toledo native. It is so named because it was served for many years at the Tally Ho Restaurant. It is served as a main course side dish, even though it is sweet.

TALLY HO TOMATO PUDDING
4 servings

1 cup light brown sugar
1 cup tomato puree
¼ cup water

2 cups bread cubes, crusts removed
½ cup melted butter

Combine brown sugar, tomato puree and water and cook 5 minutes. While tomato mixture is cooking, put bread cubes in a casserole and pour butter over. Add tomato mixture. Bake in a 325°F oven 50 minutes.

Woodene Merriman

Pittsburgh Post-Gazette / Pittsburgh, Pennsylvania

Exactly where Pittsburgh Potatoes originated is a mystery, but the dish is a local specialty that turns up consistently on hotel menus. Chefs tell me that it is just a recipe that was handed down from chef to chef, and that everybody knows how to make it.

PITTSBURGH POTATOES

8 servings

Salted water
4 cups peeled and cubed
    potatoes
1 medium onion, chopped

3 pimientos, chopped
2 cups medium white sauce
    (see any basic cookbook)
1 cup grated mild cheese

Bring a large pot of salted water to a boil. Add potatoes and onion. Cook for 5 minutes. Add pimientos and continue cooking for 7 minutes. Drain.

Turn mixture into a buttered 2-quart baking dish. Cover with white sauce and cheese. Bake in a 350°F oven 15 to 20 minutes, or until potatoes are tender.

Anne Byrn Phillips

The Atlanta Journal-Constitution / Atlanta, Georgia

Georgia's Vidalia onions are becoming more famous each year, competing with those from Maui and the Northwest. This is a delicious way to prepare Vidalias. It is excellent with steaks or roast beef.

VIDALIA ONION CUSTARD

4 servings

2 pounds Vidalia onions, sliced thin
3 tablespoons butter
1 cup milk
2 eggs
1 egg yolk
1 teaspoon salt
¼ teaspoon ground nutmeg
Pepper, to taste

Cook onions in butter in a large skillet over moderate heat, stirring occasionally, for 30 to 40 minutes, or until golden and soft. Let onions cool.

Whisk together milk, eggs, egg yolk, salt, nutmeg and pepper in a large bowl. Beat mixture until well combined. Stir in onions. Transfer to a well-buttered baking dish.

Bake in a 325°F oven 40 to 50 minutes, or until lightly golden and a skewer inserted in the center comes out clean. Serve hot or at room temperature.

Bernie Arnold

Nashville Banner / Nashville, Tennessee

When you say you're from the South, people just automatically think of hot biscuits and grits. I don't want to disappoint anybody, so here's one of my family's favorites.

GARLIC CHEESE GRITS

8 *servings*

½ cup grits (not instant)
2 cups water
½ teaspoon salt
½ cup butter or margarine

1 stick (6 ounces) garlic cheese spread, cut into chunks
1 egg
Milk

Combine grits, water and salt in a saucepan. Cook over medium heat until slightly thick. Add butter and cheese. Stir over low heat until both are melted. Break egg into a measuring cup; add enough milk to make ⅔ cup. Stir egg mixture into grits and mix well.

Pour into a greased 13x9x2-inch baking dish. Bake in a 350°F oven 20 minutes, watching carefully, or until golden brown. Allow to stand 10 to 15 minutes to thicken. Serve warm.

Louise Dodd

The Courier Herald / Dublin, Georgia

Probably any grits dish is Southern through and through, but this one is appreciated by Yankees, too. A friend served this at a meal following a concert by the World's Greatest Jazz Band; these much-traveled musicians loved it and took the recipe and bags of grits back "Nawth" with them.

CAVIAR-TOPPED BAKED GRITS

12 *or more servings*

2 cups quick-cooking grits
1 cup milk
4 eggs, beaten
1 package (3 ounces) cream cheese
6 tablespoons butter
1 pound bacon, cooked and crumbled

1 can (8 ounces) water chestnuts, drained and chopped
1 can (8 ounces) mushroom pieces, drained
½ cup chopped pecans
3 cans (4 ounces each) red caviar

Cook grits according to package directions. Add milk, eggs, cream cheese and butter; blend well. Stir in bacon, water chestnuts, mushrooms and pecans, blending well. Spoon into greased, shallow 2-quart baking dish. Bake in a 350°F oven 20 to 30 minutes. Spread caviar on top. Serve hot.

243

Donna Segal

The Indianapolis Star / Indianapolis, Indiana

Indiana is one of the major corn-producing states. Come July, residents have difficulty waiting until it is time to pull and cook the wonderful ears of goodness.

We love corn fixed every way, but especially roasted over a charcoal grill or gently boiled only minutes after it has been pulled.

When I was growing up, my parents were known for their large cookouts, featuring hamburgers and roasted corn. While my Dad, Gib Salle, soaked the ears, my Mom, Sarah, made the patties and put her famous green beans on to cook.

GIB'S ROASTED CORN
6 servings

1 dozen ears of corn in the shuck
1 bucket water
Grill, heated until the coals are white

Pull back shucks just enough to remove silks from ears. Don't worry if all the silks can't be removed. Reclose shucks tightly around kernels. Put ears, stem-side up, vertically in bucket of water. Let corn soak at least 30 minutes. (It can soak up to two hours.)

When coals are hot, remove corn from water, shaking each ear thoroughly to remove excess water. Place ears on grill; do not stack. Thoroughly wet a large towel and tightly wring it out. Place towel over corn, so that ears are completely covered. Be sure towel covers ears and does not rest on grill.

Let corn cook on one side for 5 to 8 minutes. Remove towel and place in bucket of water to soak. Using large tongs, turn ears. The husks on the cooked side should be nicely roasted. Wring out towel and again place on ears. Cook 8 to 10 minutes, or until ears are roasted on the other side. If ears are really large, the corn may have to be turned again to ensure all sides are cooked.

Keep ears warm in a low oven if they are not to be served immediately.

To serve, pull back husks and break off stem.

Note: The ears are so good, butter and salt are not needed, although most people do add a little. I like them just the way they are.

Ann Criswell

Houston Chronicle / Houston, Texas

Jalapeños are a part of Texas cooking. The addition of these hot peppers to rice gives this casserole a Texas flavor.

JALAPENO PEPPER RICE   *4 to 6 servings*

1 cup regular long-grain rice, cooked
2 cups dairy sour cream
1 can (4 ounces) jalapeño peppers, seeded and chopped
   (see note)
½ cup grated Cheddar cheese

Blend cooked rice with sour cream in a bowl; stir in jalapeños. Place mixture in a buttered 1¾- or 2-quart baking dish, or a shallow casserole dish. Top with grated cheese. Bake in a 350°F oven 20 minutes, or until heated through.

Note: Always be careful when working with hot peppers, fresh or canned, because the peppers and the fumes they release when cut can be irritating to the eyes and skin. Some cooks prefer to wear rubber gloves when handling jalapeños. Seed the peppers, then chop; or buy canned, seeded peppers. Do not put your hands near your eyes after working with peppers. Green chilies may be substituted for jalapeños for a milder taste.

When August and September come to the Sonoran Desert in Southern Arizona, it's time to gather the purple-red fruit of the prickly pear cactus and make it into jelly and other good foods. Juiced in a blender, it goes into gelatin salads or drinks. Or cut up the fruit (after carefully removing the peel and stickers, and the seeds), and use it in fruit-nut bread. Or, boil and mash the fruit, then strain the juice to make a gorgeous red jelly.

Experienced hands always use a pair of tongs to avoid the stickers when picking the ripe fruit.

USING THE FRUIT OF THE PRICKLY PEAR CACTUS

To juice: Wash the fruit in the sink, drain and transfer 7 or 8 good-sized fruit to the blender, using tongs. Slice the fruit in half with a long knife, add ¾ to 1 cup water and blend for a few seconds. Strain through cheesecloth to remove the stickers, peel and seeds. (No, the stickers absolutely will not go through the cheesecloth!)

Use the juice to flavor and color any fruit drink or punch, or use as any other juice to make gelatin dishes, being certain to add a little lemon juice to enhance the flavor.

To make jelly: Slice pears in half (without peeling) into a large kettle and add water to barely cover. Boil until tender, about 25 minutes. Press with potato masher and strain through jelly bag or two thicknesses of cheesecloth. (Stickers will not go through.) At this point, juice may be frozen for making jelly later.

To 2½ cups juice, add one 1¾-ounce package powdered fruit pectin. Bring to fast boil, stirring constantly. Add 3 tablespoons lemon or lime juice and 3½ cups granulated sugar. Bring to a hard boil. Cook for 3 minutes at a rolling boil (or until mixture sheets from a metal spoon). Remove from heat, skim off any foam, ladle into sterilized canning jars. Adjust 2-piece lids. Invert jars for a few seconds; return upright and let cool out of drafts. Test for seal. Label and store in cool, dry, dark place.

Breads

Barbara Gibbs Ostmann

St. Louis Post-Dispatch / St. Louis, Missouri

Alligator Rolls may not be originally from St. Louis, but local folks tend to think they are the creation of the Stix, Baer and Fuller Tea Room. This recipe isn't from Stix (a department store), but the resulting rolls are similar to those served there.

ALLIGATOR ROLLS

16 rolls

Rolls:
3¾ cups unbleached all-
    purpose flour, or more,
    as needed, divided
2 cups lukewarm water,
    divided
1 tablespoon active dry yeast
1½ teaspoons salt
    Yellow cornmeal

Crunchy Topping:
2 tablespoons active dry yeast
1 cup lukewarm water
4 teaspoons granulated sugar,
    divided
2 tablespoons safflower or
    corn oil
1⅔ cups rice flour (see note)
1½ teaspoons salt

For rolls: Measure 2½ cups flour into a large mixing bowl. Make a well in center of flour and pour in ⅓ cup lukewarm water. Sprinkle yeast over water, stir to dissolve. Cover with a tea towel and let stand until yeast is foamy. Gradually add remaining 1⅔ cups water, beating in flour until well blended. Beat vigorously about 3 minutes until air bubbles form. Cover batter with tea towel and let rest 30 minutes, or as long as 8 hours.

Sprinkle salt over batter; stir in. Gradually beat in remaining 1¼ cups flour to make a stiff dough. Turn out onto lightly floured board and knead at least 10 minutes, or until smooth and pliable but still soft, adding additional flour only as needed. Form into a smooth ball, place in lightly floured bowl and sprinkle top lightly with flour. Cover with plastic wrap and a lightly dampened terry towel. Let stand at room temperature 1½ to 2 hours, or until double in bulk.

Punch down, knead briefly (about 1 minute), cover with tea towel and let rest 10 minutes. Divide into 16 equal portions, about 2 ounces each. Form into smooth balls; cover with tea towel and let rise 1 hour.

With palm of hand, flatten each ball slightly, fold in long edges as if forming a loaf, and shape into ovals; reshape into smooth balls. Arrange on a greased baking sheet that has been sprinkled with cornmeal. Cover with tea towel and let rise 45 minutes, or until almost double in size. (At this point, they're ready to bake.)

For topping: About 20 minutes before rolls are ready to bake, sprinkle yeast over water, stir in 1 teaspoon sugar and let stand until foamy. Stir in remaining 3 teaspoons sugar, oil, rice flour and salt. Beat well; set aside.

Place a shallow pan on bottom shelf of oven and preheat oven to 375°F. Just before baking, beat topping and dip each ball of dough in mixture to coat upper one-third. Place each roll, dipped-side up, on baking sheet. (Beat topping several times during process to make sure it remains well mixed.)

Pour ½ cup water into heated pan in oven. Place baking sheet of rolls on rack above pan. Bake in the preheated 375°F oven 20 minutes, or until golden, removing water pan after first 10 minutes. Transfer rolls from baking pan to wire rack. Serve warm.

Note: Don't buy sweet rice flour; it's not the baker's kind. The appropriate rice flour is available in stores selling Oriental foods, or try a natural foods store.

Janice Okun
Buffalo News / Buffalo, New York

Roast beef on "weck" is very big in Buffalo. "Weck" is short for kummel-weck—German for caraway and Buffaloese for a four-sectioned caraway-and-salt-topped bun. Kummelweck rolls are the base of the famous roast beef on weck sandwiches served in bars around Buffalo. The roast beef is sliced very thin before your eyes and piled on the roll. The sandwich is served with horseradish.

KUMMELWECK ROLLS
16 *rolls*

4½ to 5½ cups unsifted all-purpose flour, divided
2 tablespoons granulated sugar
2 teaspoons salt
1 package active dry yeast
3 tablespoons margarine, softened
1½ cups hot water (120°F to 130°F)

1 egg white, at room temperature
Melted butter
2 teaspoons kosher or other coarse pure salt, or to taste
2 teaspoons caraway seeds, or to taste

Combine 1⅓ cups flour, sugar, salt and dry yeast in a large bowl. Mix thoroughly. Add margarine. Gradually add hot water, mixing as you go, then beat 2 minutes at medium speed with an electric mixer, scraping bowl occasionally. Add egg white and another cup of flour (enough to make a thick batter). Beat at high speed 2 minutes, scraping bowl occasionally.

Stir in enough additional flour to make a soft dough. Turn out onto a lightly floured board. Knead until smooth and elastic, 8 to 10 minutes. Place in greased bowl and turn to grease top. Cover and let rise in warm place until double in bulk, about 45 minutes. (Test by pushing fingers into top of dough. If indentation remains after fingers are removed, dough is ready.)

Punch down dough and turn onto floured board. Knead gently for a minute or two. Divide dough into 2-ounce pieces (a little less than ¼ cup). You should have about 16 pieces. Form pieces into balls. Let them stand, covered, on the board for 15 minutes.

Many modern rolls are shaped by machine and have a different form, but this is how to form the rolls the "correct," or old way. Swab a small amount of melted butter on top of each round. Using a ½-inch dowel (use the handle of a wooden spoon), press across middle of each round firmly, almost to the board. Then make another crease at right angles to first crease, forming 4 equal segments. Dough, where pressed in center, will now be thin enough to almost see through it.

Gently squeeze each creased roll back together with hands. Place, buttered-surface down, on greased baking sheet. Repeat with each roll. Cover rolls and let rise in warm place until double in size, about 35 minutes.

Mix coarse salt with caraway seeds (adjust amounts to suit taste). Rub through fingers to combine flavors.

Turn each risen roll face up. With a pastry brush, lightly brush top of each roll with water, then sprinkle with caraway-salt mixture.

Place pan containing ½-inch water on bottom rack of oven. (This creates steam, which will allow rolls to bloom, which means just what it sounds like: The quartered segments will spread out gently like a flower, with a rounded rather than a peaked top.) Place rolls on rack above (or put one pan beside pan of water, if necessary). Bake in a preheated 375°F oven 25 to 30 minutes. Open oven door carefully; the steam is hot.

Cool rolls on racks, then store in as dry a place as you can find. Do not store in refrigerator, or they will weep and become soggy.

Note: A good kummelweck not only lacks the peak, it should break naturally into its four divisions with plenty of topping on each.

Phyllis Hanes

The Christian Science Monitor / Boston, Massachusetts

The Parker House, established in 1855, is one of Boston's finest hotels, where many famous people, including Charles Dickens, often stayed. It is still flourishing today and is famous as the home of Parker House Rolls, considered one of the most patrician of dinner rolls.

PARKER HOUSE ROLLS
30 rolls

1 package active dry yeast	3 tablespoons butter
¼ cup warm water	6½ to 7 cups sifted all-purpose
2 cups milk	flour, divided
2 tablespoons granulated sugar	1 egg, well beaten
1 teaspoon salt	Melted butter

Dissolve yeast in warm water. Combine milk, sugar, salt and butter in a saucepan; scald, then cool to lukewarm. Stir in yeast mixture, then add 3 cups of the flour, beating very hard, until smooth and creamy. Cover with a tea towel and place in a warm spot. Let rise until light and bubbly, about 1 hour. Mix in egg and enough of remaining flour to make a kneadable dough. Knead well, cover again, and let stand in a warm place until double in size, about 1½ hours.

Roll dough to ⅓-inch thickness on a lightly floured board. Dough will spring back at first. Cut with a 3-inch round cookie cutter. Brush each circle with a little melted butter, crease center with back of a table knife to make one straight crease across the center, then fold over in half, pinching edges together. Place rolls 1 inch apart on ungreased baking sheets. Let rise again in a warm place until almost double in size, about 45 minutes. Bake in a preheated 450°F oven 12 to 15 minutes.

Donna Segal

The Indianapolis Star / Indianapolis, Indiana

In late October, when the leaves have changed to their vibrant colors and there is just a hint of a nip in the air, we take our annual trek to Southern Indiana to enjoy Brown County. After hiking around the lake, taking in the breathtaking colorama of the hills and browsing through the quaint shops, we take our place in line at the Nashville House to wait for one of my favorite dinners.

This restaurant is an Indiana tradition, and it is always busy. It is known for its pan-fried chicken, mashed potatoes, gravy and fried biscuits with homemade baked apple butter.

This recipe is adapted from one for Nashville House biscuits. The batter makes a lot. I usually use half the dough for fried biscuits and refrigerate the rest to use later for rolled and baked biscuits. When sprinkled with confectioners sugar, the fried biscuits are similar to the famous New Orleans beignets, only the dough is heavier.

HOOSIER FRIED BISCUITS
4 to 5 dozen biscuits

1 package active dry yeast
2 tablespoons warm water
2 tablespoons granulated sugar
2 cups milk
1 teaspoon salt (optional)

About 3 cups all-purpose
  flour, divided
¼ cup vegetable oil
Vegetable oil for deep-frying

Dissolve yeast in warm water. Add sugar and stir thoroughly. Heat milk slightly. Put milk and yeast mixture in a large mixing bowl or bowl of an electric mixer. Stir to mix.

Stir salt, if used, into 1 cup of the flour. Gradually add flour mixture to yeast mixture, beating well. While beating, add ¼ cup oil and enough of the remaining 2 cups flour to make a soft workable dough. Beat with a dough hook or knead dough until it is smooth and elastic.

Grease a large bowl; add dough and turn to coat all sides. Cover with waxed paper and a cloth. Let rise until double in bulk.

Punch down dough. Have oil heated to hot, but not smoking. Oil should be deep enough for deep-frying. Pinch off dough, about the size of a large walnut for small biscuits, and roll lightly in palms of hands to make a round ball. Drop balls, a few at a time, into hot oil. Balls will sink to the bottom and then rise. Cook until golden brown on one side, then turn to cook other side (sometimes balls turn by themselves in oil). Cook until biscuits are golden brown. Drain on paper towels.

Serve fried biscuits with apple butter, honey, butter, jelly or a sprinkling of confectioners sugar.

Note: If desired, fry half of dough. Cover and refrigerate remaining dough. Use refrigerated dough within two to three days. For rolled biscuits, punch down dough, then roll on a flour-dusted board to about ½-inch thickness. Cut into 3-inch rounds. Place on a greased baking sheet and let come to room temperature. Bake in a 400°F oven 10 to 15 minutes.

Kitty Crider
Austin American-Statesman / Austin, Texas

History doesn't tell us just which Southern belle was responsible or what circumstances caused her to tamper with the traditional biscuit recipe and add yeast as well as baking powder or baking soda. Maybe the family's blue ribbon cooking was at stake, or perhaps she figured if Pillsbury could refrigerate a biscuit, she could do the same.

Whatever her motives, puffy golden angel or "riz" biscuits are the result of this hybrid recipe that Alabama cooks have been stirring up for some twenty-five years. (A check through a score of cookbooks, both national and regional, found angel biscuits hidden only in Alabama recipe collections.)

Alice Jarman, who served as the director of Martha White test kitchens in Nashville for twenty-seven years, first encountered angel biscuits in the late '50s. They were called Alabama biscuits then. She renamed them "riz" biscuits and printed the recipe in a Martha White flour leaflet. Somewhere along the way, either the bread or the baker was accorded the title "angel," because the flop-proof recipe goes by that name now.

Once the biscuits are cut out, they can be allowed to rise once, for about an hour, or baked immediately. Rising will give them a roll-like texture. A bonus of angel biscuits is that the dough can be kept in the refrigerator for a week and used as needed. (Allow extra rising time if the dough is cold.)

This is my family's adaptation of a recipe from the Alabama First Lady's Cook Book. *And if you are wondering what a Texas gal is doing with this recipe, I was a food editor in Alabama ten years prior to moving to Austin. It wasn't until I got to Austin and found no one baking angel biscuits that I started checking into their history.*

ANGEL BISCUITS

About 36 large biscuits

⅓ cup granulated sugar
5 cups sifted all-purpose flour
3 teaspoons baking powder
1 teaspoon baking soda
2 teaspoons salt

1 cup solid shortening
1 package active dry yeast
2 tablespoons warm water
1½ cups buttermilk
Melted butter

Sift sugar, flour, baking powder, baking soda and salt into a large mixing bowl. Cut in shortening. Dissolve yeast in warm water in a small bowl. Add buttermilk and yeast mixture to flour mixture. Mix well. Knead mixture, adding more flour as needed.

Roll out amount of dough needed to ½-inch thickness. Using the rim of a juice glass or a 2½-inch biscuit cutter, cut out biscuits. Place on greased cookie sheet. Let rise until double in size. Brush tops with melted butter. Bake in a 450°F oven until brown, about 10 to 15 minutes, depending upon size.

Note: Dough may be stored in refrigerator for a week or longer. Unbaked cut-out biscuits may be frozen on a cookie sheet until hard. Then store in freezer in a plastic bag, taking out as many as needed for a meal.

Jane Baker

The Phoenix Gazette / Phoenix, Arizona

As a Midwesterner transplanted to the Southwest, I'm fascinated by Mexican and native American foods. Traditionally, the Mexican foods have gotten all the attention. But now the food specialties of the Hopis and Navajos have won acclaim.

One such food is blue corn, which most often is ground into cornmeal. Blue cornmeal is coarser in consistency than yellow or white cornmeal, and recipes made with it tend to be denser. Admittedly, things made with blue cornmeal are not particularly good looking. The pale blue-gray cornmeal turns teal or lavender when mixed with water and then back to a grayish color when baked or cooked.

Most consumers aren't going to find blue cornmeal on their supermarket shelves. Even in Phoenix it is not readily available, but blue cornmeal from the Hopi Indian Community in northern Arizona usually is available at the Gentle Strength Cooperative in Tempe, a suburb of Phoenix. It's more readily available in New Mexico and can be ordered by mail from some establishments.

This corn bread recipe, which is a variation of a favorite using yellow cornmeal, is the best of the recipes I've tried with blue cornmeal.

BLUE CORN BREAD   *9 squares*

1½ cups blue cornmeal
¼ teaspoon salt
1 tablespoon baking powder
1 medium onion, chopped
2 eggs, beaten
1 cup dairy sour cream

½ cup butter or margarine, melted
1 to 2 cups grated Cheddar cheese (see note)
¼ cup chopped canned green chilies

Combine cornmeal, salt, baking powder and onion in a medium mixing bowl. Make a well in center of cornmeal mixture. Add eggs, sour cream, butter, cheese and chilies; mix well. Pour into a greased 9-inch square pan. Bake in a preheated 350°F oven 40 minutes, or until knife inserted in center comes out clean. Serve warm with lots of butter.

Note: I personally like lots of cheese, so I use 2 cups grated Cheddar in this recipe. The amount used may vary, depending on your own taste. Also, you may substitute 2 tablespoons chopped jalapeño peppers for the green chilies for a hotter taste.

Janet Beighle French

The Plain Dealer / Cleveland, Ohio

At our local restored village, a rough version of Johnnycake is baked in a fireplace oven there on weekends.

HALE FARM JOHNNYCAKE

16 squares

½ cup solid shortening
1½ cups cornmeal (regular or
the finest "coarse
ground")
¾ cup unsifted all-purpose
flour

¾ cup granulated sugar
½ teaspoon salt
2 eggs
1¼ teaspoons baking soda
1 cup buttermilk (see note)

Melt shortening and allow to cool somewhat. Combine cornmeal, flour, sugar and salt in a large mixing bowl. Make a well in center. Add eggs and cooled shortening. Stir baking soda into buttermilk; add to mixture in bowl, scraping out all the baking soda. Mix well.

Pour batter into a greased 8-inch square pan. Bake in a preheated 350°F oven 40 minutes. Bread is done when top is lightly browned and firm and toothpick inserted in center comes out clean. Cool a few minutes in pan. To serve, split and butter.

Note: If desired, bake in a 9-inch round cast-iron skillet and cut into wedges.

To substitute for 1 cup buttermilk, you may use 2 tablespoons vinegar or lemon juice, mixed with ⅞ cup milk and allowed to stand 5 minutes.

Jean Thwaite

The Atlanta Journal-Constitution / Atlanta, Georgia

Spider Cake is not a cake but a corn bread which originally was cooked in a cast-iron skillet or spider. It can be used in place of rice, potatoes or grits or in place of bread. Actually, it can be used in place of both. Spider Cake is delicious with ham and red-eye gravy, but even better with butter.

I have no idea of the origin of the recipe, but I grew up with it in Texas.

SPIDER CAKE

8 to 10 servings

1 tablespoon butter or
   margarine
1½ cups white (never yellow)
   cornmeal
½ cup all-purpose flour
¼ cup granulated sugar

1 heaping teaspoon baking
   powder
1 teaspoon salt
2 cups milk
3 eggs
1 cup heavy cream

Preheat oven to 425°F. Put butter in a heavy 9-inch iron skillet or spider, or a deep-sided 1½- or 2-quart oven-proof casserole; place on center rack of oven. The butter will melt, almost brown, while you prepare the batter.

Put cornmeal, flour, sugar, baking powder and salt in a large mixing bowl. Sifting is not necessary. Add milk and stir until almost smooth. Add eggs and stir into batter. (A whisk does it very well.)

Pull oven rack forward until you are able to pour batter into spider without removing it from oven. Next, very carefully pour cream into center of batter in the spider. You should be able to see it spread out underneath a thin layer of the batter. It will form into a custard layer.

Bake in the 425°F oven 15 to 20 minutes, then turn heat down to 350°F and bake for another 20 minutes. If the rest of the meal is not ready, turn heat down to 250°F. The spider cake will hold another 15 minutes or so if necessary.

Note: Spider cake can be served in pie-shaped wedges or can be spooned onto plates. The custard layer will really set after the first wedge is cut.

Eleanor Ostman

St. Paul Pioneer Press and Dispatch / St. Paul, Minnesota

This is a recipe Evelyn Sponberg Young made famous during the thirty-two years she was food service director at Gustavus Adolphus College, St. Peter, Minnesota. It's a recipe she learned to make from her Swedish mother, a southern Minnesota pioneer. This recipe, exceptionally delicious, is typical of Swedish rye breads that Minnesota bakers treasure.

MINNESOTA SWEDISH RYE BREAD   *3 loaves*

1 cup milk	2 packages active dry yeast
1 cup water	¼ cup warm water (105°F to
2½ tablespoons solid	115°F)
shortening	1 tablespoon granulated sugar
½ cup molasses	2 cups rye flour
½ cup granulated sugar	4 to 5 cups all-purpose flour
1 teaspoon salt	Melted butter
1 teaspoon ground anise	

Scald milk. Transfer to a large mixing bowl and add water, shortening, molasses, ½ cup sugar, salt and anise. Dissolve yeast in ¼ cup warm water and 1 tablespoon sugar in a small bowl. When milk mixture is lukewarm (90°F), add yeast mixture, then rye flour; mix until smooth. Add all-purpose flour until dough is easy to handle.

Turn dough onto floured board. Knead until smooth, about 10 minutes. Place in greased bowl and turn to grease top. Cover and let rise in a warm place until double in bulk, about 1 hour.

Measure and form into three balls. Cover and let rest 15 minutes. Form into loaves and place in well-greased 9x5x3-inch loaf pans. Cover and let rise in a warm place until double in size, about 30 minutes.

Bake in a preheated 375°F oven 35 to 40 minutes. After removing from oven, brush tops with melted butter. Remove from pans and cool on racks.

Charlyne Varkonyi

Fort Lauderdale News & Sun Sentinel / Fort Lauderdale, Florida

To most Northerners, mangoes are exotic tropical fruits that occasionally appear in the supermarkets with large price tags. To South Floridians with mango trees in their backyards, mangoes are as common as peaches in Georgia.

Every year, mango lovers suffer from a condition called "mango madness." For example, one local mango lover insists that the fruit Eve was tempted with in the Garden of Eden was a mango, not an apple. Others say that because the mango is so messy to eat, the only way to eat it properly is standing in a bathtub wearing a raincoat.

But there is trouble in mango paradise. Some people are allergic to the sap of the tree or the slightly oily skin of the fruit. These are usually the same people who are allergic to poison ivy. If you aren't sure if you will react, wear rubber gloves and peel the fruit under running water; don't use the same knife to cut the fruit that you used to peel the mango.

MANGO NUT BREAD   *1 loaf*

½ cup butter or solid
    shortening
¾ cup granulated sugar
2 eggs
2 cups sifted all-purpose flour
1 teaspoon baking soda

¼ teaspoon salt
⅔ cup finely chopped raw
    mango
1 tablespoon lime juice
½ cup chopped nuts

Cream butter and sugar in a mixing bowl. Add eggs. Stir in flour, baking soda and salt. Add mango and lime juice. Mix well. Stir in nuts. Turn into a greased 9x5x3-inch loaf pan. Bake in a 375°F oven 1 hour, or until done. Do not cut bread until the next day.

Marian Burros

The New York Times / New York, New York

This cheese bread was created by Dean Kolstad, the original owner of Ms Desserts, one of the most popular food booths at Harborplace. Someone else owns the booth now, but cheese bread is still sold there. It is sold by the slice, warm, with butter.

BALTIMORE CHEESE BREAD   *12 servings*

¼ cup plus 1 teaspoon granulated sugar, divided
3 tablespoons warm water
1 package active dry yeast
2 eggs
1 cup milk
½ cup unsalted butter, melted and cooled to room temperature
1 teaspoon salt
  About 5 cups unbleached flour, divided
1 pound Svenbo, Jarlsberg or Swiss cheese, grated
1 egg, lightly beaten, for glaze

Stir 1 teaspoon sugar into warm water in a small bowl; stir in yeast and set aside until dissolved.

Lightly beat eggs in a large bowl. Mix in remaining ¼ cup sugar, milk, butter and salt. Blend in yeast mixture. Stir in 2 cups of flour to make a dough. Stir in another 1½ cups flour, turn dough onto a work surface and knead in enough of the remaining 1½ cups flour to make a soft, smooth dough. Knead dough about 15 minutes more, or until it is smooth and satiny.

Place dough in a lightly oiled bowl, turn to lightly grease top, cover with a towel and allow to rise in a warm place until double in bulk, about 1½ hours.

Thoroughly grease a 9-inch pie plate. Punch down dough and roll it into a 16-inch round. Center dough in pie pan, pressing it snugly against edges of pan and allowing excess to hang over. Mound cheese in the center and fold and pleat dough into a turban shape by gathering it into 6 or 7 equally spaced folds, stretching dough slightly as you draw each pleat over the filling. Hold ends of dough in your hand, and twist them together tightly on top. Glaze surface by brushing with lightly beaten egg. Set aside in a warm place and let rise until double in bulk, about 45 minutes.

Bake bread in center of a preheated 325°F oven 50 minutes, or until top is golden brown and bread sounds hollow when lightly tapped on the side. Cool for 15 minutes, remove from pan and let rest another 30 minutes before slicing into wedges and serving.

Charlyne Varkonyi
Fort Lauderdale News & Sun Sentinel / Fort Lauderdale, Florida

This is the perfect accompaniment to Conch Chowder (see page 22).

BIMINI BREAD   *4 loaves*

 2 packages active dry yeast, or 2 cakes (0.6 ounce each)
   compressed yeast
 ½ cup warm water (110°F to 115°F for dry yeast; 95°F for
   compressed yeast)
 ½ cup nonfat dry milk powder
 ⅔ cup granulated sugar
 ½ cup vegetable oil
 1 teaspoon salt
 2 eggs
1⅓ cups warm water
7½ cups all-purpose flour, or as needed

Soften yeast in ½ cup warm water for 10 minutes. Using a large food processor, electric mixer or wooden spoon, beat yeast mixture, dry milk powder, sugar, oil, salt and eggs until smooth. Add 1⅓ cups warm water and 2 cups of the flour; beat until smooth. Add remaining flour, a little at a time, beating well after each addition. Stop adding flour when a stiff dough is formed. Without a heavy-duty mixer or food processor, you will need to work in the last of the flour with your hands.

With dough hook or by hand on a lightly floured surface, knead until dough is smooth and elastic. Place in a greased bowl and turn to grease top. Cover and let rise until double in bulk, about 2½ hours.

Punch dough down and fold over edges, pressing until air bubbles are pushed out. Divide dough into 4 pieces. Form each piece into a loaf or ball. Place in greased 8x4-inch loaf pans or 8-inch round cake pans. Cover and allow to rise until double in size, about 1 hour.

Bake in a preheated 350°F oven 40 minutes, or until nicely browned and done. Remove from pans and cool on wire racks. Freeze extra loaves for future use.

Marilynn Marter

The Philadelphia Inquirer / Philadelphia, Pennsylvania

Outside of Philadelphia, putting mustard on pretzels is viewed as being just about as kinky as talking to yourself in public...a habit not too uncommon among the local folk either, come to think of it.

PHILADELPHIA SOFT PRETZELS   *16 pretzels*

1 package active dry yeast
1¼ cups warm water (110°F),
    divided
4 to 5 cups all-purpose flour,
    divided

2 teaspoons salt
4 teaspoons baking soda
    Coarse salt

Dissolve yeast thoroughly in ¼ cup warm water. Stir in remaining 1 cup warm water. Mix 4 cups flour and salt in large bowl. Add dissolved yeast and mix. Add enough additional flour to make a stiff dough. Knead 10 minutes, or until smooth and elastic.

Roll dough into a ball. Place in a greased bowl, turning to coat top. Cover with a towel. Let rise in a warm place until double in bulk, about 45 minutes.

Divide dough into quarters; then divide each quarter into 4 balls of dough. Take one of the balls of dough and roll it between your hands to form a coil 20 inches long and ¼ to ⅜ inch in diameter. Shape coil into a pretzel shape, pinching ends to shaped pretzel. Shape remaining dough into coils, then into pretzels.

Dissolve baking soda in 4 cups water; bring to a boil. Drop pretzels, one at a time, into boiling water and let boil 1 minute, or until pretzel floats. Remove and drain.

Place drained pretzels on buttered baking sheets. Sprinkle with coarse salt. Bake in a 475°F oven 12 minutes, or until golden brown. Place on rack to cool. Serve with mustard.

Desserts

Carol Brock

Daily News / New York, New York

Who can name the cook who created the Brownstone Front Cake? Despite its unknown provenance, this is doubtless the most "city" of all city dishes; chocolate inside and out, it looks like the slabs of brownstones that have come to characterize a romantic version of Little Old New York. With any luck, it'll be around just as long, too.

BROWNSTONE FRONT CAKE
12 to 15 slices

2 cups unsifted all-purpose
    flour, spooned into cup
1 teaspoon baking soda
⅛ teaspoon salt
2 squares (1 ounce each)
    unsweetened chocolate
1 cup boiling water
½ cup butter

1¾ cups firmly packed light
    brown sugar
2 eggs, well beaten
½ cup dairy sour cream
1 teaspoon vanilla extract
    Chocolate Frosting (recipe
    follows)

Stir flour, baking soda and salt in a bowl. Set aside.

Place chocolate in another bowl; pour boiling water on top. Set aside.

Beat butter in a large mixing bowl until soft and creamy; add brown sugar gradually, continuing to beat until creamy after each addition. Add eggs and beat smooth. To this mixture, add flour mixture alternately with sour cream, beginning and ending with flour. Stir chocolate mixture to blend; fold in with vanilla.

Pour batter into a greased and floured 9x5x3-inch loaf pan. Bake in a preheated 325°F oven 50 to 60 minutes, or until done. Cool 10 minutes. Turn out on rack. Cool. Frost with Chocolate Frosting.

CHOCOLATE FROSTING

2 squares (1 ounce each)
    unsweetened chocolate
2 tablespoons butter, softened
½ teaspoon vanilla extract
    Pinch salt

1 to 1½ cups confectioners
    sugar
1 egg
¼ cup milk

Melt chocolate over hot, not boiling, water.

Beat together butter, vanilla and salt in a bowl. Beat in confectioners sugar, a small amount at a time. Then beat in egg, milk and melted chocolate. Beat well until creamy.

Spoon over loaf to glaze.

Elaine Corn

The Courier-Journal / Louisville, Kentucky

Stack Cake was a traditional pioneer wedding cake that was put together right at the wedding celebration. Each guest brought a layer of cake. Applesauce made from either fresh or dried apples was spread on each layer, then the layers were stacked. The bride's popularity could be measured by the number of stacks she had and by the number of layers in each stack. It's still a popular cake in Kentucky.

KENTUCKY STACK CAKE
24 or more servings

7 to 8 cups sifted all-purpose
    flour, divided
½ cup margarine, softened
1 box (16 ounces) light brown
    sugar
1 teaspoon baking soda
1 teaspoon salt
2 teaspoons pumpkin pie
    spice, divided

1 egg
1 cup buttermilk
3 cups fresh or canned
    unsweetened applesauce
¾ cup granulated sugar, or to
    taste

Put 7 cups flour into a large bowl. Make a well in center of flour; put margarine in well. Add brown sugar, baking soda, salt and 1 teaspoon pumpkin pie spice; work into margarine with fingers. Add egg and work into margarine-sugar mixture. Gradually add buttermilk, working in flour as you go, until all buttermilk is used and a soft dough is made. Add remaining flour, if necessary.

Divide dough into 7 equal portions. Press one portion into a greased and floured 9-inch round cake pan. Bake in a 350°F oven 10 to 12 minutes. Turn layer onto a wire rack to cool. Repeat procedure for the remaining 6 portions of dough.

Combine applesauce and remaining 1 teaspoon pumpkin pie spice. Sweeten with granulated sugar. Spread applesauce between slightly warm cake layers. Do not put filling on top layer.

Cover with plastic wrap and allow cake to age for several days for best flavor.

In Mardi Gras country, King's Cake is served from January 6, Twelfth Night, the beginning of the Carnival, until Fat Tuesday, the day before Lent begins. A tiny plastic baby or dried bean or nut is baked into each cake. (It really isn't a cake at all; it's a yeast bread, decorated in Mardi Gras colors of purple, green and gold.) The person who finds the bean, baby or nut in his slice of cake is king of the Twelfth Night Ball or of the party at which the cake is served; he chooses his queen—or the other way around.

In recent years, it has become a custom for office groups to buy a King's Cake on Twelfth Night, and the person who gets the bean furnishes the cake the next week, and so on each week until Lent begins. Or in groups of friends, the bean-finder will have the next party.

NEW ORLEANS KING'S CAKE   *12 to 15 servings*

- 2 packages active dry yeast
- 2 teaspoons granulated sugar
- ½ cup lukewarm water
- 4½ cups all-purpose flour, divided
- ½ cup granulated sugar
- 2 teaspoons salt
- 1 teaspoon ground nutmeg
- ½ cup lukewarm milk
- 1 teaspoon grated lemon peel
- 5 egg yolks
- ½ cup butter, cut into small pieces
- 2 tablespoons butter, divided
- 1 dried bean or pecan half, or small (1-inch) plastic baby
- 1 egg, beaten with 1 tablespoon milk
  Additional butter, for top of cake
  Sugar tinted green, yellow and purple, about 4 tablespoons of each color (see directions)

Sprinkle yeast and 2 teaspoons sugar over lukewarm water. Let soften. Stir, then let sit about 10 minutes, until light and bubbly. Mix 3½ cups of flour, ½ cup sugar, salt and nutmeg well. Add yeast mixture, milk and lemon peel. Work mixture together well. (An electric mixer is fine for this.) Add egg yolks and beat in well. Work in ½ cup butter and continue to beat until butter is incorporated and mixture is smooth.

Either change to a mixer dough hook, or turn dough out on floured board and knead until smooth and elastic, working in remaining 1 cup flour gradually. Dough will not be sticky when ready.

Butter a bowl with 1 tablespoon butter; put in ball of dough and turn to coat all sides. Cover with a towel, put in a draft-free place and let rise until double in bulk, about 1½ to 2 hours.

Brush baking sheet with remaining 1 tablespoon butter. Turn dough out on floured board and form into a roll about 14 or 15 inches long. (This can be done with the hands.) Put roll on prepared baking sheet and form into a ring shape, pressing ends together to seal. Push bean or baby or nut into cake from the bottom, so that it is not visible from the top. Cover with towel and put in draft-free, warm place to rise until double in size, 45 minutes to an hour.

Brush top of cake with egg-milk wash. Bake in middle of a preheated 375°F oven until brown, about 25 minutes. Slide cake onto wire rack to cool.

Butter top of cooled cake; using each color to cover a third, spread colored sugars over top of cake.

Note: Some people knead candied citron or raisins into dough. Some use a cinnamon-brown sugar filling. But the most common King's Cake is plain. Sometimes a confectioners sugar icing (white) is applied before the colored sugars are added, but most often it is not.

To tint sugar: Put a drop of desired food color into sugar (one drop for 4 tablespoons sugar) and stir until sugar is evenly colored and brightly tinted. Green, yellow and purple are the traditional colors.

Dotty Griffith

The Dallas Morning News / Dallas, Texas

Editors from opposite ends of the country sent in the recipe for Texas Sheet Cake. Where did it get its name? "Some said it was Lady Bird's recipe. Others said no, it was called Texas Sheet Cake because of its size, or because it is rich. Whatever the reason, it is well worth baking, especially in the summer when large parties abound," wrote Janice Okun of the Buffalo (New York) News. *"The cake is quite well known in Pennsylvania and Ohio, judging from reader responses to a recent request. The cake is ultra-easy to put together. You can have the whole thing frosted and ready to go in half an hour. But it also keeps well. It is a moist, heavy cake."*

This is Dotty Griffith's version, from deep in the heart of Texas.

TEXAS SHEET CAKE

Fifteen 3-inch squares

2 cups granulated sugar	½ cup buttermilk
2 cups all-purpose flour	2 eggs, slightly beaten
½ cup margarine	1 teaspoon baking soda
½ cup solid shortening	1 teaspoon vanilla extract
4 tablespoons cocoa powder	Icing (recipe follows)
1 cup water	

Sift together sugar and flour in a large bowl. Combine margarine, shortening, cocoa and water in a saucepan. Bring to a rapid boil, then pour over flour-sugar mixture; stir well. Add buttermilk, eggs, baking soda and vanilla; mix well. Pour batter into a greased 15½x10½-inch baking pan (jelly roll pan). Bake in a 400°F oven 20 minutes.

Five minutes before cake is done, prepare Icing. Spread icing on cake while it is still hot and in the pan.

ICING

½ cup margarine	1 box (16 ounces) confectioners
4 tablespoons cocoa powder	sugar
⅓ cup milk	1 teaspoon vanilla extract
	1 cup chopped pecans

Combine margarine, cocoa and milk in a saucepan and cook over low heat until margarine is melted. Then bring to a boil, remove from heat and add confectioners sugar, vanilla and pecans. Beat well. Use to ice cake as directed.

Barbara Gibbs Ostmann

St. Louis Post-Dispatch / St. Louis, Missouri

The mighty Mississippi rolls alongside the Arch and St. Louis, and gives its name to a regional specialty: Mississippi River Mud Cake (also called Mississippi Mud Cake). This is a good one for chocoholics.

MISSISSIPPI RIVER MUD CAKE

12 average-size or 24 small servings

1 cup butter or margarine
2 cups granulated sugar
4 eggs
¼ cup cocoa powder
¾ teaspoon salt
1½ cups all-purpose flour
1 teaspoon vanilla extract
1½ cups flaked coconut
1½ cups chopped nuts
     (preferably pecans)
1 jar (9 ounces)
     marshmallow cream, or
     miniature marshmallows
     as needed

Frosting:
⅓ cup cocoa powder
½ cup butter or margarine
½ teaspoon vanilla extract
⅛ teaspoon salt
⅓ cup light cream or milk
1 box (16 ounces)
     confectioners sugar

Cream butter and sugar in a large mixing bowl. Beat in eggs, one at a time. Sift cocoa, salt and flour, then add to egg mixture. Stir in vanilla, coconut and chopped nuts.

Pour batter into a greased and floured 13x9x2-inch pan. Bake in a 350°F oven 30 to 35 minutes, or until toothpick inserted in center comes out clean. Remove from oven and, while hot, either spread with marshmallow cream or cover with miniature marshmallows and spread them after they have melted. Let cake cool, then frost with frosting.

For frosting: Beat cocoa, butter, vanilla, salt, cream and confectioners sugar in a medium mixing bowl until fluffy. Spread over marshmallow cream on cake.

Note: No baking powder or baking soda is needed in this recipe.

Barbara Durbin

The Oregonian / Portland, Oregon

Filberts—better known in Europe as hazelnuts—are strictly a product of the Northwest, in terms of U.S. production. The Oregon crop accounts for ninety-eight percent of those grown in the States, according to the Oregon Filbert Commission.

This filbert recipe, shared by a reader, Linda Dau Gray-Fellows of Hillsboro, is an old family favorite.

FILBERT CREAM CAKE
12 servings

5 eggs
½ cup butter or margarine
½ cup solid shortening
2 cups granulated sugar
1 teaspoon baking soda
1 cup buttermilk
2 cups all-purpose flour, sifted twice

1 can (3½ ounces) flaked coconut
1 cup finely chopped or ground filberts (using a blender makes this easy)
1 teaspoon vanilla extract
Cream Cheese-Filbert Icing (recipe follows)
Whole filberts, for garnish

Separate eggs. Beat egg whites in a mixing bowl until stiff. Set aside.

Cream butter and shortening in a large mixing bowl; add sugar. Add egg yolks, one at a time, beating well after each addition. Dissolve baking soda in buttermilk; add alternately with flour to creamed mixture. Beat well. Add coconut, nuts and vanilla. Fold in stiffly beaten egg whites.

Pour batter into three greased and floured 9-inch cake pans, using about 2 cups batter for each pan. Bake in a preheated 350°F oven 25 minutes. Let cool, then remove from pans; cool completely.

Prepare icing. Spread icing between cake layers and on top of cake. Garnish top of cake with whole filberts, if desired.

CREAM CHEESE-FILBERT ICING

1 package (8 ounces) cream cheese, softened
½ cup margarine
1 box (16 ounces) confectioners sugar

½ teaspoon almond extract
¼ cup finely chopped or ground filberts

Combine cream cheese, margarine, sugar, almond extract and filberts in a bowl; beat well. Use to ice cake, as directed.

Ginger Johnston

The Oregonian / Portland, Oregon

This recipe was shared with us more than ten years ago by a former local blueberry grower. Although there are only roughly six hundred acres of land in Oregon in blueberry production, 1983 brought in an estimated $2 million to growers.

MELT-IN-YOUR-MOUTH BLUEBERRY CAKE   *9 servings*

2 eggs, separated
1 cup granulated sugar,
    divided
½ cup solid shortening
¼ teaspoon salt
1 teaspoon vanilla extract

1½ cups sifted all-purpose
    flour, divided
1½ cups fresh or unthawed
    frozen blueberries
1 teaspoon baking powder
⅓ cup milk
Additional granulated sugar

Beat egg whites with ¼ cup sugar in a medium mixing bowl until mixture forms stiff, shiny peaks. Set aside.

Cream shortening in a large mixing bowl. Add salt and vanilla. Gradually add remaining ¾ cup sugar. Add egg yolks. Beat until light and creamy.

Take a small amount of flour and toss gently with blueberries so they won't settle to the bottom; set aside. Sift remaining flour with baking powder. Add to batter alternately with milk. Fold in reserved beaten egg whites and blueberries. Pour batter into a greased 8-inch square pan. Sprinkle top of batter lightly with additional sugar. Bake in a 350°F oven 50 to 60 minutes, or until cake springs back when lightly pressed in center.

Barbara Gibbs Ostmann

St. Louis Post-Dispatch / St. Louis, Missouri

Gooey Butter Coffee Cake is a St. Louis specialty that no one else seems to have heard of or enjoyed. This is difficult for generations of St. Louisans to believe. The popular cake features a rather dry base that is more than compensated for by the deliciously gooey topping. Gooey Butter Coffee Cakes are available at most local bakeries and supermarkets, but homemade from scratch is hard to beat. Here's how to make your own.

GOOEY BUTTER COFFEE CAKE

2 cakes (18 servings)

Sweet Dough:
- ¼ cup granulated sugar
- ¼ cup solid shortening
- ¼ teaspoon salt
- 1 egg
- 1 cake (0.6 ounce) compressed yeast
- ½ cup warm milk
- 2½ cups all-purpose flour
- 1 tablespoon vanilla extract

Gooey Butter:
- 2½ cups granulated sugar
- 1 cup butter, softened
- Dash salt
- 1 egg
- ¼ cup light corn syrup
- 2¼ cups all-purpose flour
- ¼ cup water
- 1 tablespoon vanilla extract
- Confectioners sugar

For sweet dough: Mix sugar with shortening and salt. Add egg and beat with an electric mixer for 1 minute until well blended. Dissolve yeast in warm milk. Add flour, then milk-yeast mixture and vanilla to sweet dough batter. Mix for 3 minutes with a dough hook.

Turn dough out on floured board and knead for 1 minute. Place in a lightly greased bowl, cover with a towel and set in a warm place to rise for 1 hour.

For gooey butter: Combine sugar, butter and salt. Add egg and corn syrup. Mix enough to incorporate. Add flour, water and vanilla.

To assemble: Divide dough into two pieces. Place in two well-greased 9-inch square pans. Crimp edges halfway up side of pans so gooey butter will not run out underneath. After dough is spread out, punch holes in dough with a fork (to keep dough from bubbling when baking).

Divide gooey butter into two equal parts. Spread over dough in each pan. Let cakes stand for 20 minutes. Then bake in a 375°F oven 30 minutes. Do not overbake; topping will not be gooey if cakes are baked too long.

After cakes are cool, sprinkle tops with confectioners sugar.

GOOEY BUTTER COFFEE CAKE
(Convenience Method)

12 servings

1 box pound cake mix, or a
    2-layer yellow cake mix
4 eggs, divided
½ cup butter, melted
1 package (8 ounces) cream
    cheese

1½ tablespoons vanilla extract
1 box (16 ounces)
    confectioners sugar,
    divided

Blend cake mix with 2 eggs and melted butter; pour into a 12x8x2-inch baking dish. In another bowl, combine cream cheese, remaining 2 eggs, vanilla and confectioners sugar, minus 2 tablespoons. Mix well and spread over batter in dish. Bake in a 300°F oven 15 minutes. Remove cake from oven and sprinkle reserved 2 tablespoons confectioners sugar on top. Return to oven and continue to bake 25 minutes longer. Do not overbake; topping will not be gooey if cakes are baked too long.

Note: This coffee cake is good cold, but much better warm. And yes, this one coffee cake really does require one entire box of confectioners sugar; so don't skimp.

Charlotte Hansen
The Jamestown Sun / Jamestown, North Dakota

This is a Norwegian Apple Cake that is well liked in our area.

EPLE KAKE

6 to 8 servings

1 cup butter, melted
1 box (7 ounces) zwieback, crushed
1 cup granulated sugar
4 to 6 apples, peeled and sliced

Heat butter in a skillet until it becomes a deep brown but is not burned. Mix zwieback crumbs and sugar in a bowl; add browned butter.

Place a layer of apples in a greased 9-inch casserole, then a layer of crumb mixture; repeat until casserole is filled, reserving enough of crumb mixture to cover top of casserole. Mixture should be about 3 to 4 inches deep.

Bake in a 350°F oven 1½ hours. Serve hot or cold with whipped cream or ice cream.

Janet Beighle French

The Plain Dealer / Cleveland, Ohio

Not far east of Cleveland, the Concord grape vineyards begin. They stretch across Pennsylvania and New York, and perfume the air for miles with an aroma that brings Welch's to mind. (Indeed, that company uses most of the production.)

Geneva, Ohio, has an annual Grape Festival, which features homemade grape pies and kuchens and jams and jellies, and which has certainly popularized such recipes locally.

Actual recipes are hard to nail down, however, and inevitably they require separating the pesky skins and seeds from the pulp. After several tries, we developed a kuchen which is "faster" than previous versions, and is really quite delicious.

What is kuchen? The word may mean cake in German, but in Cleveland, it tends to mean coffee cake, with or without yeast.

FASTER CONCORD GRAPE KUCHEN   *12 servings*

Puree:
1½ cups Concord grapes,
    stems removed
¼ cup granulated sugar
1 tablespoon all-purpose
    flour
¾ teaspoon lemon juice

Batter:
3 cups unsifted all-purpose
    flour, divided
1 package active dry yeast
¾ cup milk

¼ cup water
½ cup butter
½ cup granulated sugar
1 teaspoon salt
2 eggs
½ cup dairy sour cream

Streusel:
¼ cup all-purpose flour
2 tablespoons light brown
    sugar
⅛ teaspoon ground cinnamon
2 tablespoons butter

For puree: Remove grape skins by pinching each grape at end opposite stem end. Save skins. Put pulp (with seeds) in a saucepan. Carefully cook over low heat until soft. Do not boil or delicate flavor will be destroyed. Put pulp through a food mill or sieve to remove seeds.

Return grape pulp to pan. Add skins. Stir in sugar, flour and lemon juice. Cook and stir over low heat until thickened. Remove from heat. Puree thickens as it stands.

For batter: Measure 1 cup flour into a large mixer bowl. Blend in yeast. In a saucepan, combine milk, water, butter, sugar and salt. Heat to 120°F to 130°F, stirring constantly.

Pour warm mixture into flour mixture. Add eggs and sour cream. Beat with an electric mixer for 30 seconds on low speed, scraping bowl constantly. Beat 3 more minutes at high speed. Stop mixer. Gradually stir in remaining 2 cups flour.

Grease a 13x9x2-inch casserole dish. Pour in batter. Cover and let stand 20 minutes.

For streusel: Mix flour, brown sugar and cinnamon. Cut in butter until crumbly.

To assemble: Top batter with half of streusel, then the grape puree, then remaining streusel. Pierce batter with skewer here and there so that puree runs down.

Cover and let rise above a bowl of warm water, in a turned-off electric oven or microwave oven or similar draft-free place, about 45 minutes, or until double in bulk.

Preheat oven to 375°F (but remove casserole before you do!). Bake 35 minutes, or until kuchen pulls away from sides of casserole and tests done with toothpick.

Janet Beighle French

The Plain Dealer / Ceveland, Ohio

Cleveland is Kolachy country, no matter how you spell it. Kolachy is tender pastry, usually cut in wedges, and rolled up with a filling made with fruit, poppy seeds or nuts. Some Kolachy is cut in rounds and filled in the center, some is cut in rounds and folded over. Many an ethnic holiday or family celebration would be incomplete without the platter of Kolachy.

One of our best and simplest recipes hails from Lillian Kriscak, who is of Slovak descent. She calls her Kolachy "rozki" (it's cut in circles). She always makes several fillings and carries the pastries to her three daughters' homes at Christmas and Easter. We like the apricot filling best.

SLOVAK KOLACHY
80 pastries

1 pound butter, softened	1 egg, beaten
1 pound cream cheese, softened	**Filling:**
4 cups sifted all-purpose flour	12 ounces dried apricots
2 egg yolks	Water
3 tablespoons milk	3 cups granulated sugar

Combine butter, cream cheese and flour in a large mixing bowl; cut together with pastry blender until like coarse crumbs.

Beat egg yolks with fork in a small bowl; add to crumbly mixture along with milk. Work together with hands until mixed well and mixture "comes off the hands." (Dough can be frozen at this point. Thaw completely; continue.)

Divide ball of dough into 8 wedges. Cut each wedge into 10 parts. Roll each part into a round ball. Place in a large pan with waxed paper between layers. Chill until firm.

For filling: Turn apricots into saucepan and cover with water. Cook over low heat until apricots are very soft and water is mostly absorbed and evaporated. Mash with potato masher. Add sugar. Bring to boil. Cool to very cold. Makes about 3⅓ cups of filling.

Remove 10 balls of dough at a time from refrigerator. On lightly floured board, roll each one out to a 4- to 5-inch circle, of ⅛-inch thickness. Put a rounded teaspoon of apricot filling on each round and spread, leaving a border. Roll up loosely. Place seam side down on greased cookie sheet. Bend into a crescent. Brush pastries with beaten egg.

Bake in a preheated 375°F oven just until golden, about 18 minutes.

Jean Thwaite

The Atlanta Journal-Constitution / Atlanta, Georgia

Just ask anyone from Georgia where the best peaches are grown and you can be sure the answer will be an emphatic, "Georgia." Cobbler is a traditional way to use this summer fruit.

GEORGIA PEACH COBBLER

6 to 8 servings

2 cups sliced fresh peaches (or any fresh fruit)
1 cup granulated sugar
½ cup butter or margarine

¾ cup self-rising flour (see note)
¾ cup milk
Ground nutmeg

Combine fruit with sugar in a bowl; set aside. Put butter in an 11x8x2½-inch baking dish. Place in 350°F oven to melt butter. Butter should be bubbly but not brown.

Combine flour and milk; pour over melted butter in pan. Spoon fruit mixture on top. Sprinkle with nutmeg. Do not stir. Return to 350°F oven and bake 1 hour, or until cobbler is golden brown.

Note: To make your own self-rising flour, add 1 teaspoon baking powder and ¼ teaspoon salt to ¾ cup all-purpose flour.

Jane Moulton
The Plain Dealer / Cleveland, Ohio

Elephant Ears and Funnel Cakes have been popular for years in Mennonite homes in northern Ohio. They have now become part of local carnivals and county fairs.

ELEPHANT EARS

16 to 20 ears

1¼ cups milk, scalded to just below boiling (see note)
½ cup butter or margarine
1 package active dry yeast
1 teaspoon granulated sugar
¼ cup warm water (110°F to 115°F)
2½ cups all-purpose unbleached flour
1 teaspoon salt
3 eggs
¾ cup granulated sugar
¼ teaspoon ground nutmeg (optional)
3 to 4 cups additional all-purpose unbleached flour
   Vegetable oil for deep-frying
   Confectioners sugar or cinnamon sugar (1 cup granulated
      sugar with ½ teaspoon ground cinnamon)
   Baked custard or vanilla ice cream (optional)

Pour milk into a mixer bowl and add butter. Cool to lukewarm (110°F to 115°F). Soften yeast and 1 teaspoon sugar in warm water for 10 minutes, or until bubbles start to form. Add yeast mixture to lukewarm milk mixture. Gradually add 2½ cups flour and salt, beating until smooth. Cover and let stand in a warm place until full of bubbles, about 30 minutes.

Beat in eggs, ¾ cup sugar and nutmeg. Add enough additional flour to make a soft dough. (Your finger will not stick to the dough when you touch it lightly, but you will think it is going to.)

Knead on lightly floured board or with dough hook of heavy-duty mixer until smooth and elastic, about 8 minutes by hand, or 4 to 5 minutes with dough hook. Cover and let rise in warm place until double in bulk, about 1½ hours.

Punch dough down; divide dough into quarters. From each quarter, make 4 or 5 pieces, each about the size of a small handball.

Heat oil for frying to 365°F in a deep-fryer or large skillet. Work with one ball of dough at a time. Pull and stretch until dough is about 10 inches long and 6 inches wide. Fry in hot fat, poking it down frequently to keep it from puffing too much. When one side is brown, turn with tongs to cook other side. Drain on paper towels. Sprinkle with confectioners sugar or cinnamon sugar.

Repeat with remaining dough. Top Elephant Ears with baked custard or vanilla ice cream, if desired.

Note: You may substitute ⅔ cup evaporated milk plus hot water to make 1¼ cups for the fresh milk.

Unfried dough can be kept tightly covered with plastic wrap in the refrigerator for 3 to 4 days. Allow to come to room temperature before stretching individual ears.

Variation: About 1 cup raisins can be kneaded into dough before shaping.

FUNNEL CAKES
8 large funnel cakes

3 eggs
½ teaspoon vanilla extract
¼ cup granulated sugar
2 cups milk
4 cups all-purpose flour
2 teaspoons baking powder
½ teaspoon salt
  Solid shortening or vegetable oil for deep-frying
  Confectioners sugar

Beat eggs and vanilla in a mixer bowl until light and fluffy. Slowly beat in sugar; beat until thick. Slowly mix in milk.

Sift together or stir well flour, baking powder and salt. Add dry ingredients gradually to egg mixture and mix well.

Heat shortening or oil to 375°F in a deep-fryer or 10-inch skillet. To make a large funnel cake, use about ½ cup batter in a funnel with a hole about ½ inch in diameter, placing your finger over the hole as you fill funnel with batter.

Release batter over center of pan and let batter flow into hot oil in a circular pattern, in rosettes or whatever shape you desire, working from the center out. You can make cakes whatever size you like. (About 9½ inches is probably as large as you can manage.)

When brown on the under side, turn and cook until other side is brown. Drain on absorbent paper. Sprinkle with confectioners sugar. Eat hot.

Janet Beighle French

The Plain Dealer / Cleveland, Ohio

Nut-filled pastries are never missing from the table during ethnic celebrations in Cleveland. This luscious version, Slovenian Icebox Potica, hails from Lillian Hlabse, a Plain Dealer *secretary who worked for the food staff for several years. On Easter, she takes it to church, along with sausage, colored eggs and fresh horseradish, for the blessing.*

SLOVENIAN ICEBOX POTICA

Six 9-inch rolls

Dough:
1 package active dry yeast
¼ cup warm water
1 teaspoon granulated sugar
4½ cups sifted Sapphire flour
   (see note)
3 tablespoons granulated
   sugar
1½ teaspoons salt
½ cup butter or margarine,
   softened
3 egg yolks, beaten
1 cup dairy sour cream

Filling:
1 cup milk

½ cup butter or margarine,
   cut in chunks
2½ pounds walnuts, ground at
   home (see note)
1 cup dairy sour cream
1½ cups granulated sugar
2 tablespoons honey
1 egg yolk, beaten
4 egg whites, beaten stiff
2 tablespoons orange zest or
   lemon zest (optional)
1½ cups golden raisins,
   plumped 10 minutes in
   hot water, then drained
   (optional)
1 egg yolk, beaten with
   1 teaspoon water

Prepare dough the day before baking.

For dough: Soften yeast in warm water. Add 1 teaspoon sugar and let stand until foamy. Sift flour with 3 tablespoons sugar and salt into a bowl. Cut in butter.

Mix egg yolks with sour cream, then add yeast mixture. Stir liquid mixture into flour mixture. Turn out on a lightly floured board and knead about 5 minutes, or until smooth.

Place in a greased bowl, turn to grease top, cover and refrigerate overnight. Next day, remove dough from refrigerator. Let stand one hour, to come to room temperature. Meanwhile, prepare filling.

For filling: In a saucepan, combine milk and butter; heat just to boiling. Remove from heat and allow to cool.

Stir together milk-butter mixture and ground nuts. Stir in sour cream, sugar, honey and egg yolk. Blend in egg whites until completely mixed in. Stir in zest, if desired.

To assemble: Divide dough into 6 parts. Roll each part to a rectangle 9 inches wide and between 14 and 18 inches long.

After each piece of dough is rolled out, spread with one-sixth of filling. Sprinkle with raisins. Roll up, starting from narrow side, and pricking top surface as you go, to prevent cracking. Do not prick top of roll.

Place in six 9x5x3-inch loaf pans that have been lined with foil and greased. Cover and let rise 1½ hours. Brush tops of rolls with egg yolk-water mixture. Bake in a preheated 325°F oven 1 hour, or until toothpick inserted comes out clean and top is golden brown. Cool in pans for 10 minutes. Then remove from pans and finish cooling on rack. Potica can be frozen.

Note: Sapphire is hard wheat bread flour, such as King Midas or Fisher's West Coast bread flour. If all-purpose flour is used, more may be needed.

Commercially ground nuts are less oily than those ground at home.

Variation: Recipe can be made in three circular rolls, baked in 10-inch tube pans, or three 15-inch rolls plus one 8-inch roll, or any combination thereof.

Ruth Gray
St. Petersburg Times / St. Petersburg, Florida

Florida's most famous dessert is a must for visitors to the Sunshine State. There are a number of recipes for it, but this one appears to be the most popular and true to the old-time Florida spirit. Use only the small yellow (when ripe) limes of the Florida Keys, and not the larger green Persian limes for a real Key Lime Pie.

Thirty minutes in the freezer will help this recipe to set. Store it in the refrigerator (not the freezer) until serving time. Lemon or calamondin juice can be substituted. Calamondins are the small, orange citrus grown on specialty trees in Florida.

KEY LIME PIE
6 or 12 servings

1 can (14 ounces) sweetened, condensed milk (not evaporated milk)
½ cup Key lime juice

3 eggs, separated
Salt
1 (9-inch) or 2 (8-inch) pie shells, baked and cooled

Chill milk overnight in refrigerator. Place in a large mixing bowl and beat at high speed of electric mixer for several minutes. Add lime juice a few drops at a time, using a spatula to scrape mixture from the sides. Mixture will begin to thicken. Add egg yolks, one at a time, and continue to beat. Beat egg whites until stiff and fold into mixture gently. Add a few grains of salt.

Pour filling into one 9-inch pie shell or two 8-inch pie shells. Chill several hours before serving.

Toni Griffin

The Tribune / San Diego, California

San Diegans usually enjoy jicama, a root vegetable, raw for low-calorie crunching. It is also a frequently used element in salads, or as a water chestnut substitute in stir-fried dishes. Local cooking teacher Jerrie Strom bakes this unusual pie with jicama, yielding a delicious source of conversation over dessert.

JICAMA PIE
6 to 8 servings

1 jicama (½ pound), peeled and shredded (about 2 cups)
½ cup sherry
½ cup water
¾ cup plus 2 teaspoons granulated sugar, divided
6 tablespoons all-purpose flour
¼ teaspoon salt
3 egg yolks
2 cups milk, divided
1 cinnamon stick
2½ teaspoons butter, divided
1 pie shell (9 inches), baked and cooled
¼ teaspoon ground cinnamon

Combine shredded jicama, sherry and water in a small saucepan. Bring to boil; reduce heat. Cover and boil gently 45 minutes, or until most of liquid has evaporated. Drain thoroughly. Set aside.

Mix ¾ cup sugar, flour and salt in a medium saucepan. Beat egg yolks and 1 cup milk in a small bowl; stir into sugar mixture. Add remaining 1 cup milk and cinnamon stick. Stir over medium heat until mixture boils and becomes very thick. Remove and discard cinnamon stick.

Add jicama mixture to milk mixture. Cook and stir 1 or 2 minutes longer, until mixture is very thick. Stir in 1½ teaspoons butter. Remove from heat and cool slightly.

Turn mixture into prepared pie shell. Sprinkle filling lightly with ground cinnamon and remaining 2 teaspoons sugar. Cut remaining 1 teaspoon butter into small pieces; place over filling. Broil pie 3 inches from heat 3 to 4 minutes, or until butter and sugar are melted and bubbly. Watch carefully and do not let crust burn. Cool pie slightly. Serve warm or at room temperature.

Ginger Johnston
The Oregonian / Portland, Oregon

Marionberries are a special variety of blackberry grown in Oregon. They are called marionberries because extensive testing to develop the cross was done in Marion County. However, any blackberry could be substituted in this pie recipe.

MARIONBERRY PIE
6 to 8 servings

1 cup granulated sugar
3 tablespoons quick-cooking
   tapioca, uncooked
½ teaspoon ground cinnamon
¼ teaspoon lemon juice

1 quart marionberries or
   blackberries, rinsed and
   picked over
Pastry for a double-crust pie

Mix sugar, tapioca, cinnamon, lemon juice and berries in a medium mixing bowl. Pour filling into pastry-lined 9-inch pie pan. Adjust top crust; seal and flute edges. Cut slits in top. Bake in a preheated 400°F oven 10 minutes, then reduce heat to 350°F and bake 45 minutes more. Cool before serving.

Clara Eschmann
The Macon Telegraph and News / Macon, Georgia

Georgia Pecan Pie is justly famous because our state has absolutely the most delicious pecans anywhere! They are large, sweet and oily. We refrigerate and freeze the fall crop for year-round use.

GEORGIA PECAN PIE
6 to 8 servings

4 eggs
1 cup granulated sugar
1 cup dark corn syrup
½ tablespoon all-purpose flour
¼ teaspoon salt

1 teaspoon vanilla extract
¼ cup butter, melted
2 cups pecan halves
1 unbaked 9-inch pie shell

Beat eggs well. Add sugar, corn syrup, flour, salt and vanilla. Beat well. Stir in melted butter and pecans. Pour mixture into pie shell. Bake in a 300°F oven 1 hour, or until knife inserted near center comes out clean. Cool on rack.

Sue Dawson

The Columbus Dispatch / Columbus, Ohio

Ohio has been credited with a unique, two-crusted lemon pie. We had run across the recipe several times, yet we had never seen or tasted it in our many years of living in this state. Why is it called Ohio Lemon Pie? The answer was found recently in a Shaker cookbook, which traces the pie to the early Ohio Shakers. It's a different way to make lemon pie—very lemony in taste and with a delightful texture.

The pie filling has only four ingredients. Paper-thin slices of whole lemons are mixed with sugar and allowed to stand for the sugar to draw out the juice. Beaten eggs and salt are added just before baking.

OHIO LEMON PIE
6 to 8 servings

2 lemons
2 cups granulated sugar
5 eggs

¼ teaspoon salt
Pastry for a double-crust pie

Wash lemons well and cut off ends. Place lemons on a cutting board over a bowl to catch juices. With a knife, slice into paper-thin slices. (A food processor won't slice them thin enough.) Combine lemon slices and juice with sugar in a bowl and let stand at room temperature at least 2 hours or overnight. Beat eggs with salt in a small bowl and stir into lemon mixture.

Roll out half of pastry and fit into 9-inch pie pan. Roll out second half of pastry and cut slits to allow steam to escape. Pour filling into pastry-lined pan and top with second crust. Trim and flute edge.

Bake in a 425°F oven 15 minutes. Reduce heat to 350°F and bake 30 to 40 minutes more, or until pastry is golden and knife inserted in vent hole comes out clean.

Karen Marshall

St. Louis Globe-Democrat / St. Louis, Missouri

Sugar Cream Pies are as basic in Indiana, where I grew up, as beans are in Boston or chili in Texas. You can buy them frozen in the supermarkets, and almost every pie baker has a version.

According to Marge Hanley, food editor of the Indianapolis News, *old-fashioned Sugar Cream Pie is a Hoosier tradition. As the colonies grew, and pioneers moved westward, they adapted recipes brought by early English settlers. Transparent, Buttermilk and Sugar Cream Pies evolved. Sugar Cream Pie is probably a variation of English Chess Tarts.*

Early Hoosier cooks made Sugar Cream Pie by first rubbing the unbaked pastry pie crust with butter and then pouring in a mixture of cream, sugar and flour, flavored with vanilla. While the pie baked, they periodically stirred the filling with their fingers to keep the flour from settling to the bottom and coating the crust. More modern versions save the fingers and suggest shaking or stirring the filling while baking.

SUGAR CREAM PIE
6 to 8 servings

1 cup granulated sugar
½ cup all-purpose flour, minus
   1 tablespoon

1 pint heavy cream
1 unbaked 9-inch pie shell
3 tablespoons butter

Mix sugar with flour in a medium mixing bowl. Add cream and stir well. Pour into pie shell and dot with butter. Bake in a preheated 500°F oven 5 to 7 minutes. Stir ingredients in shell and bake 5 minutes longer. Stir again and reduce oven temperature to 350°F. Bake about 30 minutes longer, or until knife inserted near center comes out clean. Cool before cutting.

Nancy Pappas
The Louisville Times / Louisville, Kentucky

At Derby time, "everyone" in Louisville makes rich "Derby Pie," but a local restaurant, The Melrose Inn, has convinced the natives that it owns the name. Hence, we call it the Run for the Roses Pie, named after the Derby's major race.

RUN FOR THE ROSES PIE
8 to 10 servings

1 cup granulated sugar
½ cup all-purpose flour
½ cup butter or margarine,
   melted and slightly cooled
2 eggs, slightly beaten
2 tablespoons bourbon

1 teaspoon vanilla extract
1 cup semisweet chocolate
   morsels
1 cup chopped nuts
1 pie shell (9 or 10 inches),
   unbaked

Combine sugar, flour, butter, eggs, bourbon and vanilla in a mixer bowl; beat until well blended. Stir in chocolate morsels and nuts. Pour filling into pie shell. Bake in a preheated 325°F oven 50 to 60 minutes, or until pie is set and top cracks. Cool on rack.

Jann Malone
Richmond Times-Dispatch / Richmond, Virginia

This is a dessert that's both impressive and easy. Strawberry and chocolate ice creams are used in this particular version, but you can use whatever flavor combinations you wish. The Mile-High Pies of my wide-eyed childhood, which were served at the Pontchartrain Hotel in New Orleans, were made with vanilla and chocolate ice creams.

This New Orleans classic has been transplanted to other parts of the country, and deservedly so, by visitors to the hotel or former residents of the area.

MILE-HIGH ICE CREAM PIE
8 to 12 servings

Crust:
1⅔ cups graham cracker crumbs (about ⅓ of a 1-pound box)
¼ cup granulated sugar
⅓ cup (5⅓ tablespoons) margarine

Filling:
1 pint strawberry ice cream
1 pint chocolate ice cream

Meringue:
8 egg whites (about 1 cup), at room temperature
¼ teaspoon cream of tartar
½ teaspoon vanilla extract
½ cup granulated sugar

Chocolate Sauce:
1 cup semisweet chocolate pieces
½ cup cream, divided

Before you do anything, make space in your freezer for a really tall pie.

Prepare graham cracker crust by crushing crackers into crumbs. If you have a food processor or an electric blender, this is a snap. If you don't have either one, break crackers into small pieces and put into a plastic bag. Seal bag, then roll a rolling pin back and forth across bag until crackers become crumbs.

If you're using the food processor, add sugar to crumbs and mix well; cut margarine into chunks and process until evenly distributed in the crumbs. If you're working by hand, put crumbs into a mixing bowl and stir in sugar. Soften margarine, then cut into crumbs.

Press crumb mixture into bottom and sides of a 9-inch pie pan. Be sure to use a smooth pan; if you use one with fluted edges, you may have trouble getting the pie out.

Put crust in freezer and take out strawberry ice cream to soften a bit.

When ice cream has softened, spoon it into pie crust. Smooth and pack down with a spoon so there aren't any bubbles. Return pie to freezer until ice cream is hard, about 1 hour.

When strawberry ice cream is hard, take chocolate ice cream out of freezer to soften. Spoon chocolate ice cream on top of strawberry and pack down firmly. Return pie to freezer until ice cream is hard.

When ice cream is hard, prepare meringue. Make sure the bowl and beaters are clean, without any trace of grease. Beat egg whites with cream of tartar and vanilla until soft peaks form. Gradually add sugar, about 1 tablespoon at a time, until sugar is dissolved and egg whites are stiff and glossy. Test for stiffness by turning bowl upside down; egg whites should not slide out. If they start to slide, beat them some more.

Spread meringue over pie, making sure to spread to edges to seal ice cream inside, or else ice cream will leak when pie is placed in oven. Make decorative swirls on top with the edge of a spoon.

Broil for about 1 minute, or until meringue browns.

Freeze pie overnight, or at least for 3 to 4 hours to allow ice cream to harden.

Just before serving, prepare chocolate sauce by melting chocolate pieces with ¼ cup of cream in top of a double boiler. Add enough additional cream so sauce will pour.

Use a hot knife (run it under hot water, then wipe it off) to cut pie into serving pieces. Drizzle chocolate sauce over the top of each piece.

Elaine Corn
The Courier-Journal / Louisville, Kentucky

Transparent Pie is similar to a number of other Southern pies—it's a rich pie made with staple ingredients that every cook already has in the cupboard. It's been popular through the years in Kentucky.

TRANSPARENT PIE

8 *servings*

1¼ cups granulated sugar, divided
3 tablespoons all-purpose flour
½ cup light cream or half-and-half

4 egg yolks
2 tablespoons butter, melted
1 unbaked 9-inch pie shell

Mix sugar and flour in a mixing bowl. Combine cream and egg yolks; stir well. Add to sugar mixture. Add butter; mix well. Pour into pie crust. Bake in a 350°F oven 30 to 35 minutes, or until filling is brown. Remove from oven; allow pie to cool.

Janice Okun
Buffalo News / Buffalo, New York

This exceptionally good pie is popular in a Niagara Falls restaurant, John's Flaming Hearth. This is the restaurant where Nikita Khrushchev ate a meal during a visit here. Rumor has it he never paid the bill.

JOHN'S FLAMING HEARTH PUMPKIN ICE CREAM PIE

6 to 8 servings

1 quart vanilla ice cream
1 pie shell (9 inches), baked and cooled
1 cup cooked or canned pumpkin
¾ cup granulated sugar
½ teaspoon salt
¾ teaspoon pumpkin pie spice

1 cup heavy cream, whipped
Additional whipped cream, for garnish
Syrup:
½ cup light brown sugar
¼ cup dark corn syrup
¼ cup hot water
½ teaspoon vanilla extract

Spread ice cream in pie shell. (If your pie plate is not a deep one, you might want to use a little less than 1 quart of ice cream.) Place in freezer until thoroughly hardened.

Blend together pumpkin, sugar, salt and spice in a bowl. In another bowl, whip 1 cup cream until stiff; fold whipped cream into pumpkin mixture. Spoon into frozen pie shell over the ice cream. Return to freezer until ready to serve.

Before serving, cover with additional whipped cream and drizzle syrup over the top.

For syrup: Combine sugar, corn syrup and water in a small saucepan; bring to a boil and continue to boil until it starts to thicken (but don't let it get too thick). Let cool, then add vanilla. Use to top pie as directed.

Woodene Merriman
Pittsburgh Post-Gazette / Pittsburgh, Pennsylvania

Most people know, thanks to Elaine Light and the Punxsutawney, Pennsylvania, Groundhog Club, that February 2 is Groundhog Day. If the groundhog comes out of his burrow in Punxsutawney that morning and sees his shadow, there will be six more weeks of winter. No shadow means spring is here.

Elaine Light was a reporter for the Associated Press in Pittsburgh in the late 1940s. She was sent to cover the groundhog story in Punxsutawney, but fell in love with the president of the groundhog club, married, and stayed in the little town. In the years since, she has publicized "Punxsutawney Phil" (the groundhog) throughout the country; many have heard about him through her cookbook, Gourmets & Groundhogs. *She developed a groundhog cookie and a groundhog sundae—neither of which contains groundhog—that are perfect eating every February 2. In Pittsburgh, by the way, stores sometimes sell groundhog-shaped cookie cutters just before the big day. That was Elaine Light's idea, too.*

SPICY GROUNDHOGS

12 to 15 large or 36 to 48 small cookies

2 cups sifted all-purpose
    flour
½ teaspoon salt
½ teaspoon baking soda
1 teaspoon baking powder
1 teaspoon ground ginger
1 teaspoon ground cloves
1½ teaspoons ground cinnamon
½ cup butter, softened

1 cup granulated sugar
½ cup molasses
1 egg yolk
   Granulated sugar, for
    rolling out
1 egg, slightly beaten
   Currants or raisins, for
    decoration

Sift flour, salt, baking soda, baking powder, ginger, cloves and cinnamon into a mixing bowl. Set aside.

Cream butter and sugar in a medium mixing bowl until fluffy. Blend in molasses and egg yolk. Stir in flour mixture and mix well. Form into a ball. Wrap in plastic wrap or waxed paper. Chill for 1 hour or longer.

Roll out a small amount of dough at a time on a sugar-sprinkled board. Roll to ⅛-inch thickness. Cut out cookies with a lightly floured cutter (preferably groundhog-shaped). Place cookies on a greased baking sheet. Brush with lightly beaten egg. Decorate with currants for eyes, buttons, etc. Bake in a preheated 350°F oven 8 to 10 minutes. Cool slightly before removing from cookie sheet.

GROUNDHOG SUNDAES

6 servings

1 quart vanilla ice cream, cut in 6 slices
6 Spicy Groundhogs (see recipe)
  Chocolate sauce (your favorite)

Place slices of ice cream on individual serving plates. Place a groundhog cookie in the center of each slice. Drizzle chocolate sauce across ice cream and on plate to suggest a shadow.

Moravians are members of a Protestant religious sect from Central Europe who settled in North Carolina in 1766. They brought to the Carolina wilderness a strong religious faith and close-knit way of life that has fostered long-standing traditions.

For more than two hundred years, Moravians in the Winston-Salem area have been baking special wafer-thin cookies for Christmas. These interesting cookies combine the seasonal spices of ginger, cinnamon and nutmeg with the flavor of molasses to achieve a delicate, tangy taste.

MORAVIAN COOKIES
3 to 6 dozen cookies

⅓ cup light molasses
¼ cup butter or margarine, softened
2 tablespoons granulated sugar
1¼ cups sifted all-purpose flour

½ teaspoon salt
½ teaspoon baking soda
¼ teaspoon ground cinnamon
¼ teaspoon ground ginger
¼ teaspoon ground cloves

Blend molasses, butter and sugar in a medium mixing bowl. Sift flour, salt, baking soda, cinnamon, ginger and cloves. Blend sifted dry ingredients into creamed mixture; mix well. Cover tightly with plastic wrap and refrigerate for at least 2 hours. (This dough may be kept refrigerated for several days.)

True Moravian cookies are paper thin. This delicious thinness is rather difficult to achieve at home by rolling the dough. If desired, form chilled dough into a roll about 2 inches in diameter; freeze, then slice paper thin with a sharp knife and bake as directed.

To roll cookies, stretch a pastry cloth over a large cutting board. Sprinkle cloth generously with flour; rub flour into cloth with hands and brush off excess. Remove about one-third of dough from refrigerator at a time, and roll out as thin as possible. Use only as much flour as necessary to keep dough from sticking to rolling pin. Cut with round, fluted-edged pastry cutter or various shaped cookie cutters.

Place cookies on a greased cookie sheet. Bake in a preheated 375°F oven 5 to 6 minutes, or until only slightly brown; be sure to check the baking cookies carefully to keep the thin cookies from burning.

Remove from oven; cool about 3 minutes. Remove cookies from pan onto cooling rack or paper towels. When cool, store in tightly covered container.

Note: The yield will vary according to whether the dough is rolled or sliced.

Barbara Gibbs Ostmann

St. Louis Post-Dispatch / St. Louis, Missouri

Growing up in the Arkansas Ozarks, I learned to appreciate "home cooking." Most of what we ate could be called Southern, but some of it was Ozark cooking.

I can remember my grandmother making potato candy—a treat to which my sisters and I looked forward. It wasn't until years later, when I attended a cooking class on Ozark foods for the newspaper, that I realized potato candy was a distinctly regional food.

GRANDMA'S POTATO CANDY   *About 72 pieces*

1 teaspoon vanilla extract
¼ teaspoon salt
¼ cup mashed potatoes,
    unseasoned

4 cups confectioners sugar
1 cup smooth peanut butter

Add vanilla and salt to mashed potatoes. Chill.

Add confectioners sugar slowly to chilled potatoes until mixture is stiff and dry. Divide mixture into 3 parts. Working with one part at a time, roll out to about a ¼-inch thickness on waxed paper (it should form a rectangle about 4″ x 12″). Spread with a thin layer of peanut butter. Roll up as for jelly roll. Repeat with remaining potato mixture and peanut butter. Chill several hours. Slice (not too thick; this is rich). Store in refrigerator.

Sandra Day

The Times-Picayune/States-Item / New Orleans, Louisiana

Pecans are abundant in Louisiana, and pecan pralines are a classic Creole candy.

PECAN PRALINES
36 small pralines

3 cups firmly packed light
  brown sugar
1 cup heavy cream
¼ teaspoon salt

¼ cup butter or margarine
2 teaspoons vanilla extract
2½ cups pecan halves or pieces

Combine brown sugar, cream and salt in a large, heavy saucepan. Place over moderate heat and stir until sugar dissolves. Cover pan and boil mixture for 3 minutes; remove lid and continue cooking without stirring until mixture reaches soft-ball stage, or 232°F on a candy thermometer. Remove from heat; add butter and cool to 200°F without stirring. Add vanilla and pecans; beat until thick and creamy.

Drop mixture by teaspoonfuls onto buttered waxed paper, allowing room to spread. Let stand at room temperature until firm.

Sue Dawson

The Columbus Dispatch / Columbus, Ohio

Buckeyes, from which Ohio gets its designation as the Buckeye State, are round, nut-like seeds that are dark brown with a light tan tip. These easy-to-make candies, which taste much like the popular peanut butter cups, are made to look like their namesake. They are extremely popular here at Christmastime. Although many versions exist, I like this one the best.

BUCKEYES
About 3 pounds candy

1 box (16 ounces)
  confectioners sugar
½ cup butter or margarine,
  softened
1 jar (18 ounces) creamy
  peanut butter

1 package (12 ounces)
  semisweet chocolate
  morsels
1 (1-inch) square paraffin
  (see note)

Combine sugar, butter and peanut butter in a large mixer bowl. Beat until mixture is well blended and begins to cling together. Roll mixture into ¾-inch balls and place balls on waxed paper.

Melt chocolate morsels and paraffin in top of a double boiler over hot water. Stick a toothpick in a peanut butter ball and dip ball in warm chocolate so that all but tip of ball is covered. Let excess chocolate drip back into pan. Place on waxed paper. Remove toothpick. Repeat until all candy has been dipped. Pinch toothpick holes closed with fingers and smooth tops. Refrigerate.

Note: The paraffin called for is household paraffin wax, as is used for sealing jelly. The paraffin makes the chocolate easier to handle and shape, and it does not affect the taste of the candy. Consumption of such a small amount is not harmful.

Jane Mengenhauser
The Journal Newspapers / Springfield, Virginia

This candy is sold along the Skyline Drive in the Shenandoah area of Virginia.

VIRGINIA APPLE CANDY   *About 32 candies*

8 medium apples
½ cup cold water, divided
2 cups firmly packed light
    brown sugar
2 envelopes unflavored gelatin

1 cup chopped nuts (walnuts
    or pecans)
1 tablespoon fresh lemon juice
½ cup confectioners sugar
1 tablespoon cornstarch

Peel, core and chop apples. Place apples in a saucepan and add ¼ cup water. Cook until tender; put through a food mill or a sieve. Return to saucepan and add brown sugar. Cook over low heat until thick, about 30 minutes, stirring often.

Soften unflavored gelatin in remaining ¼ cup cold water. Mix into hot apple mixture; stir until dissolved.

Chill mixture until thickened, then stir in chopped nuts and lemon juice. Pour into an 8- or 9-inch square pan to a depth of about ½ inch. Chill until firm. Cut into squares.

Combine confectioners sugar and cornstarch and sift together. Roll squares in mixture and place each square in a paper candy cup.

Janet Beighle French

The Plain Dealer / Cleveland, Ohio

Apple orchards still produce abundantly near Cleveland, offering great variety at farm markets. The Melrose, a Jonathan-Delicious cross, is available chiefly at such outlets, although it's Ohio's "official" apple.

Maple syrup is also produced in the nearby countryside, and several energetic small towns, such as Burton and Chardon, have maple syrup festivals, with the cooking down taking place on the town square, while city firemen serve pancake breakfasts in their respective firehouses.

Here is a simple recipe that combines apples and maple syrup. It had been in our files a long time before we retested it a few years ago and decided it was too good to remain hidden.

APPLES WITH MAPLE CREAM
4 servings

4 big cooking apples
1 cup maple syrup or maple-flavored syrup
½ cup water
1 tablespoon butter or margarine
1 teaspoon all-purpose flour
½ cup light cream or half-and-half
   Julienne peel of 1 lemon

Pare apples and core with an apple corer.

Combine syrup and water in a saucepan that will just accommodate apples. Boil, uncovered, for 3 minutes. Add apples. Cover. Simmer until tender, about 3 minutes. Lift apples with slotted spoon into individual dessert dishes.

Boil syrup down to ¾ cup, which takes about 2 minutes.

Melt butter in wide 2-quart pan; blend in flour. Blend in cream, then syrup. Boil, uncovered, until reduced to 1 cup, which takes about 3 minutes. Pour over apples.

Serve warm or cool, sprinkled with lemon peel.

Note: Use McIntosh, Golden Delicious, Melrose, Winesap, Jonathan, Rome Beauty or other similar apples.

Marilyn McDevitt Rubin
The Pittsburgh Press / Pittsburgh, Pennsylvania

Of all the recipes I've ever published, this is the one for which I've had the most requests.

PENNSYLVANIA APPLE PANCAKE   *4 servings*

3 eggs
½ cup flour (preferably quick-mixing flour)
½ cup milk
¼ teaspoon salt
8 tablespoons butter or margarine, divided
3 or 4 tart apples

3 tablespoons granulated sugar, or to taste (depending on tartness of apples)
Cinnamon-sugar (3 tablespoons granulated sugar mixed with 1 teaspoon ground cinnamon)
Lemon wedges

Preheat oven to 450°F while preparing batter. Beat eggs in a medium bowl; add flour, milk and salt and beat. Slightly lumpy batter makes a light pancake.

Melt 2 tablespoons butter in a large oven-proof skillet. Pour batter into skillet and immediately place in preheated 450°F oven; bake 15 minutes. Reduce oven temperature to 350°F and bake 10 minutes longer, or until crisp and golden.

While pancake bakes, prepare apples. Peel, core and cut apples into thin slices. Melt remaining 6 tablespoons butter in a large skillet. Sauté apples with sugar in butter 5 minutes, or less, just until crisp-tender. Set aside.

Remove baked pancake from oven. Transfer apples with slotted spoon and place over half of pancake surface. Fold pancake in half. Pour butter from skillet over pancake. Sprinkle generously with cinnamon-sugar. Cut pancake in wedges and serve with lemon.

Note: Make sure your skillet handle can tolerate 450°F heat or you'll have a souffléed handle.

Jane Baker
The Phoenix Gazette / Phoenix, Arizona

While visiting Santa Fe, New Mexico, I had this extraordinary bread pudding. Cheddar cheese adds a different twist. It is a favorite New Mexico dessert that is sometimes called sopa, which means dry soup and often refers to a dessert such as this. In New Mexico, it sometimes is called capirotada. Whatever the name, it has become a favorite of mine.

NEW MEXICO BREAD PUDDING   *8 to 10 servings*

1 loaf (16 ounces) white bread, sliced	2 cups firmly packed light brown sugar
1 cup raisins	3 teaspoons ground cinnamon
1½ quarts water, divided	1 teaspoon ground nutmeg
1 pound Cheddar cheese, shredded	2 tablespoons butter or margarine

Toast bread slices lightly. Remove some of the crusts, if desired. Soak raisins in 2 cups warm water until puffy. Layer bread, cheese and raisins with soaking water in a 13x9x2-inch baking dish. Start with a layer of bread and continue alternating layers until all of the bread, cheese and raisins are used. Try to end with a cheese layer.

Dissolve brown sugar, cinnamon and nutmeg in remaining 1 quart water in a large saucepan. Add butter. Bring to a boil; reduce heat and simmer for 15 minutes.

Pour hot syrup slowly over layers in baking dish until all ingredients are completely soaked. Bake, covered, in a 350°F oven 1 hour. Serve hot or chilled.

Pat Baldridge

Morning Advocate and State-Times / Baton Rouge, Louisiana

This is a classic New Orleans dessert.

BREAD PUDDING WITH WHISKEY SAUCE   *6 to 8 servings*

2 cups milk
4 cups day-old French bread
    cubes (½-inch pieces)
¼ cup butter, melted
½ cup granulated sugar
2 eggs, slightly beaten

¼ teaspoon salt
½ cup raisins
1 teaspoon ground cinnamon
    Whiskey Sauce (recipe
    follows)

Scald milk. Put bread cubes in a large bowl; pour milk over bread cubes. Cool. Add butter, sugar, eggs, salt, raisins and cinnamon; mix well. Pour into a greased 1½-quart casserole dish. Put casserole in a pan of hot water (1 inch deep). Bake in a 350°F oven 1 hour, or until knife inserted into pudding comes out clean. Serve warm with Whiskey Sauce.

WHISKEY SAUCE   *¾ cup*

½ cup butter or margarine
1 cup granulated sugar

1 egg, beaten
¼ cup whiskey

Cook butter and sugar in a double boiler until mixture is thick and sugar is dissolved. Add spoonful of mixture to egg, then stir egg into butter-sugar mixture. Cool slightly; add whiskey. Serve hot or cold over Bread Pudding.

The persimmon is to Indiana what the cranberry is to New England. The first settlers who crossed the Appalachian Mountains discovered a beautiful, amber-colored fruit tree growing wild in fields and lightly wooded areas of Ohio and Indiana—the native American persimmon.

Round to oval in shape and bright orange to almost black in color, the American persimmon is native to the entire southeastern part of the United States and grows wild over most of Southern Indiana.

Full of tannin and "puckery" when not ripe, persimmons must be left to ripen on trees before they are edible. Once they reach full color and succulent softness, they drop to the ground, ready for harvest. Some don't survive the fall, but persimmons should never be picked from trees.

Indiana settlers learned from the Indians how to add honey, cornmeal or other coarse ground meal to persimmon pulp to make simple puddings or breads. Some were cooked over the open hearth or steamed in black iron kettles. Today Hoosier cooks make everything from cakes and breads to pies, cookies, sauces, mousses and even ice cream from the legendary persimmon. Treasured persimmon puddings have become traditional Thanksgiving and Christmas desserts.

INDIANA PERSIMMON PUDDING
10 to 12 servings

2 cups persimmon pulp
  (see note)
2 cups granulated sugar
2 eggs, beaten
1¾ cups sifted all-purpose
  flour
2 teaspoons baking powder

1 cup buttermilk
1 cup half-and-half or light
  cream
1 teaspoon baking soda
⅓ cup butter
¼ to ½ teaspoon ground
  cinnamon

Combine pulp, sugar and eggs in a large mixing bowl; mix well. Combine flour and baking powder; set aside. Combine buttermilk, half-and-half and baking soda. Add alternately with flour mixture to pulp mixture.

Meanwhile, melt butter in a 13x9x2-inch baking pan; brush to coat pan. Pour remaining butter into pulp mixture. Stir in cinnamon. Pour mixture into buttered pan. Bake in a preheated 325°F oven 55 to 60 minutes, or until set. Pudding will be dark, heavy and moist with a rather leathery, shiny top and bottom. The consistency is thicker and more dense than pumpkin pie filling. Serve warm or cold.

Note: It takes six to twelve Indiana persimmons to make 1 cup pulp. To obtain pulp: Wash persimmons well; remove and discard caps and black tips. Quarter or halve persimmons, then press through a colander. Frozen pulp is available in some stores. If using frozen pulp, thaw in refrigerator overnight and then bring to room temperature before mixing pudding.

The large Japanese or Oriental persimmons raised in California and available in supermarkets are good for salads and fresh fruit desserts. These can be put through a colander to make pulp, but they don't have the intensity of flavor best for a baked pudding. It takes only two large California persimmons to make 1 cup pulp.

Woodene Merriman
Pittsburgh Post-Gazette / Pittsburgh, Pennsylvania

To salt—or not to salt—the pecans in the Toasted Pecan Balls. That is the issue in Pittsburgh. Toasted Pecan Balls are found on many restaurant menus in the city. But some use salted chopped pecans, some prefer them plain. Either way, it's a typical Pittsburgh dessert.

TOASTED PECAN BALLS

For each serving:
1 scoop vanilla ice cream
  Chopped toasted pecans,
    salted or plain

1 (or more) topping of your
  choice: chocolate or
  butterscotch sauce,
  whipped cream, etc.

Roll round scoop of ice cream in chopped nuts until well coated. Place in dessert dish. Add topping (or toppings) of your choice.

Note: For convenience, you may want to freeze the nut-coated ice cream balls until ready to serve.

They are called CCBs, these Chocolate Crumble Balls of vanilla ice cream, rolled in crushed chocolate cookies and topped with a hot fudge sauce so thick you can eat it with a fork. The stuff of which dreams are made, they are the all-time favorite food at the Scottish Rite Dormitory at the University of Texas.

It's not often that dorm food is so good that alumnae still talk about it many years later, but CCBs are the exception to the rule. CCBs have been on the dorm menu since the 1930s; students know about them before they arrive, having been cautioned by their alumnae mothers to "watch out for the desserts." The popular dessert was included in a cookbook produced by the dorm in 1982, much to the delight of UT graduates who then were able to make the recipe at home.

CCBS (Chocolate Crumble Balls)   *8 servings*

1½ cups chocolate cookie crumbs (made from creme-filled
        sandwich-style chocolate cookies, such as Oreos or Hydrox)
1½ quarts vanilla ice cream
    Hot Fudge Sauce (recipe follows)

Crush or grind cookies (with filling) to make fine crumbs. Using a medium scoop, make 8 balls of ice cream. Roll ice cream balls immediately in crumbs, place in serving dishes and top with Hot Fudge Sauce.

If preferred, after balls have been rolled in cookie crumbs, they can be frozen on a cookie sheet until ready to serve.

HOT FUDGE SAUCE   *3 cups*

½ cup butter
1 can (5⅓ ounces) evaporated milk
2½ cups confectioners sugar, unsifted
6 squares (1 ounce each) unsweetened chocolate
1 teaspoon vanilla extract

Melt butter in a double boiler. Add evaporated milk, sugar and chocolate. Heat, stirring occasionally, until chocolate melts, about 30 minutes. Remove from heat. Add vanilla and stir vigorously.

Sauce is best when served warm or at room temperature. Sauce will keep indefinitely in refrigerator.

Note: Sauce is supposed to be thick. If you want a thinner sauce, add more milk or half-and-half. Do not add water.

Index

A

Alligator rolls, 248
Almond(s)
  cheese pie, 144
  French fried, 159
  Hungarian, 160
  lemon torte, 140
  paste, for Danish kringler, 107
  smoky cocktail, 159
Angel biscuits, 254
Anticuchos (marinated skewered beef), 218
Antipasto, holiday, 23
Appetizers
  artichoke squares, Mimi's, 19
  Benedictine (cucumber and cream cheese spread), 158
  blue cheese dressing, 163
  bowknots, 24
  Buffalo chicken wings, 162
  cheese balls, zippy, 16
  chicken paté, 8
  chicken roll-ups, curried, 17
  crab mold, summer, 18
  crab puffs, 10
  crayfish, 164
  curried mayonnaise, 164
  curry dip, 13
  dill dip in bread bowl, 15
  eggplant, 22
  egg-shrimp divine, 18
  gougère bourgignon, 16
  holiday antipasto, 23
  Hungarian almonds, 160
  lime fruit dip, 20

  Louisville rolled oysters, 165
  love letters, 11
  Manhattan cocktail, 166
  meatballs, sweet and sour, 21
  mint julep, 166
  mushroom, 20
  mushroom sandwiches, hot, 12
  olive-cheese balls, 10
  onion sandwiches, 158
  poultry mousse, 14
  salmon roll, 24
  shrimp spread, 22
  smoked fish dip, 163
  smoky cocktail almonds, 159
  spinach frittata, 9
  Swiss crusts, 14
  Texas cheese dip, 160
  toasted ravioli, 161
  vegetable hot dip, 13
Apple(s)
  cake, Norwegian (eple kake), 274
  candy, Virginia, 293
  pancake, German, 148
  pancake, Pennsylvania, 295
  pie, naked, 121
  with maple cream, 294
Artichoke(s)
  chicken sauté with, 60
  crab meat casserole, 60
  squares, Mimi's, 19
Asparagus salad, Chinese, 35
Avocado, hearts of palm, and endive with caper vinaigrette, 44

B

Bacon, hot dressing, for spinach salad, 181
Baked Alaska, birthday, 120
Baltimore cheese bread, 260
Banana bread, Hawaiian, 114
Barbecue
    Delmarva chicken, 208
    Memphis, 235
    sauce, basic, for Texas pit barbecue, 214
    sauce, LBJ, 215
Bass with fennel butter, broiled sea, 74
Beans, dry
    chili mac, Toledo style, 222
    New England baked beans, 238
    ranch-style beans (frijoles a la charra), 239
    red beans and rice, 199
    Spanish bean soup (potaje de garbanzos), 175
    white beans and tasso, 202
Beef
    Burgundy, budget, 72
    Chickasaw baked steak, 216
    chicken-fried steak, Texas, 211
    chili con carne, 223
    chili mac, Toledo style, 222
    chili, Texas chuck wagon, 217
    Cincinnati chili, 221
    Cousin Jack pasties, 204
    Delmonico steak, 212
    marinated skewered (anticuchos), 218
    meatballs, sweet and sour, 21
    meat loaf (pâté Americain), 63
    Philadelphia cheese-steak, 230
    picadillo (stew), 173
    pot roast, sweet-sour, 71
    ribs, rave-bringing, 71
    shredded filling, for chimichangas, 76
    skirt steak in tortillas, marinated (fajitas), 213
    steak and kidney pie, 57
    tamale pie, hot, 220
    tenderloin, sherried, 56
    vegetable soup, 26
Beer-battered fish, 196
Benedictine (cucumber and cream cheese spread), 158
Bimini bread, 261

Biscuits
    angel, 254
    for strawberry-raspberry shortcake, 122
    Hoosier fried, 253
Blackberries, marionberry pie, 283
Blueberry
    butter cake, Grandma's, 128
    melt-in-your-mouth cake, 271
    soup, chilled, 30
Blue corn bread, 255
Bluefish, Boston baked, 72
Boil
    fish, Door County, 195
    low-country, 194
Bourbon balls, 132
Bowknots, 24
Bran bread, whole wheat cranberry, 110
Brandy Alexander soufflé, 137
Bread
    alligator rolls, 248
    angel biscuits, 254
    Baltimore cheese, 260
    banana, Hawaiian, 114
    bimini, 261
    blue corn, 255
    bowknots, 24
    corn, Mother's, 110
    dill dip in bread bowl, 15
    garlic, Joe's, 105
    graham, Grandma's, 104
    Hale farm Johnnycake, 256
    herb butter-spread, 117
    Hoosier fried biscuits, 253
    kringler, Danish, 107
    kummelweck rolls, 250
    mango nut, 259
    Minnesota Swedish rye, 258
    molasses raisin rye, Mother's, 104
    Parker house rolls, 252
    Philadelphia soft pretzels, 262
    pizza, 116
    pudding, New Mexico, 296
    pudding, pioneer, 133
    pudding with whiskey sauce, 297
    spider cake, 257
    squaw, Osage, 114
    Swiss crusts, 14
    Swope, 113
    treacle, Irish-American, 108
    whole wheat, Québec style, 118
    whole wheat cranberry bran, 110
    whole wheat honey, 106
    whole wheat zucchini, 111

Breakfast burritos, 227
Broccoli
    broccoli-tomato casserole, 86
    salad, 45
    stir-fry chicken with, 54
Brownies
    butterscotch, 148
    chocolate, for birthday baked Alaska, 120
    saucepan Indians, 144
Brownstone front cake, 264
Buckeyes (candies), 292
Buffalo chicken wings, 162
Bundt cake, 150
Burritos
    breakfast, 227
    smothered, 227
Butter
    blueberry cake, Grandma's, 128
    fennel, for sea bass, 74
    herb butter-spread bread, 117
Butternut squash soup, 31
Butterscotch brownies, 148

C

Cabbage
    cole slaw, tangy, 35
    peanut crunch salad, 46
    skillet, 87
Cactus, prickly pear, using fruit of, 156
Caesar salad, original, 36
Cake
    blueberry butter, Grandma's, 128
    booze, Swedish, 126
    brownstone front, 264
    bundt, 150
    chocolate, Mrs. America, 136
    Concord grape kuchen, 274
    cupcakes, chocolate chip, 129
    filbert cream, 270
    fruitcake, keepsake, 143
    funnel, 279
    Georgia peach cobbler, 277

gooey butter coffee, 272
    convenience method, 273
Kentucky stack, 265
melt-in-your-mouth blueberry, 271
Mississippi river mud, 269
New Orleans king's, 266
Norwegian apple (eple kake), 273
nutmeg, 141
pecan and peach upside-down, 135
poppy seed tea, 132
raisin, holiday, 146
Slovak kolachy, 276
strawberry-raspberry shortcake, 122
Texas sheet, 268
white fruitcake, Mrs. Harvey's, 130
California baked chicken, 210
Candied carrots, 93
Candy
    buckeyes, 292
    Grandma's potato, 291
    Mexican pecan, 126
    pecan pralines, 292
    Virginia apple, 293
Caper vinaigrette, 44
Carrot(s)
    candied, 93
    good way, 100
    marinated, 93
    salad, 38
    soufflé, 95
    with ginger and cumin, 96
Casserole
    broccoli-tomato, 96
    chicken, 51
    chicken, King Ranch, 206
    chicken breasts with Gruyère and
        mushrooms, 61
    chicken with rice (paella), 59
    chili relleno, 219
    crab meat, 60
    grits, Pete's, 87
    potatoes au gratin, 97
    ratatouille, 91
    rosemary parsnip, 98
    spinach, 99
    sweet potato, 85
Cauliflower
    continental salad, 46
    fresh salad, Mrs. Poole's, 41
Caviar-topped baked grits, 243
CCBs (chocolate crumble balls), 300
Cheese
    almond pie, 144

and chilies, toasted, 227
ball, zippy, 16
blue cheese dressing for Buffalo chicken
    wings, 163
blue corn bread, 255
bread, Baltimore, 260
Chicago stuffed spinach pizza, 225
chili relleno casserole, 219
chicken breasts with Gruyère and
    mushrooms, baked, 61
dip, Texas, 160
egg-shrimp divine, 18
garlic grits, 243
garlic Parmesan rolls, 113
gougère bourguignon, 16
grits, casserole, Pete's, 87
in chicken pocket, 66
Louisville hot brown, 231
olive-cheese balls, 10
onions, baked, 86
Philadelphia cheese-steak, 230
pimiento-cheese sandwiches, 236
pumpkin angel squares, 123
pumpkin pie cheesecake, 145
ricotta cassata, 134
salmon roll, 24
sandwich buns, homemade, 115
sauce, for devonshire sandwich, 235
scalloped potatoes, Mother's, 82
soufflé, brunch, 62
spinach frittata, 9
spinach lasagna, 50
Swiss crusts, 14
Cheese-steak, Philadelphia, 230
Chicago deep-dish pizza, 224
Chicago fish soup, 171
Chicago hot dogs, 233
Chickasaw baked steak, 216
Chicken
    and sausage gumbo, 205
    booyah (thick soup), 176
    breasts with Gruyère and mushrooms,
        baked, 61
    California baked, 210
    casserole, 51
    casserole, with rice (paella), 59
    cheese in chicken pocket, 66
    Country captain, 207
    crazy (el pollo loco de tu cocina), 209
    curried roll-ups, 17
    Delmarva barbecued, 208
    Iron Skillet's Hoosier fried, 210
    King Ranch casserole, 206

Louisville hot brown, 231
love letters, 11
marinated broiled, 76
mystery, 66
oven-fried, 75
pâté, 8
poultry mousse, 14
salad with champagne dressing, 64
sauté with artichokes, 60
sweet-sour pineapple, 48
wings, Buffalo, 162
with broccoli, stir-fry, 54
Chicken-fried steak, Texas, 211
Chili
    Cincinnati, 221
    con carne, 223
    mac, Toledo style, 222
    relleno casserole, 219
    Texas chuck wagon, 217
Chilies and cheese, toasted, 227
Chimichangas (meat- or bean-filled
    tortillas), 226
Chocolate
    brownies, for birthday baked Alaska, 120
    cake, Mrs. America, 136
    chip cupcakes, 129
    crumble balls (CCBs), 300
    frosting, for brownstone front cake, 264
    hot fudge pudding, 130
    Mississippi river mud cake, 269
    Run for the Roses pie, 285
    sauce, mile-high ice cream pie, 286
    saucepan Indians, 144
    torte, Ventana, 142
Chrysanthemum salad, 40
Cincinnati chili, 221
Cinnamon rolls, Aunt Ruth's, 109
Cioppino (fish and shellfish stew), 174
Clam(s)
    cakes, Rhode Island, 189
    chowder, New England, 169
    Portuguese pork and, 65
Cobbler, Georgia peach, 277
Cod fillets, poached, 58
Coffee cake
    faster Concord grape kuchen, 274
    gooey butter, 272
        convenience method, 273
Cole slaw, tangy, 35
Conch chowder, 172
Concord grape kuchen, faster, 274
Cookies and small cakes
    Bourbon balls, 132

butterscotch brownies, 148
chocolate brownies for birthday baked
    Alaska, 120
chocolate chip cupcakes, 129
chocolate crumble balls (CCBs), 300
everyday, 131
fruit balls, Christmas, 149
Moravian, 290
pumpkin angel squares, 123
saucepan Indians, 144
spicy groundhogs, 289
sugar, Abbie's, 125
Coriander, bay scallops with, 70
Corn
    custard, 102
    Gib's roasted, 244
    low-country boil, 194
    pudding, 90
Corn bread
    blue, 255
    Mother's, 110
    spider cake, 257
Cornmeal crust, 220, 224
Country ham and red-eye gravy, 199
Cousin Jack pasties, 204
Crab
    cakes, 185
    casserole, 60
    imperial, 184
    low-country boil, 194
    puffs, 10
Cranberry bran bread, whole wheat, 110
Crawfish étouffée, 192
Crayfish appetizers, 164
Crazy chicken (el pollo loco de tu cocina),
    209
Cream cheese-filbert icing, for filbert cream
    cake, 270
Cream gravy, for chicken-fried steak, 211
Crust. See Pastry
Cucumber(s)
    dilled, 95
    salad, Nana's, 42
    soup, chilled, 28
Cumberland Island shrimp, 193
Cumin, carrots with ginger and, 96
Cupcakes, chocolate chip, 129
Curried mayonnaise, 164
Curry
    chicken roll-ups, 17
    dip, 13
    potatoes with mustard and, 89
Custard

corn, 102
Vidalia onion, 242

D

Danish kringler, 107
Delmarva barbecued chicken, 208
Delmonico steak, 212
Desserts. See Brownies; Cake; Candy;
    Cookies; Fruit; Ice cream; Pie; Pudding;
    Soufflé; Torte
Devonshire sandwich, original, 234
Dill
    cucumbers, dilled, 95
    dip in bread bowl, 15
    pickles, fried, 240
Dinner rolls, 112
Dip
    curry, 13
    dill, in bread bowl, 15
    lime fruit, 20
    smoked fish, 163
    Texas cheese, 160
    vegetable, hot, 13
Door County fish boil, 195
Dove in Madeira sauce, 79
Dressing
    bacon, hot, for spinach salad, 181
    blue cheese, for Buffalo chicken wings,
        163
    caper vinaigrette, 44
    champagne, for chicken salad, 64
    for eggs Pontchartrain, 179
    French, for Cobb salad, 178
    soy mayonnaise, for Oriental shrimp
        salad, 40
Drinks
    Manhattan cocktail, 166
    mint julep, 166
Dumplings, liver (leberknaefly), 203

E

Egg(s)
    brandy Alexander soufflé, 137

brunch soufflé, 62
egg-shrimp divine, 18
Hangtown fry, 185
Pontchartrain, 179
spinach frittata, 9
trail ride (huevos Mexicanos), 58
Eggplant appetizer, 22
Elephant ears, 278
Endive, hearts of palm, and
avocado with caper vinaigrette, 44
English tea muffins, ice box, 116
Eple kake (Norwegian apple cake), 273

F

Fajitas (marinated skirt steak in tortillas), 213
Fennel butter, for sea bass, 74
Fettucine Florentine, 88
Filbert cream cake, 270
Filling
almond paste, for Danish kringler, 107
for lemon zucchini pie, 124
for ricotta cassata, 134
Fish
beer-battered, 196
Boston bluefish, baked, 72
chowder, Maine, 168
cod fillets, poached, 58
dip, smoked, 163
Door County boil, 195
fillets amandine, broiled, 80
Lake George shrimp (perch), 73
lutefisk, 190
orange-tuna-macaroni salad, 34
salmon, grilled rice-stuffed, 190
salmon roll, 24
sea bass with fennel butter, broiled, 74
smelts in orange sauce, baked, 79
soup, Chicago, 171
stew (cioppino), 174
see also Seafood
Frankfurters, red devil, 77
French dressing, 178
French leek soup, 30
Frijoles a la charra (ranch-style beans), 139

Frittata, spinach, 9
Frosting/icing
chocolate, 136, 264
cream cheese-filbert, 270
for Mississippi river mud cake, 269
for Texas sheet cake, 268
Fruit
apple cake, Norwegian (eple kake), 273
apple candy, Virginia, 293
apple pancake, German, 148
apple pancake, Pennsylvania, 295
apples with maple cream, 294
banana bread, Hawaiian, 114
blackberries, marionberry pie, 283
blueberry butter cake, Grandma's, 128
blueberry cake, melt-in-your-mouth, 271
Christmas balls, 149
Concord grape kuchen, faster, 274
dip, lime, 20
Georgia peach cobbler, 277
Key lime pie, 281
kiwifruit salad, 39
lemon pie, Ohio, 284
lemon torte, almond, 140
lemon zucchini pie, 124
mango nut bread, 259
marionberry pie, 283
orange-tuna-macaroni salad, 34
peach and pecan upside-down cake, 135
pears with raspberries and cream,
poached, 147
persimmon pudding, Indiana, 298
pineapple pie, fresh, 139
strawberries, peppered, 127
strawberry-raspberry shortcake, 122
Fruitcake
keepsake, 143
white, Mrs. Harvey's, 130
Fry bread, Navajo, 229
Fudge sauce, hot, for CCBs, 300
Funnel cakes, 279

G

Garlic
bread, Joe's, 105

cheese grits, 243
Parmesan rolls, 113
Gazpacho, 27
salad, molded, 42
Georgia peach cobbler, 277
Georgia pecan pie, 283
German apple pancake, 148
German potato salad, 34, 182
German-style venison roast, 78
Gib's roasted corn, 244
Ginger
carrots with cumin and, 96
pumpkin slices, gingered, 140
Goetta (Cincinnati variation on scrapple), 200
Gooey butter coffee cake, 272
convenience method, 273
Gougère bourguignon, 16
Graham bread, Grandma's, 104
Grandma's graham bread, 104
Grandma's potato candy, 291
Gravy
cream, for chicken-fried steak, 211
red-eye, for country ham, 199
Greek-style pilaf, 90
Grits, 243
Grits casserole, Pete's, 87
Groundhogs, spicy (cookies), 289
Gumbo
chicken and sausage, 205
okra, 98

Herb butter-spread bread, 117
Hollywood Brown Derby Cobb salad,
original, 178
Honey bread, whole wheat, 106
Hoosier fried biscuits, 253
Hot dogs, Chicago, 233
Hot fudge sauce, for CCBs, 300
Hot tamale pie, 220
Huevos Mexicanos (trail ride eggs), 58
Hungarian almonds, 160

I

Icebox potica, Slovenian (pastries), 280
Ice cream
baked Alaska, birthday, 120
chocolate crumble balls (CCBs), 300
groundhog sundaes, 289
mile-high ice cream pie, 286
pumpkin ice cream pie, John's
Flaming Hearth, 288
strawberries, peppered, 127
toasted pecan balls, 299
Icing. See Frosting/icing
Indiana persimmon pudding, 298
Irish-American treacle bread, 108
Iron Skillet's Hoosier fried chicken, 210
Italian salad, 180

H

Hale Farm Johnnycake, 256
Ham
and oyster pie, 188
and red-eye gravy, 199
mystery chicken, 66
sandwich, in homemade buns, 115
Southern Maryland, stuffed, 197
Tennessee country, how to cook, 198
Hangtown fry, 185
Hawaiian banana bread, 114
Hearts of palm, endive, and avocado with
caper vinaigrette, 44

J

Jalapeño pepper rice, 245
Jicama
pie, 282
salad, 180
Johnnycake, Hale Farm, 256
John's Flaming Hearth pumpkin ice cream
pie, 288

K

Kentucky stack cake, 265
Key lime pie, 281
King Ranch chicken casserole, 206
King's cake, New Orleans, 266
Kiwifruit salad, 39
Kolachy, Slovak, 276
Kringler, Danish, 107
Kuchen, Concord grape, 274
Kummelweck rolls, 250

L

Lake George shrimp (perch), 73
Lasagna
    spinach, 50
    Steve's favorite, 49
LBJ barbecue sauce, 215
Leberknaefly (liver dumplings), 203
Leek soup, French, 30
Lemon
    almond torte, 140
    lemon-butter sauce for fish fillets
        amandine, 80
    pie, Ohio, 284
    sauce, for pioneer bread pudding, 133
    zucchini pie, 124
Lime
    fruit dip, 20
    pie, Key, 281
Liver
    dumplings (leberknaefly), 203
    poultry mousse, 14
Louisville hot brown, (chicken or turkey
    sandwich), 231
Louisville rolled oysters, 165
Low-country boil, 194
Lutefisk, 190

M

Madeira sauce, for dove or quail, 79

Maine fish chowder, 168
Mango nut bread, 259
Manhattan cocktail, 166
Maple cream, apples with, 294
Marinade
    for anticuchos, 218
    for fajitas, 213
Marinated carrots, 93
Marinated chicken, broiled, 76
Marionberry pie, 283
Mayonnaise, curried, 164
Meatballs, sweet and sour, 21
Meat loaf (pâté Americain), 63
Melt-in-your-mouth blueberry cake, 271
Memphis barbecue (barbecued pork
    sandwich), 235
Meringue, for mile-high ice cream pie, 286
Mexican pecan candy, 126
Mile-high ice cream pie, 286
Minestrone Siciliano, 29
Minnesota Swedish rye bread, 258
Minnesota wild rice soup, 170
Mint julep, 166
Molasses
    raisin rye bread, Mother's, 104
    treacle bread, Irish-American, 108
    whole wheat bread, Québec style, 118
Moravian cookies, 290
Mousse
    poultry, 14
    sausage, for pork loin, 52
Muffins, ice box English tea, 116
Mushroom(s)
    appetizers, 20
    baked chicken breasts with Gruyère and,
        61
    sandwiches, hot, 12
    sauce, 51
    soup, brown, 31
Mussels, saffron, 62
Mustard
    potatoes with curry and, 89
    ring, 44
Mystery chicken, 66

N

Navajo fry bread, 229
Navajo tacos, 228

New England baked beans, 238
New England clam chowder, 169
New Mexico bread pudding, 296
New Orleans king's cake, 266
Norwegian apple cake (eple kake), 273
Nut bread, mango, 259
Nutmeg cake, 141

O

Ohio lemon pie, 284
Okra gumbo, 98
Olive-cheese balls, 10
Onion(s)
    baked, 86
    custard Vidalia, 242
    sandwiches, 158
Orange
    orange-tuna-macaroni salad, 34
    rolls, 113
    sauce, for baked smelts, 79
Oriental shrimp salad, 40
Osage squaw bread, 114
Oyster(s)
    and ham pie, colonial, 188
    Hangtown fry, 185
    loaf, 187
    Louisville rolled, 165
    scalloped, 186

P

Paella (chicken and rice casserole), 59
Pancake(s)
    apple, German, 148
    apple, Pennsylvania, 295
    potato, 101
Parker House rolls, 252
Parsnip casserole with rosemary, 98
Pasta
    fettucine Florentine, 88
    lasagna, Steve's favorite, 48
    orange-tuna-macaroni salad, 34
    pilaf, Greek-style, 90

ravioli, toasted, 161
Southwest salad, 43
spaghetti primavera, 92
spinach lasagna, 50
toasted ravioli, 161
Pasties, Cousin Jack, 204
Pastry
    Ann's, 138
    elephant ears, 278
    funnel cake, 279
    gougère bourgignon, 16
    for lemon zucchini pie, 124
    nut, for pineapple pie, 139
    ricotta cassata, 134
    Slovenian icebox potica, 280
    for turkey pot pie, 68
Pâté
    Americain (meat loaf), 63
    chicken, 8
Peach and pecan upside-down cake, 135
Peanut
    crunch salad, 46
    soup, creamy, 177
Pears with raspberries and cream, poached,
    147
Pecan(s)
    balls, toasted, 299
    candy, Mexican, 126
    pie, Georgia, 183
    pralines, 192
    pumpkin angel squares, 123
    upside-down cake, peach and, 135
    white fruitcake, Mrs. Harvey's, 130
Pennsylvania apple pancake, 295
Perch (Lake George shrimp), 73
Persimmon pudding, Indiana, 298
Philadelphia cheese-steak, 230
Philadelphia soft pretzels, 262
Picadillo (beef stew), 173
Pickles, fried dill, 240
Pie
    almond cheese, 144
    apple, naked, 121
    colonial oyster and ham, 188
    Georgia pecan, 283
    hot tamale, 220
    jicama, 282
    John's Flaming Hearth pumpkin ice
        cream, 288
    Key lime, 281
    lemon zucchini, 124
    marionberry, 283
    mile-high ice cream, 286

Ohio lemon, 284
pineapple, fresh, 139
pumpkin cheesecake, 145
ricotta cassata, 134
Run for the Roses, 285
steak and kidney, 57
sugar cream, 285
transparent, 287
turkey pot, Maggie Steffen's, 68
Pilaf, Greek-style, 90
Pimiento-cheese sandwiches, 236
Pineapple
  chicken, sweet-sour, 48
  pie, fresh, 139
Pittsburgh potatoes, 241
Pizza
  bread, 116
  Chicago deep-dish, 224
  Chicago stuffed spinach, 225
Poppy seed tea cake, 132
Pork
  brunch soufflé, 62
  Cousin Jack pasties, 204
  loin, with sausage mousse, 52
  marinated skewered (anticuchos), 218
  meat loaf (pâté Americain), 63
  Memphis barbecue, 235
  Portuguese, with clams, 65
  satay, 74
  white beans and tasso, 202
Portuguese pork and clams, 65
Potaje de garbanzos (Spanish bean soup),
  175
Potato(es)
  candy, Grandma's, 291
  casserole au gratin, 97
  golden stuffed baked, 94
  pancake principle, 101
  Pittsburgh, 241
  salad, German, 34, 182
  scalloped, Mother's, 82
  stuffing, mashed, 84
  with mustard and curry, 89
Poultry mousse, 14
Pralines, pecan, 292
Pretzels, Philadelphia soft, 262
Prickly pear cactus, using fruit of, 246
Pudding
  bread, pioneer, 133
  bread with whiskey sauce, 297
  delight, 124
  hot fudge, 130
  Indiana persimmon, 298

New Mexico bread, 296
rice, ultimate, 138
Tally Ho tomato, 240
Pumpkin
  angel squares, 123
  gingered slices, 140
  ice cream pie, John's Flaming Hearth, 288
  pie cheesecake, 145

Quail in Madeira sauce, 79
Québec style whole wheat bread, 118

R

Raisin(s)
  booze cake, Swedish, 126
  holiday cake, 146
  molasses rye bread, Mother's, 104
Ranch-style beans (frijoles a la charra), 239
Raspberries
  strawberry-raspberry shortcake, 122
  with poached pears and cream, 147
Ratatouille, 91
Red beans and rice, 199
Rhode Island clam cakes, 189
Rice
  jalapeño pepper, 145
  pilaf, Greek-style, 90
  pudding, ultimate, 138
  red beans and, 199
  salmon, grilled rice-stuffed, 190
  with vegetables, stir-fry brown, 83
Ricotta cassata, 134
Rolls
  Alligator, 248
  cinnamon, Aunt Ruth's, 109
  dinner, 112

garlic Parmesan, 113
Kummelweck, 250
orange, 113
out-of-this-world, 112
Parker House, 252
sandwich buns, homemade, 115
sour cream yeast, 112
tea muffins, ice box English, 116
Rosemary
broiled shrimp with, 69
parsnip casserole with, 98
Run for the Roses pie, 285
Rye bread, Minnesota Swedish, 258

S

Saffron mussels, 62
Salad
asparagus, Chinese, 35
broccoli, 45
Caesar, original, 36
carrot, 38
cauliflower, Continental, 46
cauliflower, fresh, Mrs. Poole's, 41
chicken with champagne dressing, 64
chrysanthemum, 40
Cobb, original Hollywood Brown Derby, 178
cole slaw, tangy, 35
cucumber, Nana's, 42
eggs Pontchartrain, 179
gazpacho, molded, 42
hearts of palm, endive, and avocado with caper vinaigrette, 44
Italian, 180
jicama, 180
kiwifruit, 39
mustard ring, 44
orange-tuna-macaroni, 34
peanut crunch, 46
potato, German, 34, 182
shrimp, Cumberland Island, 193
shrimp, Oriental, 40
Southwest, 43
spinach, with hot bacon dressing, 181

zucchini, zippy, 38
Salmon
grilled, rice-stuffed, 190
roll, 24
Sandwich(es)
ham, in homemade buns, 115
Louisville hot brown, 231
Memphis barbecue, 235
mushroom, hot, 12
onion, 158
original Devonshire, 234
Philadelphia cheese-steak, 230
pimiento-cheese, 236
Springfield horseshoe, 232
Sandwich buns, homemade, 115
Sauce
barbecue, basic, 214
barbecue, LBJ, 215
caper vinaigrette, 44
cheese, for Devonshire sandwich, 235
chocolate, for mile-high ice cream pie, 286
hot fudge, for CCBs, 300
lemon, for pioneer bread pudding, 133
lemon-butter, for broiled fish fillets amandine, 80
Madeira, for dove or quail, 79
mushroom, 51
orange, for smelts, 79
Welsh rarebit, for Springfield horseshoe, 233
whiskey, for bread pudding, 297
white, for turkey divan, 67
Saucepan Indians, 144
Sausage
and chicken gumbo, 205
goetta, 200
low-country boil, 194
red beans and rice, 229
Scallops, with fresh coriander, bay, 70
Scrapple, 201
Seafood
bay scallops with fresh coriander, 70
chicken and rice casserole (paella), 59
cioppino (fish and shellfish stew), 174
clam cakes, Rhode Island, 189
clam chowder, New England, 169
conch chowder, 172
crab cakes, 184
crab imperial, 184
low-country boil, 194
pork and clams, Portuguese, 65
saffron mussels, 62

shrimp, Cumberland Island, 193
shrimp De Jonghe, 191
shrimp étouffée, 192
see also Crab; Fish; Shrimp
Sheet cake, Texas, 268
Shrimp
  Cumberland Island, 193
  De Jonghe, 191
  egg-shrimp divine, 18
  étouffée, 192
  low-country boil, 194
  salad, Oriental, 40
  spread, 22
  with rosemary, broiled, 69
Slovak kolachy, 276
Smelts in orange sauce, baked, 79
Smoked fish dip, 163
Smothered burritos, 227
Soufflé
  brandy Alexander, 137
  brunch, 62
  carrot, 95
Soup
  bean, Spanish (potaje de garbanzos), 175
  beef vegetable, 26
  blueberry, chilled, 30
  butternut squash, 31
  Chicago fish, 171
  chicken booyah, 175
  conch chowder, 172
  cucumber, chilled, 28
  fall-vegetable, cream of, 32
  gazpacho, 27
  leek, French, 30
  Maine fish chowder, 168
  minestrone Siciliano, 29
  Minnesota wild rice, 170
  mushroom, brown, 31
  New England clam chowder, 169
  peanut, creamy, 177
  squash, 28
  tomato madrilene, 27
  zucchini, 26
Sour cream yeast rolls, 112
Spaghetti primavera, 92
Spanish bean soup (potaje de garbanzos), 175
Spicy groundhogs (cookies), 289
Spider cake (corn bread), 257
Spinach
  casserole, 99
  fettucine Florentine, 88
  frittata, 9

lasagna, 50
pizza, Chicago stuffed, 225
salad with hot bacon dressing, 181
Springfield horseshoe (meat sandwich with cheese sauce), 232
Squash
  no-noodle spaghetti, 55
  puff, 96
  ratatouille, 91
  soup, 28
  soup, butternut, 31
  tomatoes and, 99
  see also Zucchini
Squaw bread, Osage, 114
Stack cake, Kentucky, 265
Stew
  fish and shellfish (cioppino), 174
  ground beef (picadillo), 173
Stir-fry
  brown rice with vegetables, 83
  chicken with broccoli, 54
Strawberries
  peppered, 127
  strawberry-raspberry shortcake, 122
Stuffing, mashed potato, 84
Sugar
  cookies, Abbie's, 125
  cream pie, 285
Sundaes, groundhog, 289
Swedish booze cake, 126
Swedish rye bread, Minnesota, 258
Sweet and sour meatballs, 21
  pineapple chicken, 48
  pot roast, 71
Sweet potato
  casserole, 85
  balls, 88
Swiss crusts, 14
Swope bread, 113

T

Tacos, Navajo, 228
Tally Ho tomato pudding, 240
Tamale pie, hot, 220
Tea cake, poppy seed, 132

Tea muffins, ice box English, 116
Tennessee country ham, how to cook, 198
Texas cheese dip, 160
Texas chicken-fried steak, 211
Texas chuck wagon chili, 227
Texas pit barbecue, basic barbecue sauce
     for, 214
Texas sheet cake, 268
Toasted pecan balls, 299
Tomato(es)
     and squash, 99
     broccoli-tomato casserole, 86
     madrilene, 27
     pudding, Tally Ho, 240
Topping for alligator rolls, 248
Torte
     almond lemon, 140
     chocolate, Ventana, 142
Trail ride eggs (huevos Mexicanos), 58
Transparent pie, 287
Treacle bread, Irish-American, 108
Tuna-orange-macaroni salad, 34
Turkey
     divan, 67
     Louisville hot brown, 241
     original Devonshire sandwich, 234
     pot pie, Maggie Steffen's, 68

U

Upside-down cake, pecan and peach, 135

V

Vegetable(s)
     antipasto, holiday, 23
     artichokes, chicken sauté with, 60
     artichoke squares, Mimi's, 19
     asparagus salad, Chinese, 35
     beef soup, 26
     broccoli, stir-fry chicken with, 54

broccoli salad, 45
broccoli-tomato casserole, 86
brown rice with, stir-fry, 83
butternut squash soup, 31
cabbage skillet, 87
cabbage (peanut crunch) salad, 46
carrot salad, 38
carrot soufflé, 95
carrots, candied, 93
carrots, ginger and cumin, 96
carrots, marinated, 93
carrots the good way, 100
cauliflower salad, Continental, 46
cauliflower salad, Mrs. Poole's, fresh, 41
cole slaw, tangy, 35
corn custard, 102
corn, Gib's roasted, 244
corn pudding, 90
dill pickles, fried, 240
eggplant appetizer, 22
endive, hearts of palm and avocado with,
     44
gazpacho, 27
gazpacho salad, molded, 42
grits casserole, Pete's, 87
hot dip, 13
jalapeño pepper rice, 245
leek soup, French, 30
Minnesota wild rice soup, 170
mushroom soup, brown, 31
onion custard Vidalia, 242
onion sandwiches, 158
onions, baked, 86
parsnips casserole, rosemary, 98
pilaf, Greek-style, 90
ratatouille, 91
spaghetti primavera, 92
spinach casserole, 99
spinach frittata, 9
spinach pizza, Chicago stuffed, 225
squash and tomatoes, 99
squash puff, 96
squash soup, 28
tomato casserole, broccoli, 86
tomato madrilene, 27
tomato pudding, Tally Ho, 240
watercress, spicy minced, 94
zucchini salad, zippy, 38
zucchini soup, 26
see also Pasta; Potatoes; Salad; Sweet
     Potatoes
Venison
     backstrap, wine-roasted, 76

roast, German-style, 78
Ventana chocolate torte, 142
Vidalia onion custard, 242
Vinaigrette caper, 44
Virginia apple candy, 293

White beans and tasso, 202
White sauce, for turkey divan, 67
Wild rice soup, Minnesota, 170
Wine
  beef Burgundy, budget, 72
  beef tenderloin, sherried, 56
  champagne dressing, for chicken salad, 64
  chicken pâté, 8
  Madeira sauce, for dove and quail, 79
  onions, baked, 86
  pears with raspberries and cream,
    poached, 147
  venison backstrap, wine-roasted, 76

W

Walnuts
  nut crust, for pineapple pie, 139
  saucepan Indians, 144
Watercress, spicy minced, 94
Welsh rarebit sauce, for Springfield
  horseshoe, 233
Wheat
  whole wheat bread, Québec style, 118
  whole wheat cranberry bran bread, 110
  whole wheat honey bread, 106
  whole wheat zucchini bread, 111
Whiskey sauce, for bread pudding, 297

X Y Z

Zucchini
  pie, lemon, 124
  salad, zippy, 38
  soup, 26
  whole wheat bread, 111
  see also Squash